Indigenous People

and Poverty

in Latin America

An Empirical Analysis

WORLD BANK

REGIONAL AND

SECTORAL STUDIES

Indigenous People

and Poverty

in Latin America

An Empirical Analysis

EDITED BY

GEORGE PSACHAROPOULOS

HARRY ANTHONY PATRINOS

The World Bank
Washington, D.C.

The World Bank Regional and Sectoral Studies series provides an outlet for work that is relatively limited in its subject matter or geographical coverage but that contributes to the intellectual foundations of development operations and policy formulation. Some sources cited in this paper may be informal documents that are not readily available.

The findings, interpretations, and conclusions expressed in this publication are those of the authors and should not be attributed in any manner to the World Bank, to its affiliated organizations, or to the members of its Board of Executive Directors or the countries they represent.

The material in this publication is copyrighted. Requests for permission to reproduce portions of it should be sent to the Office of the Publisher at the address shown in the copyright notice above. The World Bank encourages dissemination of its work and will normally give permission promptly and, when the reproduction is for noncommercial purposes, without asking a fee. Permission to copy portions for classroom use is granted through the Copyright Clearance Center, Inc., Suite 910, 222 Rosewood Dr., Danvers, Massachusetts 01923, U.S.A.

The complete backlist of publications from the World Bank is shown in the annual *Index of Publications,* which contains an alphabetical title list and indexes of subjects, authors, and countries and regions. The latest edition is available free of charge from Distribution Unit, Office of the Publisher, The World Bank, 1818 H Street, N.W., Washington, D.C. 20433, U.S.A., or from Publications, The World Bank, 66, avenue d'Iéna, 75116 Paris, France.

George Psacharopoulos is senior adviser to the vice president of the Human Resources Development and Operations Policy Department. Harry Anthony Patrinos is an economist in the Education and Social Policy Department.

Library of Congress Cataloging-in-Publication Data

Indigenous people and poverty in Latin America: an empirical analysis/
    edited by George Psacharopoulos and Harry Anthony Patrinos.
        p. cm. — (World Bank regional and sectoral studies)
    Includes bibliographical references.
    ISBN 0-8213-2958-8
    1. Indians—Economic conditions. 2. Indians—Social conditions.
3. Latin America—Economic conditions—1982– 4. Latin America—
Social conditions—1982– I. Psacharopoulos, George.
II. Patrinos, Harry Anthony. III. Series.
E59.E3I53   1994
330.98'0089'98—dc20   94-26584
                                                            CIP

Contents

Figures

Boxes

Foreword

Indigenous people make up a large and distinct portion of Latin America's population. In some countries, the majority of the population is indigenous. In Bolivia, for example, more than half of the total population is of indigenous origin. Indigenous people are more likely than any other group of a country's population to be poor. To a very large extent, being of indigenous origin goes hand in hand with poverty.

While the incidence of poverty is high in Latin America, it is particularly severe and deep among the indigenous population. In Bolivia, more than half of the total population is poor, but over two-thirds of the indigenous population is poor. In Guatemala, over two-thirds of the population is poor, but almost 90 percent of the indigenous population is poor.

There is a very strong correlation between schooling attainment and ethnicity, and between schooling attainment and poverty incidence. The indigenous population possesses considerably lower endowments of human capital. In Guatemala, for example, indigenous male workers average only 1.8 years of schooling.

This report documents that equalization of income-generating characteristics would boost the productivity of the indigenous population in their market and non-market activities and lead to a considerable reduction in inequality and poverty. This suggests that the socioeconomic condition of indigenous people can be improved since policy-influenced variables such as education are largely responsible for differences in observed earnings. This unrealized potential provides considerable hope for the future. The challenge that remains, however, is to devise the means by which to enhance the human capital endowments of the indigenous population and create the circumstances by which the indigenous population can derive the maximum benefit from their productivity-enhancing attributes according to their individual and collective predisposition.

Sri-Ram Aiyer
Director, Technical Department
Latin America and the Caribbean Region

Acknowledgments

We have benefitted from the comments and encouragement received from people who read earlier versions of our work and participated in meetings at the World Bank and conferences organized by the Comparative and International Education Society and the Canadian Economics Association. In particular, we thank Simon Brascoupé, Renee Dankerlin, David Hughart, Zafiris Tzannatos and Eduardo Velez for their helpful comments; Sandra Rosenhouse for her comments and for material that was incorporated into the Bolivia chapter; Haeduck Lee for preparing a background study; Johanna Coenen for contributing a background study, formatting and editing an earlier version of this document and providing useful feedback throughout the study's preparation; and Faraaz Siddiqi for his help in editing and formatting the final manuscript. This study could not have materialized without the guidance, comments and encouragement received from Shelton Davis. Financial support from the Bank's Research Committee is gratefully acknowledged.

Executive Summary

At a time when there is growing international interest in bringing indigenous people more into the development process, there is also a realization that apart from casual observation, little is known about their socioeconomic condition. Extensive research by anthropologists documents that indigenous people are among the poorest of the poor. But so far, economists have ignored this problem because of a lack of quality microdata that include information on the ethnic origins of individuals. What have been missing are the economic studies—other than a few country analyses—that investigate the depth and pervasiveness of the poverty and the reasons behind it.

In an effort to answer these questions, especially on a regional level, and to complement the rich body of anthropological research at hand, the present study uses economic methods in an attempt to document the socioeconomic situation of the estimated 34 million indigenous people in Latin America (8 percent of the region's population). The results confirm that indigenous people are a seriously disadvantaged group, and in areas such as education, even worse off than expected. But the results also show that policymakers can help indigenous people improve their situation by strengthening human capital. Policies to reduce the educational gaps between indigenous and non-indigenous persons could make a very large dent in earnings differentials and lead to a considerable decline in poverty among indigenous people.

Although definitions of indigenous people differ from country to country due to the use of different survey instruments, the study relies on three variables to identify the indigenous and non-indigenous populations: language spoken, self-perception and geographic concentration. For Bolivia and Peru, language is the defining characteristic. In Bolivia, it is possible to distinguish between monolingual and bilingual (Spanish and indigenous language) individuals, while in Peru, only monolingual indigenous or Spanish speakers can be isolated. For Guatemala, self-identification or self-perception is the key, whereas in Mexico, language and geographic concentration are used.

The results of this study show that most indigenous people in Latin America, as distinguished from the non-indigenous or Spanish-speaking population, live in conditions of extreme poverty. The major findings follow.

Principal Conclusions

Poverty among Latin America's indigenous population is pervasive and severe. In Bolivia, while more than half of the total population is impoverished, over two-thirds of the bilingual indigenous population and almost three-quarters of the monolingual indigenous population is poor.

The majority, 66 percent, of the population of Guatemala is poor, and 38 percent of all households are below the extreme poverty line. The indigenous population, however, is disproportionately poor; 87 percent of all indigenous households are below the poverty line and 61 percent are below the extreme poverty line.

In Mexico, the indigenous population density in a *municipio* strongly correlates with the incidence of poverty. In *municipios* where less than 10 percent of the population is indigenous, the poverty headcount index is 18 percent; in *municipios* that are 10 to 40 percent indigenous, 46 percent of the population is poor; and in *municipios* that are more than 70 percent indigenous, over 80 percent of the population is poor.

Most of the indigenous people of Peru are poor, at 79 percent, and more than half are extremely poor. In fact, indigenous people are one and a half times as likely to be poor than non-indigenous people, and almost three times as likely to be extremely poor. Consequently, indigenous people account for 11 percent of the sample population, yet they comprise 19 percent of poor and 27 percent of extremely poor Peruvians.

In Guatemala, the degree of income inequality among the combined indigenous and non-indigenous population in each region is greater than the estimated income inequality for separate groups. This proves that income inequality is clearly an interethnic problem.

The results of a statistical analysis of the determinants of poverty in Mexico indicate that a 1 percent increase in a *municipio's* indigenous population increases an individual's probability of being poor by approximately 0.5 percent. This variable has considerable impact given the potential range of indigenous population concentration, 0 to 100 percent. Living in a 50 percent indigenous *municipio* increases one's probability of being poor by a substantial 25 percent, marking a greater increase in the marginal probability of being poor than is possible with any other observed factor.

In a similar exercise for Bolivia, it is found that being indigenous increases the probability of being poor by 16 percent. The probability of poverty increases by almost 45 percent for household members whose household head is unemployed. This suggests that employment is a more important factor than being indigenous in reducing poverty. Among indigenous heads of household, participation in the labor force leads to a 40 percent reduction in the incidence of poverty.

Closely related to poverty status, the living conditions of the indigenous population are generally abysmal, especially when compared to those of the non-indigenous population. The Guatemala study reveals that the majority of the population does not have access to such public services as water, sanitation and electricity. Less than one-third of all indigenous households have water piped to their homes for their exclusive use, compared to almost half of non-indigenous households. The study also shows that approximately half of all indigenous households have no sanitary services, and three-fourths have no electricity.

There is a very strong correlation between schooling attainment and indigenous origins, and between schooling attainment and poverty category. In Bolivia, the schooling levels of indigenous people are approximately three years less, on average, than for non-indigenous individuals. The difference is even greater for indigenous females, suggesting that they are the most disadvantaged in Bolivian society. In Guatemala, the majority of indigenous people have no formal education, and of those who do, the majority have only a primary education. On average, indigenous people have only 1.3 years of schooling and only 40 percent are literate.

Each country analysis reveals that parents' skills and educational attainment are reflected in the schooling and other human capital characteristics of their children. For example, 9 percent of non-indigenous children and 21 percent of indigenous children are reported as being employed. The children of indigenous origins are born with many socioeconomic disadvantages and are unable to keep up with their non-indigenous peers. Indigenous children are more likely to repeat grades at the primary level and to drop out of school altogether.

Much of the earnings disadvantage of indigenous workers is due to lower human capital endowments. While the returns to schooling are lower for the indigenous population, an increase in schooling attainment would lead to a significant increase in earnings in most countries. The relative magnitude, however, differs from country to country. In Bolivia, non-indigenous men experience higher returns than indigenous men, and the average schooling attainment for the indigenous male labor force is about seven years. In Guatemala, the returns to schooling are 14.5 percent for non-indigenous male workers versus 9.1 percent for indigenous male workers, who average only 1.8 years of schooling. In Mexico there is very little difference in the returns to schooling for individuals in more or less indigenous *municipios*, the rate being about 9 percent. Workers in less indigenous *municipios* average 7.3 years of schooling, while workers in more indigenous *municipios* average only 3.8 years of schooling. Estimates of earnings functions in Peru show that the average returns to schooling for Spanish-speaking workers are three times those of indigenous workers. Since higher levels of education provide higher earnings, obtaining some level of university education is the most significant factor leading to increased earnings for indigenous men in Peru.

A greater percentage of all indigenous persons participate in the labor force compared with their non-indigenous counterparts, and a higher percentage of the indigenous population in the labor force is employed. A bilingual indigenous individual in Bolivia is more likely to have a second job and work more hours than a non-indigenous person. Yet bilingual indigenous workers earn, on average, less than two-thirds the salary of non-indigenous persons. Therefore, a high proportion of the indigenous poor are "working poor."

In Guatemala, 68 percent of indigenous workers are earning the majority of their income from agriculture (as compared to 35 percent of non-indigenous workers)—and wages in agriculture are lower than in any other sector. Overall, indigenous workers earn only 55 percent of non-indigenous earnings. Both the indigenous and non-indigenous workforces in Guatemala are composed primarily of males; indigenous workers are more likely than non-indigenous workers to be self-employed. In Peru, the agricultural sector depends heavily upon the labor of indigenous people: 65 percent of indigenous female workers and 58 percent of indigenous male workers are involved in agricultural activities. Yet, on average, total labor market earnings of indigenous women and men are only one-third the earnings of non-indigenous workers employed in agriculture.

In Bolivia, approximately one-half of the indigenous population is self-employed, while the majority of non-indigenous individuals work as employees. Poorer individuals are more likely to be self-employed and less likely to be employees or business owners. Approximately 40 percent of both bilingual indigenous and monolingual Spanish-speaking employees work in the public sector, while the remaining 60 percent work in the private sector. Monolingual indigenous people, however, are far more likely to work in the private sector. Also, public sector employees are less likely to fall below the poverty line than private sector employees.

Indigenous people have less education than non-indigenous people. Equalizing education levels would result in a considerable increase in relative earnings. The issue addressed in this study is whether the equalization of human capital and other productive characteristics would result in the virtual elimination of economic inequalities based on indigenous origins, or whether the support of affirmative action programs would have the desired effect of nullifying those inequalities. Differential outcomes, of course, may be due to outright discrimination. Discrimination against indigenous people may work to deleteriously affect their access to schooling, the quality of schooling they receive and their labor market performance.

The statistical decomposition of earnings differentials between indigenous and non-indigenous workers produces mixed, but promising, results. In Bolivia, for example, the portion of the overall earnings differential due to disparities in the productive characteristics of indigenous and non-indigenous working males is 72 percent. In other words, based on observed characteristics, the earnings differential between indigenous and non-indigenous working males would narrow by 72 percent if each group were endowed with the same income-generating characteristics. A considerable proportion of the earnings differential would decrease if indigenous workers' schooling and other human capital variables were increased.

The remaining 28 percent difference in earnings is "unexplained," and reflects both measurement error and unaccounted factors such as disparities in ability, quality of education, labor force participation, culture and labor market discrimination. Therefore, discrimination could only account for 28 percent of the overall earnings differential between indigenous and non-indigenous workers in the urban Bolivian labor market. In Guatemala, however, about half of all the overall earnings differential between indigenous and non-indigenous workers is unaccounted for by productive characteristics. Therefore, up to 50 percent of the overall differential could be due to discrimination against the indigenous working population. For both Mexico and Peru, the proportion of the overall earnings differential that is due to the productive characteristics of individuals is 50 percent.

There is, fortunately, an unrealized potential; this is evident, for example, in the case of Bolivia, where the educational level of the population has been increasing rapidly over the last few decades. The average educational level of indigenous males has increased continuously over time, with a sharp rise for individuals born in 1959 and later. For indigenous women, the increase is even more dramatic, particularly for the post-1952 Revolution population. The statistical results show that by equalizing human capital characteristics, much of the earnings differential between indigenous and non-indigenous workers would disappear. This provides considerable hope for the future. The question that remains, however, is how to improve the productive capabilities of the indigenous population. One obvious solution is to raise the educational level.

Knowledge of the indigenous population can aid in determining the location of new schools, targeting those with poor performance and—if appropriate and in demand—providing bilingual education. The apparent strong influence of education to ameliorate poverty and increase earnings, especially in indigenous areas, conveys a need to focus on improving access to education as an important development issue with significant and beneficial long-term socioeconomic gains. One of several frequently noted methods of improving access to education among the indigenous population is the implementation of bilingual education.

The involvement of indigenous people can aid in the improvement of the design and implementation of development projects. First, agreement on what must be done should be reached between the interested parties. It is necessary to decide on the goal of the intervention from the outset. Is it reform? And if so, what is meant by reform? In the case of indigenous people, is the goal assimilation, integration and the erasure of indigenous culture? Or the preservation of indigenous culture through policies designed with the participation of indigenous people? In the case of education, the lack of meaningful participation by indigenous people could result in severe loss of native culture and language.

Institutional issues associated with the functioning of labor markets are also important considerations. To some extent, indigenous people receive lower earnings and have a higher incidence of poverty because they are locked into the secondary sector of the economy. This information can aid in the creation of appropriate employment generation schemes. While many poor and non-poor workers may be located in the informal sector of the economy, the location of the indigenous poor in this sector is especially important. This information points to an appropriate sector to target in any poverty reduction strategy.

The health problems of indigenous groups are severe. More detailed knowledge about indigenous populations can aid in the design of health interventions in the region. In Bolivia, indigenous people are more likely to have been sick or injured in the previous month than are non-indigenous people. There is a greater tendency for an indigenous individual to have a disability that is sufficiently severe to keep them out of work for more than a week. Furthermore, indigenous persons are less likely to seek medical help for their ailments.

In Peru, indigenous people are more likely to become ill than non-indigenous people, but they are much less likely to consult a physician. Perhaps as a result of poor initial health, or as a result of neglecting treatment, the duration and severity of illness are greater among the indigenous population. The proportion of indigenous people hospitalized is almost twice that of the Spanish-speaking population. Although the average cost of both hospitalization and medicine is less for indigenous people, only 57 percent of them purchase medicine for their illness, as compared to 81 percent of the non-indigenous population.

Access to medical care for pregnant women is essential for the preservation of the mother's life and the healthy development of the child. In Bolivia, indigenous women are in a substantially inferior position with regard to comprehensive maternal care. Surprisingly, while the poor are less likely to receive professional attention at birth in a medical establishment, effectively targeted programs through public clinics have actually led to higher provision rates for certain preventive health care procedures—such as tetanus vaccination—for poor women than for non-poor women.

A very important finding is that education has the strongest effect in reducing fertility levels in urban Bolivia. More importantly, ethnicity and household income levels are not significantly associated with fertility once education is controlled for. This implies that fertility behavior is not an insurmountable cultural datum but rather is susceptible to change through policy-based interventions such as increased access to education.

The findings presented in this study suggest that if policymakers concentrate on equalizing the human capital characteristics—that is, ensuring that indigenous people can obtain better schooling, training and health services—much of the income differential between indigenous and non-indigenous people would disappear. This, in turn, would help alleviate poverty among a large segment of the Latin American population.

Future Research

The priority for future work in the area of ethnicity and socioeconomic conditions should be a link between empirical and qualitative work. There is a lack of empirical studies regarding the socioeconomic conditions of Latin America's indigenous population. Important issues to be addressed include defining the target population, solving the problem of scarce data and designing appropriate research methodologies.

To identify the reference population in this study, it was necessary to make do with surveys that provide single indicators. However, what are truly needed are multiple indicators—as used in the United States and Canada censuses. The whole range of indicators is necessary, including language, self-identification or self-perception, geographic location or concentration, ancestry and, possibly, dress (as in the Guatemala 1993 census).

Better data are needed so that in the future researchers can undertake more in-depth analyses and include a larger number of countries. In addition, longitudinal research should be conducted; that is, an attempt should be made to answer certain questions. "What was the level of discrimination 10, 20 and 30 years ago?" "What will it be 5, 10, 15 years from now?" "What were the effects of past policies and programs?" "What will be the effects of present policies and programs?"

A future research project on indigenous people should combine the quantitative approach taken here with qualitative analysis, such as the participatory-observation research approach (or participatory poverty assessment). The idea is to combine comprehensive empirical work with fieldwork and micro-survey techniques. For example, if it is found that indigenous people in the cities of Bolivia are working as self-employed individuals who earn less than non-indigenous individuals with the same level of education, then in-depth interviews with these groups of individuals should be conducted to ascertain the reasons for the income discrepancy. Without this qualitative data, probable reasons for the discrepancy, including race, access to training, and cultural values, are merely speculative. Such sophisticated differences are difficult to assess using only empirical analysis, generally based upon less than perfect data sets.

Many indigenous groups living in urban areas maintain ties with the rural communities to their mutual advantage. Resources are constantly exchanged between town and country. This transfer of resources is important and not always adequately captured in household survey data. The complex social networks can only be examined with a qualitative research approach. An examination of informal safety nets can be accommodated through a participatory research exercise.

1

Introduction

George Psacharopoulos and Harry Anthony Patrinos

The indigenous people of Latin America live in conditions of extreme poverty. While this may be common knowledge, this study represents an initial attempt at documenting the socioeconomic conditions of indigenous people using empirical data from national survey sources. Standard economic techniques are applied, while taking into account the important cultural and behavioral differences across ethnolinguistic groups.

Study Objective

It is well known that indigenous people worldwide are in an inferior economic and social position vis-à-vis the non-indigenous, or "mainstream," population. Yet not much documentation exists regarding their exact position. Concerning Latin America, obtaining reliable indigenous population estimates is difficult (but see below) and reliable poverty indicators almost impossible. Such documentation would provide the vital information needed to assist in designing poverty reduction strategies.

If ethnicity is intimately associated with poverty and disadvantage in many developing countries, then an important challenge is to understand how, by how much and under what circumstances (Klitgaard 1991: 200; Birdsall and Sabot 1991). Furthermore, this must be considered in light of the possibility that ethnic inequalities are affected by public policies regarding education, employment, infrastructure, markets and affirmative action. In this study, the focus is primarily on this challenge. The goals are:

1. To determine the extent of poverty among Latin America's indigenous population;
2. To compare the living conditions of the indigenous population with the non-indigenous population;

3. To examine differences in educational and occupational attainment between the indigenous and non-indigenous populations;
4. To estimate what part of the difference between indigenous and non-indigenous workers' earnings cannot be explained by differences in their respective productive characteristics; and
5. To review the findings with the aim of developing policy suggestions that can contribute to the alleviation of poverty while taking into account the indigenous dimension and suggesting areas for further research.

Previous work in the area of indigenous people in Latin America and the Caribbean has concentrated on issues related to land rights, tenure and the environment (Wali and Davis 1992; Davis 1993; Hicks et al. 1990). In contrast, the aim of the present study is to empirically investigate the socioeconomic conditions of the indigenous people of the Americas and to identify the correlates of poverty. The work that has been carried out in this area to date suggests the need for more in-depth analyses of the living conditions of indigenous people in Latin America. In addition, hypotheses regarding the position of indigenous people in the Americas will be tested. The specific areas of investigation are enumerated below.

The study's ultimate purpose is to assist in the design of poverty alleviation activities in Latin America and the Caribbean. The results can feed into country poverty assessments and can aid in the creation of employment generation schemes. Much can be learned from the empirical examination of interethnic education and income differences, the results of which can be used by policymakers. In the area of health, the project contributes to our knowledge of fertility issues, infant mortality and demographic change. In the area of education, the results of the analysis can aid in the planning of school construction by helping to determine where to target indigenous populations, and to what extent. Targeting activities could also be improved by knowing more about the schooling performance of indigenous children, including age-grade progress, repetition and dropout rates.

The Problem

Latin America's indigenous peoples are descended from the hundreds of Amerindian ethnic groups that lived throughout the hemisphere before the Spanish conquest. Indigenous people are ethnically, culturally or socially distinct from the politically dominant society. Although the Latin American ethnic spectrum is very diverse, this study—by necessity—for the most part categorizes the region's population into two broad groups: indigenous and non-indigenous. These two groups do not represent homogenous communities; both include a variety of cultures, identities, languages, traditions, faiths and beliefs. Furthermore, some indigenous communities are better off than others, and some are more integrated than others.

A study of the socioeconomic conditions of indigenous people is an auspicious development. The General Assembly of the United Nations declared 1993 as

International Year of the World's Indigenous People. Multilateral development institutions have begun to focus on indigenous people. The Inter-American Development Bank has established an Indigenous Peoples Fund to support the self-development processes of indigenous peoples, communities and organizations of Latin America. The World Bank recently formulated a policy towards indigenous people, becoming the first multilateral organization to do so. The first international organization to begin examining issues related to indigenous people is the International Labour Organisation (ILO), which commissioned a series of studies on indigenous workers in 1921 (Cycon 1991: 781). The ILO published the first compendium surveying indigenous populations throughout the world and summarizing various national and international actions in support of indigenous people (ILO 1949, 1953), and, in 1953, established the Andean Programme, designed to contribute to improving the living conditions of the indigenous populations of Bolivia, Peru and Ecuador (and subsequently those of Colombia, Chile and Argentina), with a view of integrating them into their respective national communities (Rens 1961, 1963).

The socioeconomic situation of North America's indigenous people is described as being similar to that of less developed countries, but "distilled, concentrated, raised to a power" (Hagen 1962: 471). If this is true, then the abysmal situation of indigenous people in less developed countries must be raised to an even greater power. In many countries, due to a variety of factors, including language, lack of provision of social services, geographic location and discrimination, being an indigenous person is associated with, among other things, extreme poverty and illiteracy (see, for example, Kelley 1988; Stephen and Wearne 1984; del Aguila 1987). This is especially the case in rural, isolated areas (IFAD 1992). Sources indicate that indigenous people worldwide have less schooling and are concentrated in lower-paying jobs with fewer opportunities for advancement as compared to non-indigenous people. Moreover, indigenous people are much less likely to be employed in the public sector, often excluded on the basis of their lack of education. In the United States, the secondary school dropout rate of indigenous people is twice the national average, while in Guatemala illiteracy among the rural indigenous population is estimated at over 80 percent (Waggoner 1991; del Aguila 1987; Burger 1987).

A recent UNICEF report, *Children of the Americas* (1992), states that to a large extent indigenous children suffer the consequences of discrimination against their parents. Many die from lack of clean water, food or health care. In some Bolivian communities, one in three dies in childhood. The lives of the survivors are often difficult, with few chances to study in their native language and/or be supported by their native traditions. Indigenous people suffer from high rates of maternal and child mortality, while the children experience high dropout rates and an alarmingly high incidence of malnutrition. The report goes on to say that governments often press for the assimilation of indigenous people on the grounds that their cultural differences impede their development. Modernization, however, often fails to create a better life. Indigenous people are forced to give up their language, along with their knowledge of botany and ecology, and receive nothing in return (UNICEF 1992: 38).

The western model of development views traditional cultures as poor, so that efforts stemming from this archetype are directed at improving the standard of living (Brascoupé 1992; Bodley 1990). This is based on the ideology that all cultures must achieve a certain level of material acquisition in order to be developed. There is the belief that tribal cultures are unable to satisfy the material needs of their people. Some argue that all people share a desire for what is defined as material wealth, prosperity and progress. Others, it is believed, have different cultures only because they have not yet been exposed to the superior technological alternatives offered by industrial civilization.

The problem with this reasoning is that the materialistic values of industrial civilization are not cultural universals. Indigenous populations *are* different, and taking this into account means not imposing non-indigenous values. It is possible to learn from indigenous people in areas such as the environment and sustainable development, as is suggested in the report of the World Commission on Environment and Development (1987), *Our Common Future* (the Brundtland Report). Any attempt to improve the conditions of indigenous populations must be grounded in their own traditional customs and expertise.

There are also many examples of indigenous people taking control of and using technology to benefit their communities in accordance with their cultural preferences. For example, the Cree of Canada own and operate an airline company; the Aborigines of Australia broadcast television programs in their language; the Blackfoot Indians of the United States established the first indigenous financial institution; the Cordillera people of the Philippines are managing their own development projects; and the Shuar people have produced educational radio programs since 1972 in Amazonian Ecuador (Burger 1990: 148). Highly successful examples of self-managed indigenous craft production enterprises in Ecuador, Mexico and Panama prove that indigenous values are compatible with commercial success without assimilation or dependency on the mainstream culture (Stephen 1991).

In the next chapter a review of the relevant literature is presented. This includes the international literature on ethnicity and socioeconomic differences, followed by a review of the North American literature on the socioeconomic characteristics of indigenous people. A brief review of the empirical work on indigenous populations of Australia and New Zealand is included because of its quality and relevance. The review is completed with an overview of the Latin American literature on indigenous people. Chapter 3 presents an overview of the number and conditions of the indigenous people of Latin America using census and other published sources. Chapter 4 presents the methodology that is applied in the empirical work, a description of the data that are analyzed, the definitions used, the areas of analyses, and the hypotheses tested. Chapters 5 through 8 present the results of the empirical analysis of household surveys as country case studies, covering Bolivia, Guatemala, Mexico and Peru. The conclusion, Chapter 9, summarizes the findings, discusses the lessons learned from the analysis and presents a series of priority research issues for the future.

2

The Costs of Ethnicity:
An International Review

Harry Anthony Patrinos

In many countries there exist diverse ethnic groups with very different levels of educational and economic opportunities. The ethnic concentration of poverty has been increasingly recognized in the development literature (see, for example, Klitgaard 1991). The relationship between ethnicity and economic inequality in developing countries has come to the fore in recent years (see, for example, Birdsall and Sabot 1991). Empirical analyses of ethnic earnings differentials concentrated in the past on black-white differences in the United States. Some researchers have examined the experiences of other ethnic groups, but much less research has been undertaken regarding ethnic groups in developing countries. Very little investigation has been made into the different economic experiences of the indigenous population within a society, but as shall be seen in the brief review that follows, the body of this particular literature is growing. In many countries of the world, there is a "cost" to being an ethnic or racial minority; for the few countries where the situation of the indigenous population has been investigated, a substantial cost in terms of earnings, poverty and social development has been estimated. It is thus very important to consider ethnicity in discussions about economic development.

A Global Perspective

The empirical investigation of black/white economic differences began in the early 1960s. Siegel (1965) estimates the "cost" of being black in the United States. Although much of the earnings differential is due to occupation, quality of education and educational attainment, equalization of such characteristics would not lead to equality of earnings. After controlling for productivity-enhancing characteristics, about two-fifths of the difference in average earnings of whites and blacks is the "cost" of being black in the United States. Smith and Welch

(1977) present evidence to show that black-white earnings differentials are narrowing over time and that parity will eventually occur. Gains are being made, particularly by the young and educated new entrants to the labor market. The authors find that increased schooling is a major cause of equality of earnings, thus lending support to human capital theory. Furthermore, Smith (1984) presents evidence to show that as the human capital of blacks increases relative to that of white workers, so do their relative earnings. While the existence of discrimination in the labor market is not denied, it generally occurs early in the individual's career. Smith (1984) lends support to Becker's (1971) original hypothesis that ethnic wage differences are a short-run, disequilibrium phenomenon.

This explanation, however, is criticized for its inability to account for enduring differences in earnings between whites and non-whites. Darity (1982) reviews the main economic theories purporting to explain ethnic differences in earnings and concludes that they are inadequate. The main assumption of such theories, that differences in income are due to the lower productivity of non-whites, is questioned. Evidence shows that non-whites with similar characteristics and measures of "productivity" do not receive equal wages with whites (Darity 1982).

More recently, researchers document a widening in black-white earnings and employment gaps among young men in the United States, covering the period from the mid-1970s through the 1980s. The earnings gaps increased most among college graduates. The reasons for this include demand shifts, falling real minimum wages, the deunionization of the labor force, the growing supply of black graduates and increased crime among high school dropouts (Bound and Freeman 1992). The proportion of individual black wage earners receiving more than $35,000 fell by 22 percent during the 1980s. There has been an increase in the number of blacks in poverty, as well as an increase in poverty incidence among employed blacks. This is also true for those with four or more years of college. The growth in low-wage employment for blacks is most pronounced for men between the ages of 25 and 34 (Harrison and Gorham 1992). In an examination of different ethnic groups, including Hispanics, Amerindians, Asians and different white ethnic groups, Farley (1990) finds that blacks are the most disadvantaged group in terms of earnings, education and, through decomposition of differences, returns to characteristics. Of the sample, only Amerindians, Vietnamese (mostly foreign-born), and Puerto Ricans approximated blacks' disadvantaged state.

Other researchers examine the economic inequality between whites and other ethnic groups in the United States. Hirschman and Wong (1984) find that education explains much of the difference in earnings between whites and Hispanics. Equality in years of schooling between these groups would not totally eliminate the gap, but this variable has the strongest impact on inequality compared to every other variable analyzed. Wong (1982) studies the "cost" of being Asian in the United States and finds substantial inequality when examining such factors as generational status, educational attainment and occupational status. Japanese and Filipino Americans have reached earnings parity with whites given equal rates of education and other personal characteristics. Still, the "cost" of being Asian remains substantial; for example, the individual Chinese-American male cannot expect to earn as much as an Anglo male with the same generational status, years of schooling completed and general level of experience (Wong 1982: 76).

Reimers (1983) examines the earnings differential between white, black and Hispanic men. She finds that much of the difference between whites and Puerto Ricans, blacks, Central and South Americans and other Hispanic men is overwhelmingly due to discrimination, while much of the differential between whites and Mexican American and Cuban men is not due to discrimination.

Ethnicity and socioeconomic differences in other countries have also been examined. Knight and Sabot (1982) investigate earnings differentials by ethnicity and gender in Tanzania. Decomposition analysis reveals that the gross ethnic earnings differentials are mainly the result of wage and job discrimination (see also Armitage and Sabot 1991).

Race and inequality over a long time period (1914–1976) in Kenya is the subject of an analysis by Bigsten (1988). This paper documents how the Africans' share of national income evolved over time, whereby it increased as discrimination against them declined. Decomposition analyses show that the share of inequality due to inequality between ethnic groups peaked in 1936, and then gradually fell.

Evidence of decreased discrimination against blacks and other non-white groups in South Africa has been estimated over time. Moll (1992) estimates earnings functions for whites and "colored" individuals using data for 1970 and 1980, and decomposes the gross earnings differential into "explained" and "unexplained" components. He also estimates the effect of job discrimination—the relative representation of different ethnic groups in particular jobs. A decrease in discrimination is detected over time, benefitting in particular the younger cohort of workers. Lachman and Berenson (1992) examine the interracial distribution of income and find that income inequality in South Africa is overwhelmingly the result of income differentials between the races.

Discrimination against blacks (Africans) in South Africa has also been investigated in more macro terms. Lundahl (1992) argues that racial segregation in South Africa led to a skill bottleneck in the manufacturing sector that acted as a brake to further expansion of the economy. The skill bottleneck was produced as a result of the fact that too many skilled jobs were reserved for whites and that the education system prevented the majority of the population from competing for the higher-level positions.

Caste discrimination in the labor market in India has been empirically examined (Banerjee and Knight 1985; Bhattacherjee 1985; Dhesi and Singh 1989). Banerjee and Knight (1985) decompose the gross wage difference between "scheduled" and "non-scheduled" castes into its "explained" and wage and job discrimination components. They find that discrimination exists, and that it operates through job assignment with the scheduled castes entering poorly paid, "dead-end" jobs.

The demographic and socioeconomic composition of China's ethnic minorities is described in Poston and Shu (1987). Ethnic minorities compose about 7 percent of the total population. While most groups are assimilated into mainstream Han-dominated society, there is still a lack of socioeconomic advancement in a few cases.

Several evaluations of the socioeconomic effects of Malaysia's New Economic Policy (NEP), designed in the 1970s to overcome the disadvantages of the largest ethnic group, the *bumiputra*, appear in the literature (see, for example, Klitgaard and Katz 1983; Hirschman 1983). Reverse discrimination in higher education, as part of a policy to promote the interests of the *bumiputra* against the Chinese and the Indians has also been examined. Tzannatos (1991) finds that such policies have not reduced inequality and that the poor have been hurt in the process. Concerning the primary and secondary level, however, a recent study by Hammer, Cercone and Nabi (1992) demonstrates that public education expenditures have been progressive during the two decades of the NEP. The study shows that Malay children attend school at significantly higher rates than Chinese, Indians and other races. In a seminal work on poverty in Malaysia, Anand finds that the bulk of poverty is not due to ethnicity, but that about 90 percent of the inequality in Malaysia is due to the very large discrepancies in income within each racial group (Anand 1977).

Ethnic inequalities also exist in Japan. The educational and socioeconomic disadvantages of Japan's minority populations have been examined. This includes both the *burakumin* minority and the *Ainu*, the latter being the indigenous population of Japan (Shimahara 1984; Hawkins 1983). The *Ainu* suffer from a large living standards gap between them and the rest of the population. For example, among the *Ainu*, almost 7 percent are dependent on welfare payments, which is much higher than the rate for the rest of the population at only 1 percent (Takaaki 1987: 147).

Semyonov (1986) decomposes the socioeconomic gaps between noncitizen Arab workers and Israeli citizens employed in Israel. While age and education can explain much of the Arabs' segregation at the bottom of the occupational ladder, these factors cannot fully explain their lower earnings.

For Brazil, wage differences between white and non-white males remain after controlling for education and estimated experience (Webster and Dwyer 1988). In fact, the income gap between the two groups widens with increased schooling. Silva (1985) estimates a significant cost to being non-white irrespective of being mulatto or black; non-whites are equally discriminated against in Brazil relative to whites.

The growing international literature on ethnic and racial socioeconomic differences confirms what has been established in studies on the United States: ethnicity and race matter. Ethnic and racial minority groups in countries in all regions of the world have very different levels of educational and economic opportunities. In many cases, there is an ethnic (or racial) concentration of poverty. Empirical analyses of these socioeconomic differentials are increasingly being conducted in countries around the world.

Indigenous People of North America

By far the greatest attention paid to the socioeconomic disadvantages of indigenous people has been by sociologists and economists exploring the situation of

Amerindians in the United States (see Gwartney and Long 1978; Trosper 1980; Sandefur and Scott 1983; Sandefur 1986; Sandefur and Sakamoto 1988; Snipp and Sandefur 1988a; Chiswick 1988; Snipp 1988; Sandefur et al. 1989; Sandefur and Pahari 1989). Still, there is little empirical research on the inequalities between indigenous and non-indigenous people in the United States and Canada. Consequently, little is known about indigenous people's socioeconomic conditions and the policy responses necessary to improve the relative status of indigenous people in the labor market. The available studies reviewed here suggest that both labor market discrimination and lower levels of human capital endowments are responsible for the observed differentials. The experiences of indigenous people in the United States and Canada, however, point to divergent policy responses vis-à-vis the roles of investment in human capital and other actions.

There are a number of differences in economic behavior between indigenous and non-indigenous people, many of which are not easily grasped or observed. This is evident when trying to analyze important economic events such as "unemployment." The problem of measuring unemployment among indigenous people is discussed by Kleinfeld and Kruse (1982), who argue that standard measures of unemployment do not adequately take into account the job search activities of Native Americans. Many indigenous people in the United States do not actively look for work because they know it is not available. Many voluntarily drop out of the labor market for community and family obligations. To take these and other factors into account, the United States Bureau of Indian Affairs claims that all adults without a wage job are unemployed, thus providing estimates of unemployment rates varying between 50 and 80 percent. These are, however, overestimates; a true measure of unemployment among indigenous people can only be ascertained through surveys specially designed to uncover the reasons for not working or not looking for work. Most labor force surveys do not usually ask indigenous people if they prefer intermittent participation in the wage economy, and many indigenous people will not openly state that they prefer this for fear of being classified as not wanting work. Nevertheless, statistics on the intermittent worker effect are required. Kleinfeld and Kruse (1982) present the results of studies designed to properly estimate indigenous unemployment.

Snipp and Sandefur (1988a) examine the effects of residence in metropolitan areas on the earnings of Amerindians and Alaskan Native householders. The results indicate that the earnings of metropolitan Amerindians are markedly higher than those of nonmetropolitan Amerindians, but that the earnings of nonmetropolitan-to-metropolitan migrants are not much higher than those of nonmetropolitan stayers. The difference in earnings between metropolitan and nonmetropolitan Amerindians is due to better opportunities in metropolitan areas and to the interaction between these opportunities and the higher levels of human capital of metropolitan Amerindians (see also Sandefur 1986). Urban residents earn more than rural residents, but the urban advantage is less than many policymakers believe, and the short-term benefits are found to be insignificant (Snipp and Sandefur 1988b). Sandefur and Jeon (1991) examine the rate of interstate migration of Amerindians and other minority groups in the United States over time (1960–

1980) to test whether they are converging with the rates of migration of whites. They find some support for convergence, which is consistent with the view that members of minority groups are gaining access to national labor markets.

Sandefur and Sakamoto (1988) find that differences in household size are important in explaining Amerindian/non-Amerindian differences in income. Among female-headed households, household size accounts for more of the black-white income difference than the Amerindian-white difference. Parental education is more important than family structure in accounting for differences in schooling among whites and Amerindians (Sandefur et al. 1989). The same study finds that family structure and parental education are equally important in accounting for differences between whites and blacks. Amerindians living in traditional areas and on reservations are more likely to be poor than Amerindians living in other areas; the greatest improvement has occurred among those outside traditional areas (Sandefur and Pahari 1989: 209).

Numerous of studies have been published on the determinants of indigenous workers' earnings and differences with the white population of the United States. In their analysis, Gwartney and Long (1978) examine Amerindian/white earnings differences for 1959 and 1969. In 1959, Amerindian earnings as a portion of white earnings were 0.67. A decomposition of earnings differentials finds that personal characteristics explain 57 percent of the gross earnings differential; the residual 43 percent is "unexplained." This is not too different from the situation prevailing in 1969, when the overall earnings differential was 0.68, and the portion due to personal characteristics was 58.3 percent, 41.7 percent remaining "unexplained." This lack of improvement occurred despite an increase in the educational characteristics of Amerindians over the decade. Trosper (1980) finds that the returns to education that Amerindians receive are lower than those for whites and that differences in characteristics explain about half the average difference in earnings between whites and Amerindians. Chiswick (1988) also examines the returns to schooling and the schooling attainment of Amerindians in the United States, along with other ethnic/racial groups, using data for the 1970s. In general, those ethnic groups with low levels of schooling attainment also experience low returns to schooling; indigenous people have among the lowest schooling attainment levels and returns to schooling.

In contrast, Sandefur and Scott (1983) find that Amerindians receive more favorable returns to human capital variables than whites. However, Amerindians have fewer of these variables, suggesting that discrimination occurs at an earlier point in their lives. Still, according to the authors, much of the earnings differential between Amerindians and whites would disappear if Amerindians had the same human capital, regional and job characteristics as whites. In fact, about 75 percent of the difference in earnings between Amerindians and whites in the United States in 1976 was due to personal characteristics (Sandefur and Scott 1983: 63). A relatively very small portion of the observed gross differential was due to what can be classified as discrimination in the labor market.

More recently, improvements in educational attainment have a significant impact on the reduction of the Amerindian earnings disadvantage. The percentage increase in earnings that would result if the educational characteristics of Amerindians were equal to those of white men are as follows: in 1959, 20 percent; in 1969, 15.7 percent; and in 1979, 7.7 percent (Sandefur and Pahari 1989: 214). The percentage increase in earnings that would result if the characteristics of Amerindian men received the same "returns" as those of white men are calculated to be: in 1959, 45.1 percent; in 1969, 35.8 percent; and in 1979, 13.4 percent (Sandefur and Pahari 1989: 215). The results appear to suggest that the reduction in earnings inequality from 1959 to 1979 was due to the decline in the negative effect of being Amerindian on the earnings structure over time in the United States. In a study using the 1980 United States census, Snipp (1988) finds that *all* of the indigenous/ non-indigenous earnings differential is explained by productivity characteristics.

There is little research on indigenous people's earnings in Canada, although concern over educational and earnings disparities is strong. The gross earnings differential between Aboriginals and non-Aboriginals in Canada is large (Hull 1987: 128–129; Armstrong et al. 1990) and occupational segregation, whereby the indigenous working population is concentrated in low-skill, low-wage occupations, exists (Lautard 1982). Evidence of a positive correlation between years of schooling and *reserve* (official indigenous community settlement) per capita income is reported for the 1960s (Hawthorn 1967: 103; but see Deprez 1973 for a discussion).

While little research has been published on the effects of education and other productivity-enhancing characteristics on the Aboriginal earnings structure, the existing literature shows that human capital attributes have a sizable effect on indigenous people's earnings structure. Clatworthy (1981a) finds that education has a positive effect on Aboriginal labor force participation. Education is highly correlated with occupational status attainment, but the effect is large only for individuals completing 11 or more years of schooling. Evidence also shows that post-secondary schooling leads to higher earnings (Clatworthy 1981a: 24). Education has an especially strong positive effect on Aboriginal female labor force participation rates (Clatworthy 1981b). Evidence suggests the existence of the "dual labor market" and labor market segmentation (Clatworthy 1981a, 1981c). Gerber (1990) documents the low educational attainment of indigenous females in Canada in a study of gender and ethnic differences.

Researchers have presented results from their studies of northern Canadian labor markets (Stabler 1989, 1990; Kuo 1976). Stabler (1989) attempts to determine the extent to which native people in the Northwest Territories continue to participate in the traditional sector and to ascertain whether there is a queue in which people wait for a job in the modern economy. Utilizing the dual labor market methodology, the author finds that for many indigenous people, participation in traditional pursuits is a way of keeping occupied while waiting in the queue for a job in the modern economy. The degree of discrimination against indigenous people in the primary sector is high. For native people, however, increased levels of education lead to considerable reductions in discrimination.

In the first study of its kind for Aboriginal people in Canada—albeit for a remote northern area of Canada's territories—Kuo (1976) uses 1970 data to estimate the effect of education on Aboriginal earnings. At that time, Aboriginal earnings ranged from 16 to 46 percent of white workers' earnings and the schooling level of the Aboriginal population ranged from 2 to 6 years as compared with more than 9 years for the white working population. Kuo (1976) compares the results with white worker earnings in the area and finds that most of the earnings differential between whites and Aboriginal (Amerindian, Métis and Inuit) workers is due to education, age, duration of employment, size of the labor market and marital status. A mere 13 to 16 percent of the gross differential is due to "unexplained" factors.

In the first national study of the subject, Patrinos and Sakellariou (1992, 1993) use the 1986 Canadian Labour Market Activity Survey to decompose the earnings differential between Aboriginal and non-Aboriginal workers living off-*reserve* in Canada. At this time Aboriginal earnings were about 80 percent of non-Aboriginal workers' earnings and schooling differences were only 1 year, at 11.9 and 12.9 for Aboriginal and non-Aboriginal workers, respectively. When both full- and part-time workers are included in the analysis, the portion of the gross earnings differential due to productive characteristics is 17 percent (Patrinos and Sakellariou 1993). The remaining difference in wages, 83 percent, is unaccounted for and attributed to unmeasured factors such as discrimination. When the analysis is limited to full-time workers, the portion of this differential that is due to productive characteristics increases to 41 percent (Patrinos and Sakellariou 1992). Among the explanations offered for the large difference in explained earnings differentials between full-time and part-time employment is that Aboriginal people working part-time may be involved in low wage, low productivity, "dead-end" jobs (Patrinos and Sakellariou 1993). Also, those Aboriginals working part-time may be "target workers," or "traditional" persons who are in the labor force only as long as necessary to obtain a predetermined, fixed sum of wages (Patrinos and Sakellariou 1992, 1993).

This brief review of North American studies on indigenous/non-indigenous socioeconomic differences shows that discrimination, or the "unexplained" component, increases as the educational level of Aboriginal people increases in Canada, but that the same is not true in the case of Amerindians in the United States. In the United States, the evidence suggests that the effect of being indigenous is declining over time; also, the "unexplained" portion of the differential is relatively smaller. When recent results are compared to the Northwest Territories study conducted in the 1970s, discrimination in Canada appears to be increasing over time. The "unexplained" component of the earnings differential is larger for indigenous people in Canada than for indigenous people in the United States.

Indigenous People of New Zealand and Australia

Indigenous people in other countries of the world are also the topic of study. However, there is little empirical research on this subject. A notable exception is the research related to the Maoris of New Zealand and the Aborigines of Australia.

Empirical studies based on the Aboriginal populations of Australia and New Zealand are important and relevant as they offer insights into the experiences of indigenous people in the non-indigenous labor force.

Brosnan (1984) examines the earnings differential between the native population of New Zealand, the Maoris, and the non-native, white population. Age and education account for only a small part of the overall earnings differential (17 percent); the remainder is due to factors associated with being indigenous. Maoris receive lower returns to schooling investments and receive less schooling. Brosnan and Hill (1983) examine earnings differentials between Maori and non-Maori males and females, as well as occupational segregation. They confirm that Maoris receive lower earnings, although this differential varies significantly by occupation examined. Occupational segregation is a major factor explaining substantial earnings differentials between the Maori and non-Maori populations.

The economic situation of Australia's Aboriginal population is also examined (Miller 1989; Junankar and Kapuscinski 1991a; 1991b; Welch 1988). Differential rates of unemployment between Aboriginal and non-Aboriginal youth in the Australian labor market have been examined (Miller 1989) . The unemployment rates for Aboriginal youth are three times the average for non-Aboriginal youth (see also Junankar and Kapuscinski 1991a,b). Even after controlling for education, age and other factors—such as family status, children, location—the unemployment rate of Aboriginal youth is predicted to be about two and one-half times greater than that of other groups (Miller 1989: 48). Decomposition of the differential unemployment rates reveals that only a very small portion is due to differences in marketable skills between the two groups (Miller 1989: 50).

In a study of the earnings of Aboriginals using the 1976 census, Treadgold (1980) finds that per capita income is only about half that of the Australian population as a whole. Though the Aboriginal population is younger with more children, their mean income is less than two-thirds that of non-Aboriginals, even for those over 15 years of age. Also, a greater number of Aboriginals are unemployed or out of the labor force and face other occupational and educational disadvantages (Treadgold 1980).

Indigenous People of Latin America

There is little empirical analysis of the socioeconomic conditions of Latin America's indigenous people. This section makes use of the available literature on poverty, inequality and social indicators, as it relates to indigenous people.

Indigenous, ethnic and tribal populations make up a significant portion of the rural poor (IFAD 1992). These groups live on the periphery in marginal areas, and are often landless. In Latin America, indigenous people make up about 27 percent of the rural population (IFAD 1992: 49). A rural poverty mapping documents that in 11 of 18 cases (countries), the indigenous population is listed among the main groups of the rural poor (IFAD 1992: 98–102).

Prior to the revolution of 1944, indigenous migrant labor in Guatemala was recruited by a variety of coercive techniques including labor drafts (*mandamientos*), debt servitude and, after the abolition of debt servitude in 1936, restrictive vagrancy legislation (Swetnam 1989). While indigenous people no longer face such institutionalized forms of discrimination, their human capital disadvantages are severe, representing a considerable barrier to competing in the labor market on an equal basis with the non-indigenous population.

The functional and educational alienation of indigenous people is documented. The majority still use their languages and are unable to communicate in Spanish. For example, 70 percent of rural Bolivians communicate only in Quechua or Aymara (IFAD 1992). In rural Peru, where the majority of the population is indigenous, 70 percent of Quechua-speaking people over the age of 5 have never received any schooling, relative to only 40 percent of non-indigenous Peruvians (Hernandez 1988: 126). In Argentina, 56 percent of the Mapuche people have no schooling, while the same is true for only 7 percent of the non-indigenous population (Hernandez 1988: 125).

A study of the indigenous, education and earnings connection in Guatemala and Bolivia finds that those who are indigenous have much lower levels of schooling, receive lower earnings and experience lower rates of returns to schooling than do those who are non-indigenous (Psacharopoulos 1993). Kelley (1988) analyzes the "cost of being Indian" in rural Bolivia using a 1966 survey of about 1,000 male household heads. He decomposes the differential between indigenous and non-indigenous individuals in terms of education, occupation and income. With information on father's and son's education and occupation, Kelley concludes that the overall (between 95 and 100 percent) differential is due to "class" components (family background, education and occupation). In other words, equalizing the human capital and family backgrounds of individuals would result in virtual elimination of socioeconomic inequalities, based on indigenous origins.

The effect of being indigenous is controlled for in a study of education and earnings in Peru using census data for 1961 and 1972. Toledo (Carnoy 1979) finds that while the percentage of Quechua/Aymara speakers in the labor force fell, their relative income increased substantially. Results of log earnings functions for the two periods reveal a considerable decrease in the penalty associated with speaking a native language over time.

Still there is much unknown about the work activity of indigenous people, especially those residing in rural areas. The unpaid but productive activities of indigenous people living and working in rural communities in countries such as Peru and Guatemala are often misrepresented as unemployment or underemployment (Swetnam 1989; Brush 1977). Many peasants, such as those living in the highlands of Guatemala, are involved in a variety of activities that provide income and benefits, although these are not easily observed with aggregate household data (see Box 2.1). In the northern Peruvian Andes, peasants are involved in many tasks besides agricultural pursuits on a day-to-day basis. These include house building and maintenance, distributive activities of trade and exchange, craft production, firewood collection and community work projects (Brush 1977: 77).

Apparently idle peasants are in most cases heavily involved in many activities, but these are not easily categorized. This has led some observers to write about "disguised employment" (Swetnam 1980).

The children of indigenous parents are born with many socioeconomic disadvantages and are unable to keep up with their non-indigenous peers. In a study of child schooling performance in Guatemala and Bolivia, Patrinos and Psacharopoulos (1992) find that indigenous children are more likely to repeat grades at the primary level. Rojas (1991) reports that being non-white significantly affects educational attainment in Guatemala (see also Lourie 1982). A similar finding is reported in a study using Peruvian data (Patrinos and Psacharopoulos 1993). In fact, being rural and indigenous is the best predictor of grade repetition for Peruvian primary school students.

Box 2.1: Indigenous Education and the Environment

Research on the links between human capital and the environment concludes that schooling reduces tropical deforestation. Conventional estimates of the social rates of returns to rural schooling neglect these positive externalities, thus underestimating the benefits to rural indigenous people. Recent research on the Sumu Indians of Nicaragua illustrates the pathways by which schooling promotes conservation.

Sumus with a formal education and the ability to speak the language of the larger society have become the best brokers of their forest communities. Several development programs in the area grew out of the lobbying efforts of educated Sumus.

Education reduces rural indigenous people's dependence on the forest through three indirect channels: it increases the ability of foragers to leave the countryside; it improves the use of agricultural land through the adoption of new, and the better application of old, technologies; and it reduces family size.

Education assists Sumus in their efforts to obtain non-farm jobs. It provides them with the required credentials, increases their ability to obtain information about the job market, and it leverages their bargaining power by increasing their ability to speak Spanish. Education-induced migration helps forest conservation in the long run, but may produce short run damage to rural areas if either the remittance earnings or the increased wages of the remaining rural dwellers are used to purchase superior forest goods (timber and game) and/or invested to clear forest land for cattle grazing. However, with proper planning, the increased wealth can be invested without environmental ramifications.

Another important advantage of education, particularly for indigenous people, is realized in the farming sector. Numerous studies show education to benefit farmers. Not only does schooling produce cognitive skills which make it easier for farmers to seek, find and manage information about agricultural technologies, but it also helps farmers better manage their inputs, command higher prices for their products, pay lower prices for their inputs, and better cope with political and legal matters. In the long run, agricultural modernization helps forest conservation. For example, greater fertilizer use is found in nations with lower rates of deforestation. These findings are also verified with ethnographic evidence on the Sumu Indians.

The long run implications of education are positive and not exclusive to the labor market. As one Sumu reverend put it, "Education is for the future, not for the present."

Source: Godoy 1992.

The appalling state of indigenous people in terms of fertility and infant mortality rates is documented. Fertility levels of indigenous women tend to be higher than those of non-indigenous women for a number of reasons. Indigenous couples prefer a larger than average family size (Rosenhouse 1992). Although income disparities between indigenous and non-indigenous groups may account for part of this effect, anthropological studies have documented cultural differences regarding the value of children (Mondloch 1979). However, knowledge and use of modern contraceptive methods are substantially lower among the indigenous population than in either overall or rural populations (Rosenhouse 1992). This low contraceptive prevalence is correlated with low educational attainment, low access to medical attention at birth and high child mortality rates. Collins (1983) links reproductive decisions among highland Aymara people in Peru to economic, cultural and environmental factors. The Aymara typically seek a family size of five, with children spaced three years apart. Labor activities, including domestic work and childcare, are distributed across the entire family, with specific tasks assigned to children according to their age and birth order. Both parents are then free to focus on more productive endeavors. Fertility decisions thus balance the need for the labor input of children with a desire to mitigate the risk of raising more children than the productive capacity of the family can support.

In general, indigenous people have much higher mortality rates than the national averages in most countries. This is especially the case in countries where the indigenous population makes up a large proportion of the total population. In Peru, the national infant mortality rate is 169 per 1,000 live births, as compared to 269 per 1,000 live births for the indigenous population (Masferrer 1983: 600). The national under-5 mortality rate per 1,000 live births in Bolivia is 122 for Spanish language speakers, but 186 for indigenous language speakers (Institute for Resource Development 1989). In Guatemala, under-5 mortality per 1,000 live births is 120 for ladinos and 142 for indigenous people (Institute for Resource Development 1987).

Concerning health care services, indigenous people are faced with the problems of unequal access and the effects of discrimination (United Nations 1983). Unequal access is the result of three principal factors: the general isolation of many indigenous communities; widespread imbalances in the allocation of medical personnel and services which favor urban areas while most indigenous people live in rural areas; and the overall poverty of indigenous populations which limits their ability to pay for adequate services. In Guatemala, at the national level, there are 1.6 hospital beds for every 1,000 persons; there are only 0.4 hospital beds for every 1,000 indigenous persons (Masferrer 1983: 602).

Seasonal migration has serious implications for the transmission of disease within indigenous communities. Richards (1987) studies a highland Guatemalan Mayan community and finds a circular effect between high susceptibility to disease due to poverty and malnutrition, and the high transmission rate of disease resulting from seasonal migration as individuals try to supplement family income.

Scott (1992) controls for indigenous origins in her study of male/female earnings and labor market participation in Bolivia. She finds that non-

Spanish-speaking women have a lower labor force participation rate. The present disadvantaged socioeconomic position of all women in Bolivia is believed to be the result of the European conquest, prior to which women are thought to have had equality with men (Gálvez Barrera 1980). However, some researchers do not detect evidence of discrimination. Among the Bolivian Aymara, the economic contribution and value of labor of both genders are equal (Collins 1983).

Bilingual education appears to offer a solution to the problem of repetition, dropout and low educational attainment among indigenous children. Drawing on the success of employing bilingual promoters in 1965 during the *castellanizacion* program, Guatemala established a national bilingual education program (Morren 1988). Since 1979, the government of Guatemala and the United States Agency for International Development have been working together to improve the quality of education for the indigenous population. Historically, Mayan children have had less access to schooling, although they represent half the school-aged population. The national curriculum was adapted and translated for the pre-primary through grade four levels into four of the Mayan languages. The government instituted the use of the Mayan language in primary education and a national bilingual education program (PRONEBI) was created. Culturally relevant instruction in Spanish and Mayan languages is provided. This program has led to an increase in student comprehension, and has reduced failure, repetition and dropout rates. The program is operational in 400 schools with the full curriculum, and in another 400 schools the pre-primary curriculum is in place. The program serves 85,000 students, and will be adapted to 4 more Mayan languages to serve an additional 900 schools.

The success of PRONEBI can be judged from the indicators derived from the evaluations. Attendance rates, dropouts rates and promotions have improved compared to a control group of Mayan children being taught only in Spanish. The bilingual education project has had a significant impact on promotion rates; more than 9 percent higher for bilingual students relative to the control group in the first grade in 1983 (Townsend and Newman 1985). Program students receive higher scores on all subject matters, including mastery of Spanish (Morren 1988: 365). These results confirm the findings of other researchers (Modiano 1973; Dutcher 1982) who argue that the advantage of bilingual education lies in teaching students in their native tongue along with formally teaching Spanish as a second language. Bilingual education also has the support of the parents of the indigenous children (Richards and Richards 1990).

Carvajal and Morris (1989/1990), analyzing 1986 PRONEBI data from 297 communities and from a questionnaire administered to the same communities, find sizable differences *among* indigenous groups with respect to grade repetition and dropout, ranging from 30 to 46 percent in repetition rates, and 6 to 16 percent in dropout rates. The authors attempt to explain the differences with the use of community socioeconomic characteristics and differences among indigenous groups. They find that bilingualism reduces grade repetition and dropout rates.

Bilingual education has also been successful in other Latin American countries. The bilingual approach produces better results in tests of reading comprehension (Modiano 1973; Dutcher 1982; Miller 1982). That is, reading comprehension is greater for those students taught in bilingual schools where they first learn to read in their native language and then transfer their reading skill to the second language (Spanish). These are the findings of a classic study by Modiano (1973), who was instrumental in developing the materials needed to provide bilingual schooling in Mexico (Miller 1982: 801), where the indigenous school system covers about 600,000 primary level students (DGEI 1993). Children in monolingual Spanish schools learned to read in their second language as they were learning to use their second language. This double burden is probably what accounts for their poorer performance in reading tests (Dutcher 1982: 25). Education in the vernacular language also improves and develops a student's native ability to learn a second language in Ecuador (Davis 1981: 240). Without taking sides in the debate over language policy, it is worth mentioning that some advocate instructing students in their first language because the literacy skills acquired in one language can be transferred to other languages, and developing these skills is easiest in the student's native tongue (Dutcher 1982). Others argue that teaching students in their first language places them at a disadvantage for further educational opportunities. Moreover, it is not clear whether indigenous children, located mainly in rural areas, are disadvantaged educationally because of the language of instruction, or because of insufficient investment in physical facilities in school classrooms (Heyneman 1979).

Migration is an important fact of life in Guatemala. Parkyn (1989) studies the effect of prolonged culture contact between the ladinos and indigenous people of Guatemala. Indigenous people who move to urban centers begin to identify with ladinos, and identification becomes a matter of social class rather than indigenous origins. The factors identified in the study that relate to change are: family structure, work/economics, government policies, telecommunications and travel, education and religion.

An overview of internal migration in Guatemala reveals considerable differences between indigenous and non-indigenous people (Micklin 1990). On the whole, women migrate more than men, and non-indigenous people more than indigenous people. Migrants are more likely to be young, female and non-indigenous. The motivation in general is employment opportunities. There are, however, cases of forced migration: the earthquake of 1976, war, military, rebellions, and forced removals by the state during times of war—directed mostly at indigenous people (Micklin 1990).

Internal migration in other Latin American countries has also been studied (Preston 1987; Silvers 1980). Preston (1987) examines the migration experiences of five *mestizo* and indigenous communities in Highland Ecuador. Rural-rural, rural-urban and return migration are studied. The findings reveal that migrants are better educated than non-migrants and that migration is not a unidirectional phenomenon.

In their literature survey of rural income distribution in Ecuador, Luzuriaga and Zuvekas (1983) include a broad overview of case studies by region covering the living standards of a large number of indigenous populations. Over half the indigenous studies surveyed examine how the status of peasant farm laborers changed as a result of the Agrarian Reform Act of 1964. The reforms replaced the *hua-*

sipungo work system, whereby peasant labor on large landholdings was exchanged for the use of small subsistence plots (see de Villalobos and Monares 1990). The reforms formalized a wage-labor system and a land redistribution program. Inadequate subsistence allocations, however, forced farmers into seasonal migratory work.

In their survey, Luzuriaga and Zuvekas (1983) include reports on pre-reform voluntary transfers of plots to indigenous populations (Barsky 1978), on wages and economic status before the reforms (Crespi 1968), and on post-reform wage and labor changes for various regions and *haciendas* (Arcos and Marchán 1978; Sáenz Andrade 1978; IERAC, IEAG, and JUNAPLA 1965; CIDA 1965; BCE and FODERUMA 1978). Although some information is included on post-reform improvements in the living standards of indigenous people (Ecuador, Grupo de Evaluación 1977), many more studies report post-reform depreciations in living standards (Paredes Barros 1967; Martínez and Dubly 1967–68; Granja 1977; Brownrigg 1972).

Other studies mentioned by Luzuriaga and Zuvekas (1983) focus on employment and living standards of non-farming indigenous Ecuadoreans. Casagrande (1974) reports on 6 Andean communities with information on migratory labor and the weaving industry for tourist trade. An earlier study (Beghin 1964) reports on Quechua speakers in the Napo region living under conditions of debt peonage. PREDESUR (1978) examines the breakdown of traditional systems among 350 Shuar families as the incidence of wage employment increased. Walter (1976) reports similar effects among the subsistence-based "closed" indigenous community of Carabuela as young men increasingly turned to wage labor. Cornell University (1965, 1966) conducted two anthropological studies with information on employment and wages among the poorest natives in Ecuador in the Colta Lake region. In one of the few studies reporting on living conditions over time, Beals (1952, 1966) examines the employment and wages of an indigenous community on the outskirts of Quito. He finds that although living standards improved over time, the community was experiencing "increasing social disintegration" (Luzuriaga and Zuvekas 1983: 108).

Luzuriaga and Zuvekas (1983) also examine studies focusing on discrimination against indigenous people in Ecuador. Pearse (1975) and Villavicencio (1973) compare living standards and examine discrimination against indigenous people in the Otavalo region. Whitten (1976) finds increased incidence of discrimination and, as a result of increased economic activity associated with petroleum exploration in the Puyo region, disruptions to the indigenous culture and way of life.

Conclusion

This brief review indicates that relatively little empirical research on the socio-economic conditions of the indigenous people of Latin America exists. This is especially the case when compared with the rich literature on ethnicity and socio-economic conditions in developed countries. The small but growing literature on

socioeconomic differences between the indigenous and non-indigenous populations of North America is particularly interesting and informative. The results of
analyses of the socioeconomic differences between indigenous and non-
indigenous people in Canada and the United States point to divergent policy
responses, suggesting that a country by country approach be undertaken in Latin
America. The review also demonstrates the importance of taking ethnicity into
account.

The review also suggests some priority areas of research that the following
chapters attempt to address. These include estimation of the extent of poverty
among Latin America's indigenous population. In addition, the living conditions
of the indigenous population are compared with those of the non-indigenous population. The basic human capital differences between the indigenous and non-
indigenous populations are examined, as are differences in occupational attainment. The estimation and decomposition of earnings differentials allow for the
development of appropriate policy responses, as is shown in this review.

The next chapter presents an overview of the number and conditions of the
indigenous people of Latin America using census and other published sources.
This is followed by a presentation of the results found in the empirical analysis.

3

How Many Indigenous People?

Mary Lisbeth Gonzalez

Census data and other published sources are used in an attempt to provide an overview of the indigenous population of Latin America. Information covered includes population size and location, ethnolinguistic characteristics, illiteracy and schooling. The chapter opens with a discussion of operational definitions of indigenous people and examines the limitations of the available sources of information.

Although the Latin American ethnic spectrum is very diverse, this chapter categorizes the region's population into two broad groups: indigenous and non-indigenous. These two groups do not represent homogenous communities; both include a variety of cultures, identities, languages, traditions, faiths and beliefs. Furthermore, some indigenous communities are better off than others, and some are more integrated than others. However, the available data aggregate information—for the most part—across indigenous groups. Census and household surveys provide information on indigenous people as a whole without differentiating among communities.

Operational Definitions of Indigenous People

The term "ethnic group" is often used loosely, and in a similar fashion the definition of "indigenous people" is not always clear. From a broader perspective, the concept of ethnic groups relates to language, culture and territory; studies of ethnicity have focused on self-identification, ethnic consciousness and solidarity. An ethnic group is a recognizably distinct group of people embedded in a larger society (Urban and Sherzer 1992: 5). Some authors point out that the concept of "ethnicity" involves two factors. Members might share physical characteristics, faith, language and population concentration in a given region. Members might also share a sense of solidarity and might be in contact with other groups within the society (Segal 1979). The major task in defining an ethnic group is to identify its uniqueness, that is, to determine its identity and language. An ethnic group is also defined as a self-perceived group of people who hold in common a set of traditions not shared by the others with whom they are in contact. Ethnic groups share a common language, as well as cultural values, religion and identity. An ethnic group can be defined as "a self-reproducing social collectivity identified by myths of a common provenance and by identifying markers" (Smith 1990: 152). This is a two-part definition; individuals should identify themselves as members of the ethnic group, and the ethnic group may be externally identified by members of another group. Box 3.1 presents a list of variables that may be used to define an ethnic group.

There is a certain fluidity in the concept of being indigenous. Two individuals with a common heritage and same maternal language may identify as being of different ethnic groups (*ladinos* and *indios* in Guatemala; *cholos* and *indios* in Peru). Also, the concept is not fixed over time. The children of indigenous parents may not consider themselves indigenous. Self-identification may change over time, even for the same generation. In the United States during the 1980s, there was a rebirth of people recognizing their indigenous origins (Snipp 1989). The change in the proportion of the population claiming indigenous origins increased by an amount too large to be due entirely to demographics.

Indigenous people are the descendants of pre-Columbian inhabitants. Different types of indigenous tribes have been identified (Medina 1977b). "Isolated" tribes are those that have little contact with the outside world. "Intermittent" contact tribes are those found in regions that are beginning to be reached by the non-indigenous society. "Permanent" contact tribes are those that have lost their sociocultural autonomy and depend on the surrounding economy, but keep their traditional lifestyles compatible with their new status. Finally, "integrated" tribes are those that have mixed with the national population and are usually confined to portions of their former territories, but completely dispossessed of their lands.

The lack of a single and operational definition for the term "indigenous people" is a major problem for researchers. The historic relationship that some Latin

---

Box 3.1: Characteristics of Indigenous Groups

Common geographic origins
Race
Language
Religion, faith
Traditions, values, and symbols
Literature, music, and folklore
Nutrition
Social and political organizations
An internal sense of distinctiveness
An external perception of distinctiveness
Shared territory and systems of production

Source: Snipp 1989: 38–39.

American indigenous groups have maintained with the state and the dominant society has imposed problems in defining the concept. In some countries such as Peru, Guatemala and Bolivia, the concepts *indio*, *indígena* and *mestizo* have become social terms rather than "ethnic" concepts (Mörner 1970). In Bolivia, for example, the terms *campesinado* and *campesino* in common usage do not easily translate into the concept of "peasant"; instead they have replaced the terms *indio* and *indigenous people* (Hahn 1991). In 1969, Peruvian President Velasco announced an agrarian reform law, inspired by the 1952 law promulgated in Bolivia, "declaring that the former Indians and erstwhile *indígenas* were henceforth *campesinos*" (Alverson 1979). According to Smith (1990), the same has happened in Guatemala, where the state has always treated indigenous people as a class, even though indigenous people have rarely acted as a self-conscious class.

Under a broad definition, peasants are agricultural workers holding a subordinate position in a hierarchical economic and political order (Colburn 1989). The establishment of colonial labor systems like the *encomienda*, *mita*, *repartimiento* and *cuatequil* explains the use of the term *indígena* as defining social class and occupation; basically defining *campesinado*. During colonial times, the Spanish controlled the land and labor; they expropriated indigenous territories and created a landless indigenous agricultural workforce. After the *independentista* period, Latin America became the socioeconomic and political product created from the fusion of two highly structured systems—the *ancien régime* and Spanish society—both of which embrace complex social, ethnic and caste structures. With 500 hundred years of history and particularly with the social and political impact of the current century, the Latin American social spectrum is today even more complicated. Social class and ethnic elements are still interrelated. In several countries indigenous groups are peasants, but not all of the peasants are indigenous people, and not all of the indigenous people are peasants. Using an ethnic concept to define occupation or social class will narrow the analytical perspective and will restrict the capacity to understand that there are indigenous individuals within all sectors of the rural, peasantry, poor, and urban populations.

In many respects, the Latin American indigenous population is diverse. Klein (1982) shows that in Bolivia, there are major differences between the highland and the lowland groups. Evidence of the cultural diversity is abundant; Klein describes in detail the historical differences between the Tiahuanaco civilization and the Aymaras' kingdoms (Klein 1982). Although the multiethnic perspective provides a more accurate analysis, it causes some problems in terms of social research. First, comprehensive data are unavailable; second, collecting such data requires a large investment of resources; and, third, covering the whole map of cultures and identities presents an overwhelming task.

The task, nevertheless, is not only to define indigenous people, but also to define an operational indicator or set of indicators to identify them in census and sample surveys (CELADE 1992). The approaches that have been employed in some Latin America countries are: language spoken, self-perception and geographic concentration.

Language, along with ethnic unity and division of power and resources, is almost an invariable factor in determining whether the people identify with one nation state or group over another (Sagarin and Moneymaker 1979: 20). The United Nations claims that language, especially the native tongue, is a key variable in identifying ethnic groups; the underlying assumption is that language differences tend to persist unless social integration has occurred (Shyrock et al. 1976). Language is a reliable indicator given indigenous people's strong sense of identity, maintained in large part by language use (Brascoupé 1992). Language is also considered to be the most robust indicator of ethnicity over time (Modiano 1988: 314). The social meaning of languages goes beyond linguistic codes; any language may have a social value of signal distinctness and of a speaker's identification with others (Urban and Sherzer 1992: 308). It works as a marker of a social group and of an ethnic community. Language, and particularly native tongue, is the "most suitable expression of spiritual individuality" (Sagarin and Moneymaker 1979: 19). In most societies native tongue can be used as an operational indicator of ethnicity, especially in areas with a wide spectrum of ethnic groups exposed to bilingual environments.

The Spanish language and the Iberian culture are the "dominant" systems in Latin America, but they coexist with other linguistic and cultural systems (Plaza 1990: 377). Although the coexistence is not always peaceful (Munzel 1973; Urban and Sherzer 1992), some ethnic groups have developed such a level of social integration that linguistic differences and, at times, cultural differences are dispelled. The Garifunas of the Atlantic coast of Honduras provide an example of language integration. These descendants of Africa speak an Amerindian language. The African descendants of the Chota valley in Ecuador have adopted many Andean cultural features (Gnerre 1990). The indigenous people living in the Kulta territory in Bolivia are a remarkable example of cultural integration. These communities have adopted the "fiesta-cargo system" established by the Spanish colonial authorities into their culture so completely that they reinterpret it now as an indigenous cultural tradition instead of a colonial legacy (Urban and Sherzer 1992: 101–103). However, there are other indigenous groups that preserve their pre-colonial cultural patterns because they were never actively colonized. The Shuars of Ecuador, the Tukanoams of northwest Amazonia, and the Kunas of Panama are examples of groups whose cultural forms are the continuation of precontact patterns (Urban and Sherzer 1992: 3).

Since "language" has been determined to be a key indicator for identifying ethnicity and indigenous people, Latin American countries have been applying two forms of the language question. The first concentrates on native tongue, and the second on the ability to speak an indigenous language (see Table 3.1). Although the use of these questions provides useful statistics, the use of either form can lead to incomplete identification because they are likely to exclude indigenous descendants whose current operational language is Spanish and classify them as monolingual Spanish speakers.

In addition, the wide variation in the formulation of the language question sometimes impairs national and international comparisons. For example, in 1972, the Peruvian census asks: "What is your maternal language?" In the 1981 census,

Table 3.1: The Language Question in Latin American Survey Work

Language Question	Definitional Problems
Native tongue	May exclude indigenous descendants that declare Spanish as native tongue
Ability to speak an indigenous language	May exclude indigenous people who do not speak an indigenous language or deny the knowledge of it

however, the question is: "Do you speak an indigenous language?" Paraguay eliminated the language question because Guaraní, "the national language," is spoken by an extensive group of non-indigenous people.

The self-identification or self-perception method of defining the reference population has been used in Guatemala, Colombia, Paraguay and Venezuela. All these countries, except Guatemala, have applied it in combination with the geographic approach. The advantages of the self-perception approach are that it avoids language proficiency issues, allows individuals to choose and does not require special tests or genealogical investigations for determining if an individual is indigenous (Snipp 1989: 36). It is believed, however, that this method may lead to underestimation, especially when asked in the form of "Are you indigenous?" Discrimination and social prejudice in a society can lead individuals to deny any affiliation with their native origins (CELADE 1992). There is also the possibility that some individuals may believe they will receive special social benefits by declaring themselves indigenous.

The third method of identification uses geographic location or concentration of the indigenous population. In practice, it is usually used when the indigenous population is concentrated in specific territories, or in those countries with indigenous reservations. It is also used in conjunction with self-perception or language identity questions. The benefits of this approach are that it avoids individual issues of identity and problems of measurement and takes into account the community's values and opportunities. A major problem with this method is that some non-indigenous individuals may be classified as indigenous and vice versa. Table 3.2 presents some of the different identification approaches used by Latin American countries.

Depending on the country, estimates of the indigenous population are determined by individuals who (i) identify their native tongue as an indigenous language or speak an indigenous language, (ii) identify themselves as indigenous and/or, (iii) live in an indigenous territory, a reservation or an area where indigenous people are geographically concentrated.

Sources of Information

The second major problem in analyzing information on indigenous populations is the availability of data and the lack of a standard statistical classification system. Although some Latin American countries have large indigenous populations, not

Table 3.2: Some Definitions of Ethnicity Used in Latin America

Country	Sources	Ethnicity Definition
Bolivia	Census (1976) and housing survey (1988)	Language spoken
Colombia	Census (1973, 1985)	Self-perception and geographic location
Guatemala	Census (1973, 1981)	Self-perception
Honduras	Census (1988)	Language spoken
Mexico	Census (1988, 1990)	Language spoken
Panama	Census (1980, 1990)	Language spoken
Paraguay	National census (1981) and indigenous census (1982)	Geographic location and self-perception
Peru	Census (1972) Census (1981)	Maternal tongue Language spoken
Venezuela	National census (1981) and indigenous census (1982)	Geographic location and self-perception

Source: CELADE 1992.

all have collected information on indigenous people. All Latin American countries except for Uruguay and the insular countries of the Caribbean have indigenous inhabitants; in total, although estimates vary, there are approximately 34 million indigenous people, about 8 percent of the total population of the region (Gnerre 1990), but only 9 countries have a census and/or household surveys including information on the indigenous population (Table 3.2).

The Latin American Demographic Center (CELADE) recently published a demographic bulletin that includes information on indigenous people obtained from the census and national household surveys of nine Latin American countries. This publication contains valuable data used here in combination with other sources to provide a statistical overview of the indigenous people of Latin America.

Estimates of Latin America's indigenous population vary significantly according to source. Examples of these variations are provided in Tables 3.3 and 3.4. In Honduras, for example, the 1988 census estimates the indigenous population as 48,789, while other sources put it as high as 110,000 (Table 3.4). The Instituto Indigenista Latinoamericano states that in the 1970s, the Peruvian indigenous population was 9,300,000, while the 1972 census estimated it as 3,467,140 (Table 3.3). The 1981 Peruvian census calculated the indigenous population as 3,626,944, while other sources estimated 9,100,000 (Table 3.4).

Population Size and Location

This section presents an overall picture of indigenous people in terms of population size and location, ethnolinguistic characteristics, illiteracy and schooling.

Table 3.3: Estimates of Latin America's Indigenous Population, 1970s

	Census Data		Alternate Estimates	
Country	Number of Indigenous People	Percent of Total Population	Number of Indigenous People	Percent of Total Population
Argentina	..	..	350,000	1.0
Bolivia	2,514,851	65.0	4,900,000	71.0
Brazil	..	..	300,000	0.2
Chile	..	..	1,000,000	8.0
Colombia	318,425	1.5	600,000	2.0
Dominica	..	..	2,000	2.0
Ecuador	..	..	4,100,000	43.0
El Salvador	..	..	400,000	7.0
Guatemala	2,260,024	43.7	5,300,000	66.0
Honduras	..	..	700,000	15.0
Jamaica	..	..	48,000	2.0
Mexico	3,111,415	8.0	12,000,000	14.0
Nicaragua	..	..	16,000	5.0
Panama	93,809	4.8	14,000	6.0
Paraguay	..	..	100,000	3.0
Peru	3,467,140	30.5	9,300,000	47.0
Puerto Rico	..	..	72,000	2.0
Venezuela	..	..	400,000	2.0

Source: CELADE 1992; various sources cited in Jordan Pando 1990.
.. Not available.

Despite the limited scope and characteristics of the available information, this section shows that indigenous people represent a large proportion of the population of some Latin American countries. It also shows that indigenous people are poor, in the sense that indigenous communities are mostly located in rural areas and that they have high illiteracy rates. In the 1980s, over 50, 40 and 25 percent of the Bolivian, Guatemalan, and Peruvian populations, respectively, were indigenous. Approximately 80 percent of the indigenous were rural inhabitants in Bolivia and Guatemala, and about 50 percent in Peru.

Most of the indigenous people of Bolivia are Quechua and Aymara descendants and live in rural areas. In 1988, 56 percent of the population 5 years and over, and 71 percent of the rural population was indigenous (Table 3.5).

Most of Guatemala's indigenous people are Mayan descendants. In 1973, 44 percent of the Guatemalan population was indigenous, while the 1981 census estimated the indigenous population at 41 percent. The indigenous population as a proportion of the total population has been decreasing over time. According to the

Table 3.4: Estimates of Latin America's Indigenous Population, 1980s

	Census Data		Alternate Estimates	
Country	Number of Indigenous People	Percent of Total Population	Number of Indigenous People	Percent of Total Population
Argentina	..	..	360,000	1.1
Belize	..	..	27,000	14.7
Bolivia.	2,754,000	54.0	4,150,000	56.8
Brazil	..	..	225,000	0.2
Chile	..	..	550,000	4.2
Colombia	225,830	0.8	300,000	0.9
Costa Rica	..	..	26,000	0.9
Ecuador	..	..	3,100,000	29.5
El Salvador	..	..	1,000	0.02
Guatemala	2,536,523	42.0	3,900,000	43.8
Honduras	48,789	1.3	110,000	2.1
Mexico	5,181,038	9.0	12,000,000	14.2
Nicaragua	..	..	48,000	1.2
Panama	72,615	4.0	99,000	4.1
Paraguay	18,317	1.2	80,000	1.9
Peru	3,626,944	24.8	9,100,000	40.8
Venezuela	140,562	0.9	150,000	0.8

Source: CELADE 1992; various sources cited in Gnerre 1990.
.. Not available.

1921 census, indigenous people comprised 65 percent of the total population, falling to 54 percent by 1950 (see Table 3.6). High infant and crude mortality rates might explain this phenomenon, although some authors argue that the current Guatemalan classification system, based on self-perception instead of ancestry, leads to underestimation (Smith 1992).

Table 3.5: Bolivian Population Aged 5 Years and Over by Ethnicity and Region, 1988
(percent)

Region	Indigenous	Non-indigenous
Total	56	44
Urban	41	59
Rural	71	29

Source: CELADE 1992: 33–35.

Table 3.6: Indigenous Population of Guatemala, 1921–1981

Year	Percent of Population
1921	65
1940	56
1950	54
1973	44
1981	42

Source: PAHO 1990.

In terms of geographic distribution, in 1973, 77 percent of the non-indigenous population was living in urban areas, as compared with only 23 percent of the indigenous population. The concentration of indigenous people in rural areas is larger than in the urban areas; in both 1973 and 1981, about 50 percent of the rural population was indigenous (see Table 3.7).

Although historically Peru has had a substantial indigenous population, current demographic data report that approximately 30 percent of the population is indigenous. By the fifteenth century, the Peruvian indigenous population was as high as 6 to 10 million people. The population was reduced by between one-half and three-quarters during the next century (Alverson 1979: 375). In 1972, 32 percent of the Peruvian population was indigenous; in 1981, 27 percent was identified as indigenous. Most of the indigenous inhabitants have been living in the *Sierra*, a poor area traditionally known as *La Mancha India*, or the Indian strip (Alverson 1979: 372). Census data from both 1972 and 1981 reported that approximately 50 percent of the rural population was indigenous and about 80 percent of the urban population was non-indigenous (see Table 3.8).

In 1981, only 35 percent of the indigenous language speakers in Peru were monolingual and 65 percent were bilingual. Most of the bilingual speakers (88 percent) were located in urban areas, while most of the monolingual speakers (52 percent) were residing in rural regions (see Table 3.9).

Table 3.7: Population of Guatemala by Ethnicity and Region, 1973 and 1981
(percent)

Population	Non-indigenous		Indigenous	
	1973	1981	1973	1981
Total	56	59	44	41
Urban	77	75	23	25
Rural	45	50	55	50

Source: CELADE 1992: 51, 59.

Table 3.8: Population of Peru by Ethnicity and Region, 1972 and 1981
(percent)

	Non-indigenous		Indigenous	
Region	1972	1981	1972	1981
Total	68	73	32	27
Urban	81	83	19	17
Rural	50	55	50	45

Source: CELADE 1992: 105–107, 111–113.

Table 3.9: Bilingual and Monolingual Indigenous Language Speakers in Peru by Region, 1981
(percent)

Region	Bilingual	Monolingual
Total	65	35
Urban	88	12
Rural	48	52

Source: CELADE 1992: 111–113.

In absolute terms, Mexico has the largest indigenous population on the continent. According to the Instituto Nacional de Antropología e Historia (INAH), in 1980, 429 *municipios* registered the highest indigenous population density; 217 of these *municipios* were located in Oaxaca, 74 in Yucatán, 43 in Puebla, 33 in Veracruz and 26 in Chiapas (INAH 1987). This population however, has been decreasing. The 1930 census reported that 14 percent of the Mexican population was indigenous; this percentage fell to 10 percent by 1950, and to 8 percent by 1990 (see Table 3.10).

Census data show that in 1990, 80 percent of indigenous Mexicans were bilingual and 16 percent were monolingual, compared with 71 percent and 23 percent, respectively, in 1980 (Table 3.11).

Table 3.10: Indigenous Populations of Mexico, 1930–1990

Year	Percent of Total Population
1930	14
1950	10
1970	7
1980	10
1990	8

Source: INEGI 1992a, b; INAH 1987.

Table 3.11: Indigenous Populations of Mexico Aged 5 Years and Over by Language, 1980–1990
(percent)

Indigenous Population	1980	1990
Bilingual	71	80
Monolingual	23	16
Not Specified	6	4

Source: INEGI 1992b: 22–24.

Ethnolinguistic Characteristics

There are approximately 400 different indigenous languages throughout Latin America, and each country has from 7 to 200 languages. Uruguay is the only country on the continent that is Spanish-monolingual (see Table 3.12).

The major indigenous population centers are in Guatemala, Mexico, Bolivia, Ecuador and Peru. Some countries have declared an indigenous language as a second major language. In 1975, Peru stated that Spanish is the "dominant" language and Quechua the "official" language (Center for Applied Linguistics and the World Bank 1975). The Paraguayan Constitution of 1967 pronounced Guaraní as the "national" language, and the Constitution of 1992 proclaimed it an "official" language. Guaraní is spoken by both indigenous and non-indigenous people in Paraguay. This country is an exception in Latin America where Guaraní flourishes alongside Spanish, despite the virtual disappearance of the Amerindian culture (Urban and Sherzer 1992: 308). The Paraguayan relationship between language and culture shows a dichotomy as the dominant language remains Guaraní while the rest of the dominant social institutions and culture are Hispanic (Hanratty 1990: 63). In Bolivia in 1987, the Secretary of Education and Cultural Affairs approved the recognition of Tupí-Guaraní as a national language along with Spanish, Quechua and Aymara, and its inclusion into the academic curriculum of all educational levels in those urban and rural areas with large Tupí-Guaraní concentrations (Zolezzi and Riester 1987).

Bolivia is a multilingual and multiethnic country encompassing more than 30 indigenous languages within its boundaries. The major indigenous languages are versions of Quechua and Aymara (see Table 3.13). Other linguistic families such as Arawakan, Chapacuran, Uru-Chipaya, Mataco-Maca, Panoan and Tupi also exist, and some pre-Incan languages such as Uru and Puquina are still spoken (SIL 1988; Klein 1982). Aymara is spoken in the west Altiplano of the eastern Andes. Two versions of Quechua are spoken. There are also several variants of the Guaraní language (SIL 1988).

The eastern region of Bolivia covers more than half of the national territory; it includes part of the Amazonia, el Chaco and an area known as *zonas de transición*. There are in this region approximately 30 languages, 26 of which belong to 9 well

Table 3.12: Language Diversity in Latin America

Country	Number of Languages	Number with 10,000 or More Speakers
Argentina	23	9
Belize	9	8
Bolivia	38	7
Brazil	208	7
Chile	7	2
Colombia	78	7
Costa Rica	11	3
Ecuador	23	9
El Salvador	4	4
Guatemala	26	15
Honduras	10	4
Mexico	72	37
Nicaragua	9	4
Panama	6	3
Paraguay	21	5
Peru	85	27
Uruguay	1	1
Venezuela	40	5

Source: SIL 1988 for Belize, Costa Rica, El Salvador, Guatemala, Honduras, Nicaragua and Panama; Hornberger 1992: 191 for all others.

identified linguistic families, and the rest are of unknown origin (Zolezzi and Riester 1987). Among those groups, there are 16 Izoceño-Guaraní communities that emigrated from Paraguay during the fifteenth century in the *departamento* of Santa Cruz. They belong to the Tupí-Guaraní linguistic family. Depending on the

Table 3.13: Language Distribution of Indigenous Population in Bolivia, 1980s

Language	Percent of Total Indigenous Population
Quechua	39
Aymara	24
Guaraní	1

Source: SIL 1988: 86–88.

Table 3.14: Language Distribution of Indigenous Population in Guatemala, 1980s

Language	Percent of Total Indigenous Population
Quiché	15
Cakchiquel	10
Mam (Maya)	8
Tzutujil	2
Achí	2
Pokoman	1

Source: SIL 1988: 61–65.

source, there are between 20 and 30 indigenous languages in Guatemala (Richards and Richards 1990). Most belong to the Maya, the Xinca (of unknown origin), and the Garifuna or Caribe (Tujab 1987). Most of the languages are spoken by mono-lingual populations (see Tables 3.14 and 3.15).

The internal migrations from the highlands to the coastal plantations helped to develop different versions of the Quiché language (SIL 1992). The high degree of economic interaction among indigenous communities has generated a dynamic process of linguistic interchange giving Guatemala a variety of linguistic families and languages (Richards and Richards 1990). Despite the broad linguistic diversity, Mayan languages are the "languages of intra-ethnic communication" (Richards and Richards 1990: 50). There are three Mayan or Mam linguistic regions; western, southern and northern. The linguistic divergence and variety within the language are explained by the topographical characteristics of the country that

Table 3.15: Language Distribution of Indigenous Population in Guatemala, 1970s

100,000 or More Speakers	50,000–100,000 Speakers	10,000–50,000 Speakers	Less Than 10,000 Speakers
Quiché	Pokomchí	Jacalteco	Mopán
Mam	Kanjobal	Chortí	Tectiteco
Cakchiquel	Pokomam	Acateco	Uspanteco
Kekchí	Ixil	Aguacateco	Scapulteco
	Tzutujil	Garifuna or Carib	Sipacapense
			Itzá
			Lacandón
			Xinca

Source: Tujab 1987: 530.

Table 3.16: Language Distribution of Indigenous Population in Peru, 1980s

Language	Percent of Total Indigenous Population
Quechua	30
Aymara	22

Source: SIL 1988.

may have led to the isolation of the Mam speakers (Richards and Richards 1990: 28). The Mam and Quiché (K'iche'an) languages were at one time linguistically related. Their separation took place more than 1,500 years ago, and a separation within the Mam language, 400 years ago. Differences between Mam speakers involve such major cultural and linguistic features that communication among Mayan or Mam speakers is often difficult. Contrasting divisions among Quiché, Cakchiquel (Kaqchiquel) and Quechi (Kekchí) speakers are minor phonological and lexical differences (Richards and Richards 1990: 28).

In Peru, there are more than 30 different indigenous languages. The main language families are Arawakan, Aymaran, Cahuapanan, Harakmbet, Huitotoan, Jivaroan, Panoan and Quechua. Most of the indigenous individuals speak different versions of Quechua, which is widespread throughout Peru (Table 3.16). The Ancash version of Quechua is spoken in the southeast, east, and northern sides of the Ancash *departamento*. The Quechua Arequipa is spoken in the Province of Cayloma in the Arequipa *departamento*. The Quechua Ayacucho or Cahnka is spoken in the southwestern side of Ayacucho. There are also other versions of Quechua spoken in different regions.

In Mexico, the main linguistic families are the Algonkian, Hokan, Mayan, Mixe-Zoque, Mixtecan and Otopamean. There are 56 different indigenous languages in Mexico. According to the 1990 census, 23 percent of the indigenous people spoke Nahuatl, 14 percent Mayan, and 7 percent spoke Mixteco and Zapoteco (see Table 3.17). According to the INAH, approximately 90 percent of the indigenous languages were spoken in Oaxaca, Yucatán, Puebla, Veracruz and Chiapas (INAH 1987).

Literacy and Educational Characteristics

The United Nations defines literacy as the ability of a person to both read and write a short simple statement (Shyrock et al. 1976: 182). Illiteracy rates provide an approximation of the country's socioeconomic level and, if measured by subcategories of the population, can provide baseline information for comparing one segment of the population with another. For example, a cross analysis between ethnicity and education can be used as an indicator of differential educational opportunities for indigenous and non-indigenous groups.

Table 3.17: Language Distribution of Indigenous Population in Mexico, 1990

Language	Percent of Total Indigenous Population
Nahuatl	23
Maya	14
Mixteco	7
Zapoteco	7
Otomí	5
Tzeltal	5
Tzotzil	4
Totonaco	4
Mazateco	3
Chol	2
Mazahua	2

Source: INEGI 1991: 26–27.

In some countries, the variations between the two groups may be as significant or even more revealing than a comparison across countries. For instance, in Colombia, in the 1970s, only 21 percent of the non-indigenous people were illiterate, while 45 percent of the indigenous population was illiterate. In Bolivia, in the 1980s, the illiteracy rate for non-indigenous individuals was 14 percent, while illiteracy among the indigenous population was 24 percent. In Panama, the level of illiteracy also differs significantly. In the 1980s, the illiteracy rate for non-indigenous people was 14 percent and 62 percent for indigenous individuals (see Table 3.18).

Table 3.18: Illiteracy Rates by Ethnicity and Country, 1970s–1980s
(percent)

	1970s		1980s	
Country	Non-indigenous	Indigenous	Non-indigenous	Indigenous
Bolivia	23	42	14	24
Colombia	21	46	16	45
Guatemala	46	87	40	79
Panama	21	..	14	62
Paraguay	20	..	13	70
Peru	30	50	..	..

Source: CELADE 1992.
.. Not available.

The overall illiteracy rate for indigenous people in Bolivia masks the large differences in the rates for bilingual and monolingual indigenous people. In both 1976 and 1988, 98 percent of monolingual indigenous people were illiterate. In contrast, 14 percent of bilingual indigenous individuals were illiterate in 1976 and only 12 percent in 1988 (see Table 3.19).

In urban areas, in 1988, the illiteracy rate for monolingual indigenous people was 97 percent, 10 percent for Spanish speakers, and 9 percent for the bilingual population. In rural areas, the illiteracy rate for monolingual indigenous people was 93 percent, 22 percent for Spanish speakers, and 15 percent for bilingual individuals (see Table 3.20).

The difference between the illiteracy rates for the two major indigenous language communities is insignificant. In 1988, the rate for monolingual Quechua speakers was 93 percent, while the rate for monolingual Aymara speakers was about the same at 95 percent. Gender differences are also insignificant. The illiteracy rate for Quechua females in 1988 was 95 percent and for Aymara females, 96 percent. For Quechua males, the illiteracy rate was 89 percent, and for Aymara males, 94 percent (see Table 3.21).

Inequalities between indigenous and non-indigenous groups are reflected in human capital accumulation. In Guatemala, differences in illiteracy rates between indigenous and non-indigenous people are large. In 1973, the indigenous illiteracy

Table 3.19: Illiteracy Rates of Indigenous Population in Bolivia, 1976 and 1988

(percent)

Population (5 Years and Over)	1976	1988
Overall	42	24
Monolingual	98	94
Bilingual	14	12

Source: CELADE 1992: 32, 36.

Table 3.20: Illiteracy Rates by Language and Region in Bolivia, 1988

(percent)

Population (5 Years and Over)	Urban	Rural
Monolingual Indigenous	97	93
Bilingual	9	15
Spanish speakers	10	22

Source: CELADE 1992: 36.

Table 3.21: Illiteracy Rates for Monolingual Indigenous Population in Bolivia by Language and Gender, 1988
(percent)

Population (5 Years and Over)	Quechua	Aymara	Other
Total	93	95	29
Males	89	94	42
Females	95	96	22

Source: CELADE 1992: 36.

Table 3.22: Illiteracy Rates in Guatemala by Ethnicity and Region for Population Aged 30 Years and Over, 1973 and 1981
(percent)

Region	Non-indigenous		Indigenous	
	1973	1981	1973	1981
Total	46	40	87	79
Urban	27	22	72	62
Rural	67	55	89	83

Source: CELADE 1992: 53, 62.

rate was 87 percent and 46 percent for the non-indigenous group. In 1981, differences were as dramatic as in 1973; almost 80 percent of the indigenous population was illiterate, contrasting with only 40 percent for non-indigenous individuals. Furthermore, the inequalities are reflected in both urban and rural areas. Table 3.22 shows that illiteracy rates of the two groups differ significantly by region. In urban areas, 62 percent of the indigenous people were illiterate, while only 22 percent of the non-indigenous were illiterate.

In Peru, the level of illiteracy also differs dramatically between indigenous and non-indigenous populations. In 1972, the non-indigenous population had an illiteracy rate of 22 percent, while 50 percent of indigenous individuals were illiterate. Illiteracy rates by gender reveal an unequal distribution of education among indigenous people. While 65 percent of the indigenous females were illiterate, the indigenous males registered a rate of only 35 percent. In rural areas, while high illiteracy rates were found among all females, differences were more significant within the indigenous population by gender; the indigenous females' rate was 74 percent, while indigenous males registered a rate of 44 percent (see Table 3.23). Thus, in Peru, too, inequalities in human capital between indigenous and non-indigenous groups are great.

The Mexican census excludes information on indigenous illiteracy. However, statistics from the census show that general access to schooling has expanded dur-

Table 3.23: Illiteracy Rates in Peru by Ethnicity, Gender and Region, 1972
(percent)

	Non-indigenous			Indigenous		
Region	Total	Male	Female	Total	Male	Female
Total	22	17	26	50	35	65
Urban	14	11	16	31	17	46
Rural	42	32	52	60	44	74

Source: CELADE 1992: 108–110.

Table 3.24: Illiteracy Rates in Mexico by State for Population Aged 15 Years and Over, 1970 and 1990
(percent)

State	1970	1990
Mexico	26	12
Chiapas	45	30
Hidalgo	42	21
Campeche	25	15
Oaxaca	46	28
Quintana Roo	26	12
Yucatán	27	16

Source: INEGI 1992b: 33.

ing the last few decades. The national illiteracy rate decreased from 26 percent in 1970 to 12 percent in 1990. Despite this general improvement, states with high indigenous populations such as Oaxaca and Chiapas still experience high rates. According to the 1970 census, Oaxaca registered the highest illiteracy rate at 46 percent. In 1990, the national illiteracy rate was 12 percent and Oaxaca had a rate of 28 percent—more than twice the national rate. In 1970, 45 percent of Chiapas' population aged 15 years and over was illiterate, and 30 percent in 1990. Despite this improvement, Chiapas' rate was double the national proportion of illiteracy (see Table 3.24).

Conclusion

This chapter highlights the multiethnic and multilingual nature of some of Latin America's indigenous populations. There are approximately 400 different languages on the continent, with each country having from 7 to 200 different languages. While many indigenous people are bilingual, others are monolingual in their native language. Some widely spoken indigenous languages have been recognized as national or official languages, such as in Bolivia, Paraguay and Peru.

Despite this recognition, indigenous people experience higher levels of illiteracy than do non-indigenous people. This is one of the inequalities documented in this report using the available data. While many sources are used to compile the information presented, reliable and consistent data remain a problem. Better data are required in order to improve the analysis of the socioeconomic conditions of indigenous people.

The challenge is to define a set of operational indicators in order to accurately identify indigenous people in census or sample surveys. Latin American countries, in combination with indigenous organizations and specialized agencies, should review the United States and Canadian censuses in order to apply some of the indicators used by these sources. Rather than relying solely on one indicator to define indigenous populations, a combination of indicators should be used. Using a range of indicators across countries, including language spoken, self-identification, geographic location, ancestry and dress, among others, would paint a more comprehensive, reliable and accurate picture of the region's indigenous populations.

Nevertheless, the evidence reviewed here suggests that there is a strong link between being indigenous and poverty and inequality. Indigenous people are concentrated in rural areas, have low levels of human capital, and the differences between indigenous and non-indigenous groups are large. The chapter also shows that taking ethnicity into account is very important. The link between being indigenous and poverty and inequality is investigated more closely in the following chapters using more micro-level, individual data.

4

Methods and Data

Harry Anthony Patrinos

When conducting research on ethnicity and socioeconomic development, the problems that must be addressed at the outset include defining the target population, deciding which research methodologies to apply, and dealing with the scarcity of data. The approach taken here is empirical, using micro-level data from household surveys conducted in four Latin American countries.

The link between being indigenous and poverty and inequality is investigated in subsequent chapters. Here the sources of data that are used are described, operational definitions are discussed, statistical models are reviewed and the hypotheses that are directly and indirectly tested are put forward.

The Household Surveys and Definitions

While many countries in the region have sizeable indigenous populations, few include questions to identify the ethnolinguistic characteristics of individuals in their household or labor force surveys. In some cases, countries collect such information in their census but do not collect information on income characteristics. Other countries undertake a separate indigenous census, but in these cases it is difficult to make comparisons with the non-indigenous population. In any case, census data in raw form are not available, although published sources are summarized in Chapter 3.

While it would have been preferable to cover more countries in the empirical analysis, data limitations necessitate concentrating on the countries for which household surveys with information on ethnolinguistic characteristics exist and in which the indigenous population is sufficiently large both in absolute numbers and in proportion to the national population. For this reason, the analysis is limited to four countries: Bolivia, Guatemala, Mexico and Peru. It would have been preferable to include Ecuador, a country with a large indigenous population, but a household survey with ethnolinguistic information is not available. The recent census in Ecuador collected information on language but did not include income.

Indigenous people assert that they alone have the right to define what an indigenous person is. Nevertheless it is necessary that an operational definition(s) be adopted in order to carry out the study. Therefore, three approaches have been taken to identify the reference population given the nature of the data at hand. The three methods encompass (i) language spoken, (ii) self-perception and, (iii) geographic concentration/language spoken (see Box 4.1).

The four surveys used differ in coverage and methodology for defining the reference population. The Bolivian survey covers urban centers with 10,000 or more inhabitants, while the other surveys have national coverage. For Bolivia, the data come from the *Encuesta Integrada de Hogares* (EIH), conducted during November 1989 by the Instituto Nacional de Estadística (INE). The survey covers 37,864 individuals living in urban centers with 10,000 or more inhabitants. The sample of indigenous individuals was determined according to the language one usually speaks. It is possible to distinguish between monolingual and bilingual (Spanish and indigenous language) individuals. Only 1.2 percent of the sample are monolingual indigenous language speakers, while 26.4 percent are bilingual—speaking Spanish and an indigenous language such as Aymara, Quechua or Guaraní.

For Peru, data from the *Encuesta Nacional De Niveles De Vida*, conducted in October and November 1991 by the Instituto Cuanto, are used. As one of the

---

Box 4.1: The Household Surveys and Definitions

Bolivia: *Encuesta Integrada de Hogares* (EIH) conducted by the Instituto Nacional de Estadística, 1989

               Individual's ethnicity determined from question:
               ¿Qué idioma(s) habla habitualmente?

Guatemala: *Encuesta Nacional Socio-Demográfica* (ENSD) conducted by the Instituto Nacional de Estadística, 1989

               Individual's ethnicity determined from question:
               ¿Es indígena?

Peru: *Encuesta Nacional de Niveles de Vida*, conducted by Instituto Cuanto for the World Bank, 1991 (Peru Living Standards Survey (PLSS))

               Individual's ethnicity determined from questions:
               ¿Cuál es la lengua materna? and *¿Qué idioma habla?*

Mexico: *Encuesta Nacional de Ingreso - Gasto de los Hogares* (ENIGH) conducted by the Instituto de Estadística Geografía e Informática, 1989

               Individual's ethnicity determined by **geographical** concentration of indigenous people at the *municipio* level **based** on the 1990 census. The percentage of indigenous language speakers in each *municipio* was matched with the *municipios* included in the 1989 survey.

World Bank's Living Standards Measurement Studies, this survey is based on LSMS methodology and is commonly referred to as the 1991 Peru Living Standards Survey (PLSS). The survey covers about 11,500 individuals and provides household, demographic and individual level information. Unfortunately, due to difficult political circumstances at the time of the survey, certain regions of Peru were not surveyed. The survey covers households in four regions: Lima, the Urban Coast, and the Rural and Urban Sierra. The Rural Coast, the entire Selva (which includes the Amazon) and areas within the Rural Sierra were inaccessible. In addition, also due to security considerations, small farms and more remote households in the Sierra region were not surveyed. Consequently, the data from the Sierra region, and the Northern Sierra in particular, depict a population which is located in or near cities. As a result the survey accounts for about three-quarters of the Peruvian population and is, therefore, not representative of the entire country. Using PLSS information on language spoken, individuals are identified as indigenous if they speak Quechua, Aymara or another indigenous language. The resulting estimate of the Peruvian indigenous population is 11.3 percent of the total population. Quechua speakers account for the majority, or 63 percent, while Aymara speakers account for the remaining 37 percent. Only monolingual indigenous or Spanish speakers can be isolated in this survey.

Since individuals are self-identifying with a particular language or languages, it could be the case that some indigenous people are classified as Spanish-speaking monolinguals in the analysis, either through concealment of their indigenous origins or because they do not speak a non-Spanish language. This, however, is not as serious a problem as it might first appear. Those individuals who choose to identify solely with Spanish speakers may be more integrated into the Spanish-speaking society than those who still speak indigenous languages on a regular basis. An argument often encountered is that the number of indigenous people will decline over time as they become socialized through the expansion of Spanish-language schooling. This is not always correct for two reasons. First, indigenous children are less likely to attend classes conducted solely in Spanish. They have higher dropout rates in the primary grades and they experience higher rates of repetition (Patrinos and Psacharopoulos 1992; Hahn 1991; López and D'Emilio 1992). Second, the illiteracy rate for indigenous people is almost twice the non-indigenous rate, implying that Spanish-language schooling will not have as strong a socialization effect (CELADE 1992).

The Guatemalan data analyzed in this study come from the *Encuesta Nacional Socio-Demográfica* (ENSD 1989). This survey was administered by the Instituto Nacional de Estadística in (April to July) 1989 to 9,270 households including 33,262 people aged 10 years and older. The data collected include both household-level information and individual-level information. The household-level data provide information on socio-demographic indicators including the number of people in the house, the presence of water, sanitation, electricity and regional location. The individual-level data include age, level of education, income, source of income, employment and indigenous origins. The self-selection or self-perception method of identifying the indigenous population is used, as determined from the question "Are you indigenous?" Although this method *appears* more accurate, it may lead to underestimation (or overestimation) if social prejudices in a society cause individuals to deny their native origins (or some individuals believe they will receive special social benefits by declaring themselves indigenous).

The Mexican data come from the (third quarter) 1989 survey conducted by the Instituto Nacional de Estadística Geografía e Informática (INEGI), titled *Encuesta Nacional de Ingreso-Gasto de los Hogares*. The survey covers 11,545 households and contains 57,332 individual observations. The geographical coverage includes each of the 31 Mexican states, representing 260 counties (*municipios*) and the federal district. Each household is identified by the state and the *municipio* in which it is located. Income measures are determined by reported household and individual incomes, including imputed monetary value for certain in-kind income. Though the survey contains much useful information, including income, education and employment indicators, it is lacking an indigenous variable. In an attempt to overcome this, published 1990 census figures of percentages and numbers of indigenous language speakers per state and *municipio* (county) are combined with the 1989 household data. The original data set is augmented by variables that include the concentration of the indigenous population by state and *municipio* at the individual level. Therefore, instead of knowing whether each individual is indigenous, what is known is the individual's probability of being indigenous, which corresponds to the percentage of indigenous people recorded in the state and *municipio* of residence. By examining statistical characteristics of inhabitants at the state and *municipio* level and by knowing the corresponding degree to which each state and *municipio* is indigenous, general descriptive profiles of indigenous and non-indigenous people can be drawn.

To examine mean differences across different categories, the Mexican sample is divided into state and *municipio* groups by percentage of indigenous population. For example, average incomes for secondary school graduates in *municipios* under 30 percent indigenous versus graduates in *municipios* 30 percent indigenous and over are calculated. Percentage values used to divide the data are selected according to numbers of available observations. Because the vast majority of *municipios* contain only a small indigenous population (average *municipio* indigenous percentage is 6.2), care is taken to ensure that sub-samples, grouped according to indigenous percentage, retain a "healthy" number of observations for accurate analyses. Accurate is defined as at least 30 observations per mean (McClave and Benson 1991). This limitation ensures a greater probability of having a normal distribution among the observations that produce the mean score. Although 30 percent of a population does not represent a majority, it does represent a significant portion. Additional tests are conducted at different percentage levels to ensure that patterns observed between mean levels below and above the 30 percent indigenous concentration are consistent for all percentage levels. Further, the object is not to analyze "indigenous" *municipios*, but to analyze what characteristics *municipios* of varying indigenous concentration possess, and to illicit any observable correlations between indigenous concentration and socioeconomic condition.

Due to the methodology just described, for simplicity the terms "indigenous" and "non-indigenous" refer to *municipios* in Mexico that are either above or below specific percentage levels of indigenous population. For example, if the sample is divided into two sub-samples, those *municipios* below 30 percent indigenous and those 30 percent and above, the term "non-indigenous" refers to the former subsample and "indigenous" to the latter. This simplification avoids repetitive mention of percentage levels. Though most *municipio* sub-samples are created by the 30 percent indigenous population split, on occasion another percentage is used. The percentage level used is either to be explicitly stated or included in an accompanying table or figure.

Areas of Analyses

The poverty analysis includes profiles of the poor, with overall estimates of poverty rates for the indigenous and non-indigenous populations. Poverty rates by selected characteristics are presented in an attempt to better isolate the correlates of poverty. The headcount index of poverty, the proportion of the population for which income is less than the poverty line, is estimated (Ravallion 1992).

The educational attainment and earnings differentials between indigenous and non-indigenous workers are examined, and the differential returns to investments in human capital are estimated. In addition, the components of the gross wage differential that can be explained by productivity-enhancing attributes and those which are due to "unexplained" factors and labor market discrimination are empirically determined using established theoretical and applied techniques.

The dual effects of gender and being indigenous on poverty are taken into account. For example, in terms of educational and earnings attainment, comparisons between indigenous males and females, as well as between indigenous and non-indigenous females, are attempted.

The effects of language, identity and geographic concentration as they relate to indigenous people, and the social prejudices against them, are thought to be reflected in the children's experiences in terms of scholastic attainment and performance and non-school activities. For this reason, an examination of children's activities is included. The analysis looks at schooling attainment and performance, as well as child labor. Schooling performance may be poor because of indigenous origins or because of family background. Differential child schooling performance may be a consequence of parental investments in home-produced human capital. Children who have parents with higher levels of schooling, fewer siblings to compete with for parental time and other family resources, and mothers who are less likely to work usually perform better in school (Chiswick 1988). Similarly, indigenous children may be more likely to participate in the labor force because of poverty or certain indigenous values.

Main Explanations of Ethnic Socioeconomic Differences

Several hypotheses regarding the role of ethnicity in society are implicitly and explicitly tested, such as human capital theory, discrimination theories, institutional hypotheses, socioeconomic status/family background theories, theories of internal colonialism, cultural theories ("target workers") and indigenous values/ paths to development.

The significant and positive relationship between human capital and earnings is well documented in the literature (see Psacharopoulos and Woodhall 1985 for a review). The usual explanation put forward, consistent with the human capital approach, is that schooling contributes to individual productivity which, in turn, leads to higher individual earnings. The earnings advantage of the more educated relative to the less educated is subject to the laws of supply and demand: as the numbers of the more educated increase, their earnings advantage declines and the minimum qualifications for given jobs rise in line with increased relative supplies (Schultz 1961; Mincer 1974; Becker 1975). The hypothesis to be tested here is that indigenous people attain less schooling and, therefore, receive lower earnings. The indicators of schooling include years and levels attained. Other indicators of human capital may include labor market experience and health status.

Institutional hypotheses emphasize the centrality of the functioning of labor markets (Doeringer and Piore 1972). In this tradition, labor market segmentation theories view the labor market as being divided between the primary—high productivity, high wage—and the secondary—low productivity, low wage—sectors. Individuals in the secondary labor market are locked into that sector and barriers exist to their moving into the high wage, high productivity, primary labor market (Carnoy 1980). The hypothesis here is that indigenous people receive lower earnings and have a higher incidence of poverty because they are locked into the secondary sector of the economy. The key indicators here are the returns to schooling and employment in the informal sector.

Theories of internal colonialism, which have been applied to indigenous people in all parts of the world, including Australia (Welch 1988), the United States (Jensen 1984; Jorgenson 1977; Jacobson 1984), Mexico (van Ginneken 1980), Ecuador (Burgos Guevara 1970), Peru (van den Berghe 1992) and Viet Nam (Evans 1992), postulate that the conditions of colonialism can exist within a nation-state when one group dominates a previously independent nation within its borders. In such a case, a dual economy, with a dual wage and labor market, is in place. Also present are the conditions of "unfree" labor, a dual occupational structure and dual wage scales, with the more rewarding occupations reserved for the non-indigenous population. The indigenous population often plays the role of a reserve labor force. Poverty, a lower standard of living, lower expectations and a lack of knowledge of labor laws are just some of the reasons why the indigenous labor force may agree to sell its labor cheaply. Also, in many cases, indigenous workers wish to return to their families and homes and may be willing to tolerate discrimination and low wages in order to facilitate their return (similar to the "target" workers theory; see below).

The "screening" hypothesis states that, in general, employers pay higher salaries to the more educated because they use schooling level as a proxy for other characteristics that "signal" which individuals could be more productive. Thus, it is not the content of their education that makes individuals more productive, but rather that years of schooling demonstrate to employers which potential employees are more productive since the more able will attain higher levels of schooling (Arrow 1973). The hypothesis here is that indigenous people receive lower earnings because they are screened on the basis of their schooling, which reflects their ethnolinguistic characteristics. Another key indicator could be employment in the public sector.

Other explanations of outcomes are concerned with the productivity of schooling. That is, for the same level of schooling and the same level of ability, different outcomes can result due to the application of "skills" in the labor market. Individual skills may be developed both in and out of school. Group variations in rates of returns to schooling arise from differences in the ability to convert the schooling process into earnings (Chiswick 1988: 590). This may be a consequence of parental investments in the home-produced components of child quality, although one can think of many other reasons. It would appear that members of more successful ethnic groups have parents with higher levels of schooling, fewer siblings to compete with for parental time and other family resources, and have mothers who are less likely to work when young children are in the household (Chiswick 1988). Further, a positive relationship between educational attainments across generations reflects the intergenerational transmission of human wealth. In the case of indigenous people, if parents have low levels of schooling and other forms of human capital, then this will be reflected in the human capital acquisition of their children. Lower stocks of human capital will be converted into lower relative earnings and a higher incidence of poverty. A similar hypothesis states that differences are due to class background rather than discrimination (this hypothesis is verified for Bolivia in Kelley (1988), and often put forward for the case of Brazil, but has not been verified; see Webster and Dwyer 1988; Silva 1985). That is, the great differences between ethnic groups could be due to the natural working of economic forces, rather than discrimination. According to this hypothesis, an individual's socioeconomic background in terms of family income, and father's and mother's education and occupation, is a more important factor in determining present socioeconomic conditions than is ethnicity.

Differential outcomes, of course, may be due to outright discrimination against ethnic, minority or indigenous groups. Discrimination against ethnic groups may work to deleteriously affect an individual's access to schooling, the quality of schooling that individual receives and labor market performance. This leads to lower schooling levels, lower returns to schooling, lower earnings and, ultimately, higher levels of poverty. Becker's (1971) seminal work on discrimination attempts to explain segregation in the workplace. He postulates that the differential is due to individual "tastes" for discrimination against other labor market participants. Becker also predicts that competitive forces in the economy lead to a gradual elimination of wage discrimination over time. Ethnic earnings differentials then, according to this theory, are a short-term or "disequilibrium" situation that are bound to disappear as long as some employees prefer profits over prejudice. This explanation, however, has been criticized for its inability to account for enduring differences in earnings between whites and non-whites in the United

States (Darity 1982). To test for discrimination, it is necessary to control for productive differences between ethnic groups so that any remaining difference in earnings after equalizing productive characteristics becomes an estimate of the "upper bound" of discrimination in the labor market (see below for a full exposition of this methodology).

Related to the above, but coming from another social science discipline, assimilation theory, or the industrialization hypothesis, is the classical sociological theory of ethnic relations. It suggests that divisions based upon race and ethnicity will whither away in the long-run in modern societies. This outcome is supposed to reflect modern industrial organization, where social mobility is based upon achieved, rather than ascribed, status (Hirschman 1983). Also known as acculturation theories, they predict that "traditional" criteria, on which inequality is based, are being replaced by rational or legal criteria, and that "particularistic" criteria are being replaced by "universalistic" criteria such as education and ability (Weber 1947; Parsons 1954). The implication is that the significance of race and ethnicity will decline as society develops. However, there is considerable evidence of persistent ethnic inequality in many countries. The method of testing these hypotheses is similar to those regarding economic discrimination mentioned above.

It is argued that indigenous people who are "traditional" will place less importance on the labor force and will use it only to achieve a specific, short term end, such as obtaining cash to finance a lengthy period out of the labor market. Such individuals have been labelled as "target" workers: they work only as long as necessary to obtain a fixed sum of wages (Sandefur and Scott 1983: 49). The reasons put forward for this behavior include a desire to work at one's own pace and the importance of kinship and community in Amerindian society. Traditional Amerindians see themselves as members of communities first, and are driven more by the good of the community than by individual achievement. This characteristic is expected to have a negative effect on labor force attachment and, ultimately, wages. Level of education, however, is expected to lead to a decline in traditional activities (Stabler 1990: 58). Many Aymara who now live in urban environments maintain ties with the rural communities to their mutual advantage (Hardman 1981: 3). Indigenous people who reside in the cities normally maintain their rural ties and landholdings (Saavedra 1981: 21). The Aymara value education highly, which meshes with their traditional values of individualism, hard work and communal and private advancement (Hardman 1981: 6). Open competition and forceful self-expression, however, are missing from Aymara culture (Saavedra 1981: 27).

The theory of "target" workers was developed from analyses of the work behavior of peasants and has been applied to Amerindians. It is argued that peasant agricultural workers can either work more hours or work more intensely or both. They seek output adequate to meet their basic needs. Since this work often involves drudgery, their effort is not pushed beyond the point where increases in output are outweighed by the irksomeness of the extra work. A rough equilibrium is struck between the degree of satisfaction of family needs and the degree of the drudgery of labor (Chayanov 1966). Peasants may have a certain target level of income. Once this is reached, they begin consuming leisure. Thus, interventions designed to increase income might result only in an increase in the amount of leisure consumed.

Traditional community values have persisted among Amerindians. Prior to European contact, these included entrepreneurial activity, which was crushed by the European immigrants. When this entrepreneurial spirit again became active in North America, it was community- rather than individually-based (Hagen 1968). This is based on the importance indigenous people place on the kinship system, or *comuneros* in Latin America (IFAD 1992). Economic security and well-being are provided to some extent through kinship-based exchange relationships such as the institution of *compadrazgo* (Collins 1983).

Most theories, however, predict that discrimination will eventually decrease in society in the long run for a variety of reasons. These include the inefficiency associated with discrimination from the perspective of profit-maximizing employers, the process of assimilation of ethnic groups and the parity ethnic groups will achieve in terms of productive characteristics such as education, training and experience. Free markets and access to quality education should lead to less discrimination over time. Yet, segmented labor markets, as a result of such factors as ethnic and linguistic differences, can restrain the equalizing forces of competition.

Methodology

Definitions of poverty and resulting poverty indicators are numerous, and substantial disagreement exists on which are more relevant. This study, however, in its focus on the indigenous dimension, settles on a standard methodology and attempts to avoid the methodological and theoretical issues associated with designing a poverty line. In an attempt to analyze the existence and correlates of absolute poverty, a poverty line, a measure that separates the poor from the nonpoor, is used. Those whose income falls below the line are poor; those above are non-poor. Following convention, two poverty lines are used, an "upper" and a "lower" poverty line. These indicate the boundary between the poor and the very poor, respectively. The lower poverty line will be referred to as the extreme poverty line.

Absolute poverty refers to the position of an individual or household in relation to a poverty line whose real value is fixed over time. An absolute poverty line is based on the cost of a minimum consumption basket, based on the food necessary for a recommended calorie intake. The poverty line is then augmented by an allowance for non-food needs, consistent with the spending patterns of the poor (CEPAL 1991).

The country analyses in this study utilize an income-based definition of poverty, whereby individuals living on a household per capita income which is less than a given standard are classified as poor. Consumption or expenditure information was not available in all surveys. In a recent analysis of poverty in Latin America (Psacharopoulos et al. 1992), a uniform poverty line of US$60 per person per month in 1985 purchasing power parity (PPP) dollars is used following the approach taken by *World Development Report 1990* (World Bank 1990). Rather than attempting to reformulate a new poverty standard, the present study employs this same US$60 PPP poverty line in each of the four country analyses. An extreme poverty line of US$30 per person per month in 1985 PPP dollars is also utilized. While it is understood that different poverty standards may be recognized by individual countries, the reasoning behind this choice of poverty lines is *not* to establish a definitive standard of poverty. In any case, all poverty lines are arbitrary to some degree. Rather, the emphasis here is to examine poverty within the context of being indigenous in Latin America, and a poverty line of US$60 PPP per person per month serves as an effective cut-off point for assessing poverty as it relates to both indigenous and non-indigenous groups. (See Psacharopoulos et al. 1992 for individual country poverty lines in local currency.)

Most household surveys in developing countries are plagued to some degree by underreporting of income. This will tend to lower incomes across the entire distribution, though not necessarily in a uniform manner. Unfortunately, it is difficult to assess and correct this underreporting; furthermore, the income adjustment process itself may introduce new biases into the poverty analysis. However, absolute poverty statistics reflect the intersection of the income distribution with an exogenous standard, such as a poverty line. Because the value of the poverty line is determined independently from the income level of a country, the underreporting of income can cause the poverty line to intersect the income distribution at a much higher point than if there were no underreporting. The result is a poverty estimate which is highly biased in an upward direction. Therefore, the income data used in the poverty analyses in this study have been adjusted to match corresponding national account figures. National accounts are usually subject to a system of cross-checking in an effort to determine the most accurate figures possible. While these figures may contain flaws, they ordinarily represent the most accurate data available for each country. For reasons stated above, survey data tend to be less reliable for estimating total national income, though they do allow for microanalyses of income data in a way which national accounts do not (Altimir 1987). The methodology followed here is identical to that which is used in a recent study of poverty and income distribution in Latin America (Psacharopoulos et al. 1992), and is detailed extensively in that report. In this study, the poverty lines are used to examine differences in socioeconomic well-being between indigenous and non-indigenous people.

While a profile of the poor is useful and informative, it is based on only a few categories of the independent variables entering into the explanation of the poverty measure. For a more thorough investigation of the determinants of poverty, a multivariate model is used to standardize the many factors that simultaneously affect the probability of an individual being poor. A logit model is estimated since poverty incidence is a dichotomous variable. A logit model is used in attempt to capture the major determinants of poverty at the individual level. The model expresses the probability (P) of being poor as a function of various characteristics (X) such as education, employment and being indigenous.

$$P = \frac{1}{1 + e^{-\sum \beta_i X_i}}$$ (4.1)

The reported coefficients are partial derivatives indicating the change in the probability of being poor, relative to a single unit change in one of the independent variables, where ß is the logit coefficient:

$$\frac{\partial P}{\partial X_i} = \beta_i P (1 - P)$$ (4.2)

Similar logit models are used in various sections of this study to assess the determinants of such variables as educational participation and child labor.

Differential outcomes indicate the level of inequality and poverty associated with indigenous people. The higher incidence of poverty, less schooling and lower earnings reflect, in a sense, the "cost" of being indigenous in each society. It is necessary to control for the many factors that influence the various indicators of well-being before estimating how much of the difference between indigenous and non-indigenous people is due to characteristics affected by public policy and those individual characteristics that cannot be changed. In other words, the point is to calculate how much of the difference in outcomes is "explained," and how much is "unexplained," representing the potential level of discrimination in society.

On earnings differentials, the use of multivariate regression analysis allows for the simulation of alternative outcomes and the decomposition of gross differentials. The decomposition method, the technique for analyzing earnings differentials, was popularized in the economics literature by Oaxaca (1973) and Blinder (1973). It was used earlier in sociology (Siegel 1965; Duncan 1968), and before that in demography (Kitagawa 1955). Although in the economics literature it was first used to analyze the determinants of male/female earnings differentials, the decomposition technique has been used since to analyze ethnic earnings differentials, public/private sector earnings differentials, earnings differentials by socio-economic background, to test the screening hypothesis and to test the effectiveness of a job training program. Most analyses have focused on developed countries, although some studies for developing nations exist (Psacharopoulos and Tzannatos 1992; Birdsall and Sabot 1991).

The standard procedure for analyzing the determinants of earnings differentials between two groups is to fit the following two equations, or earnings functions, for employed members of the economically dominant group and employed members of the marginal group:

$$LnY_n = b_n X_n + u_n$$ (4.3)

$$LnY_i = b_i X_i + u_i$$ (4.4)

where subscripts n and i represent non-indigenous and indigenous workers, respectively; Y symbolizes labor market earnings; X represents measured productivity-determining characteristics of the workers, such as education, experience and other control variables. The regression coefficient, b, reflects the returns that the market yields to a unit change in characteristics such as education and experience. The error term, u, reflects measurement error, as well as the effect of factors unmeasured or unobserved by the researcher.

It is known that the regression lines pass through the mean values of the variables so that

$$Ln\bar{Y}_n = \hat{b}_n\bar{X}_n \tag{4.5}$$

$$Ln\bar{Y}_i = \hat{b}_i\bar{X}_i \tag{4.6}$$

where hats ($\wedge$) denote estimated values and bars ($\bar{}$) represent mean values.

If indigenous workers receive the same returns as non-indigenous workers for their endowments of wage-determining characteristics, then their average earnings would be

$$Ln\bar{Y}_i^* = \hat{b}_n\bar{X}_i \tag{4.7}$$

which are the average earnings of indigenous workers that would prevail in the absence of wage discrimination. Subtracting Equation 4.7 from 4.5 gives the difference between the average non-indigenous earnings and the average hypothetical indigenous earnings that would prevail if indigenous workers were paid according to the pay structure faced by non-indigenous workers. This difference reflects their unequal endowments of income-generating characteristics, so that

$$Ln\bar{Y}_n - Ln\bar{Y}_i^* = \hat{b}_n\bar{X}_n - \hat{b}_n\bar{X}_i = \hat{b}_n(\bar{X}_n - \bar{X}_i) \tag{4.8}$$

Subtracting Equation 4.6 from 4.7 yields the difference between the hypothetical non-discriminatory earnings of indigenous workers and their actual earnings. This difference reflects the different returns to the same income-generating characteristics:

$$Ln\bar{Y}_i^* - Ln\bar{Y}_i = \hat{b}_n\bar{X}_i - \hat{b}_i\bar{X}_i = \bar{X}_i(\hat{b}_n - \hat{b}_i) \tag{4.9}$$

Adding Equations 4.8 and 4.9 yields

$$Ln\bar{Y}_n - Ln\bar{Y}_i = \hat{b}_n(\bar{X}_n - \bar{X}_i) + \bar{X}_i(\hat{b}_n - \hat{b}_i) \tag{4.10}$$

Thus, the overall earnings gap can be decomposed into two components: one is the portion attributable to differences in the endowments of income generating characteristics (X_n-X_i) evaluated with the non-indigenous worker pay structure (b_n); the other portion is attributable to differences in the returns (b_n-b_i) that non-indigenous and indigenous workers receive for the same endowment of income-generating characteristics (*X*). This latter component is often taken as reflecting wage discrimination. In economic terms, discrimination refers to differences in economic outcomes between groups that cannot be accounted for by the skills and productive characteristics of these groups (Schultz 1991). This method, although illuminating since it allows one to determine the extent of discrimination in the labor market, does not allow one to determine the origins of discrimination. Discrimination in the labor market can be direct, affecting earnings, occupational attainment and training access, or it can be indirect, the result of unequal education and acquisition of skills (Chiswick 1987).

The use of earnings functions to estimate discrimination means that there will always be a problem of omitted variables. This type of data problem means that the "unexplained" component is not only a measure of discrimination, but also of our ignorance (Filer 1983: 84). It is because of omitted and unobserved factors that the "unexplained" component is seen as an "upper bound" estimate of wage discrimination in the labor market. Included among the omitted variables that are expected to account for some of the "unexplained" component are: the quality of labor, attachment to the labor force, lack of specific training, interrupted work careers, tastes and personality (Hill 1979; Goldin and Polachek 1987; Polachek 1975; Mincer and Polachek 1974, 1978; Filer 1983). There is also evidence to suggest that much of the discrimination against the minority group is due to occupational segregation; that is the "crowding" of the minority group into certain occupations where rates of pay and chances for promotion are low. This, of course, suggests that prior discrimination has taken place, such as lack of access to jobs, training, schooling and so on. The results of a number of studies have shown that the greater the number of variables used to control for differences in productivity-related factors, the smaller the productivity-adjusted earnings gap ("unexplained" component) relative to the unadjusted gap. However, even when an extensive list of control variables is used, most studies find some residual gap that they attribute to discrimination. When the gap is close to zero, this usually results from the inclusion of control variables whose values themselves may reflect prior discrimination (Gunderson 1989: 51).

Conclusion

In the country case studies that follow, the results obtained are evaluated by the hypotheses outlined above. The results of research based on developed countries point to the eradication of discrimination over time. Little research effort has gone into examining these issues in less developed societies, where, theoretically, discrimination is most likely due to the nature of the market and the great linguistic and ethnic differences not dissipated by schooling (Kelley 1988: 400). The fact that indigenous populations have remained distinct after centuries of assimilation policies, increasing levels of schooling and rural-urban migration, to mention a few examples, reflects the insufficiency of most theories. It is hoped that the understanding of ethnicity and being indigenous in less developed countries will increase as a result of the present study by contributing to the theoretical debate and by providing a socioeconomic overview of the importance of being indigenous in Latin America at a time when poverty reduction is paramount. The present study also indicates some priority areas for further research.

5

Urban Bolivia

Bill Wood and Harry Anthony Patrinos

Bolivia has been described as "the most Indian of the American republics" and as a society created by "imperial conquests and native adaptations" (Klein 1982:vii). Most of the indigenous people are Quechua and Aymara descendants and live in the rural regions. The rest belong to different tribes and reside in the jungles and lowlands and have chosen not to be incorporated into the rest of the country's life.

Prior to the arrival of the Spaniards, the area now known as Bolivia was dominated by the Inca empire. The Spaniards used the labor of the indigenous population to extract the precious minerals in the country. Precontact institutions were adapted by the Spaniards to benefit them in their efforts to use indigenous labor. After independence, Simon Bolívar instituted decrees designed to better the situation of indigenous people, although these decrees had to be reiterated many times up until about 1945 (Medina 1977a). Bolivia's 1952 Revolution significantly changed the country's traditional order and the status of indigenous inhabitants. One of the most notable changes was the abolition of forced labor (Serafino 1991).

Each indigenous group has its own language and distinct culture. Members of these groups speak Spanish as a second language or do not speak Spanish at all. The 5 percent of the population of Spanish descent dominates the country economically, culturally and politically. A large portion of the population is of mixed indigenous and Spanish descent.

While the majority of indigenous people in Bolivia reside in rural areas, in this chapter individual level data from a large-scale household survey conducted in urban Bolivia in 1989 are used to examine and compare the socioeconomic conditions of indigenous and non-indigenous people. Poverty, education, employment, health and population issues are also explored. The objective of this chapter is to document differences in these important areas in order to better understand the conditions and disadvantages affecting both indigenous and non-indigenous people.

The determinants of poverty are estimated, and the effects of changes in individual characteristics are simulated. It is determined that policy-influenced variables such as schooling and employment creation are important factors that can lead to a significant reduction in poverty levels. In addition, the overall earnings differential between indigenous and non-indigenous workers is decomposed into its "explained" and "unexplained" components. It is found that equalization of income-generating characteristics would boost the productivity of the indigenous population in their market and non-market activities and lead to a considerable reduction in earnings inequality in Bolivia.

The analysis focusses on indigenous and non-indigenous language individuals. Indigenous language speakers include both monolingual and bilingual (Spanish and indigenous language) speakers. In some cases, due to insufficient sample size, the monolingual and bilingual indigenous language speakers have been grouped together.

Income inequality is high throughout Latin America, and Bolivia is no exception. The bottom fifth of the urban income distribution receives only 3.5 percent of total income, while the top fifth receives 57.5 percent (Psacharopoulos et al. 1992). Individuals of indigenous background are disproportionately represented at lower income levels. While 28 percent of the urban population speaks at least one indigenous language, they comprise 38 percent of the bottom quintile and less than 17 percent of the top quintile. Income inequality is more of a between group than a within group problem. While the Gini index is 0.524 for the total urban Bolivian population, it is 0.527 for the non-indigenous population but only 0.479 for the indigenous population.

Magnitude of Poverty

Bolivia is one of the poorest countries in Latin America as measured by per capita income. The following section assesses the magnitude of poverty in the country, and its distribution by indigenous and non-indigenous population. The poverty line used in this chapter is consistent with the US$60 per person per month in 1985 purchasing power parity (PPP), which is applied throughout this study. The extreme poverty line is US$30 PPP per person per month.

Poverty Incidence and Interethnic Income Differentials

The incidence of poverty among individuals who speak at least one indigenous language is far higher than for monolingual speakers of Spanish (Table 5.1). While the overall urban poverty rate is 52.6 percent, the incidence of poverty among indigenous people is more than 15 percentage points higher than among their non-indigenous counterparts. The incidence of extreme poverty is one-half times greater among indigenous than non-indigenous individuals.

The distribution of poverty categories across ethnic groups is given in Table 5.2. Indigenous individuals are overrepresented among the poor and extreme poor relative to their population share, while monolingual Spanish speakers comprise a disproportionate position among the non-poor.

Table 5.1: Incidence of Poverty by Ethnicity
(percent)

	Indigenous		Non-indigenous	All	N
	Monolingual	Bilingual			
Not Poor	26.5	36.3	51.9	47.4	13,999
Poor	73.5	63.7	48.1	52.6	15,971
Extreme Poor	37.1	29.2	19.8	22.5	6,780
Poverty Gap Index	30.1		21.3	23.7	
FGT P_2 Index	18.3		12.6	14.2	

Source: EIH 1989.

Both the incidence and the distribution of poverty reflect the disparity in income levels found across ethnic groups. The magnitude of this disparity is apparent in Table 5.3. On average, indigenous individuals live on a per capita income that is less than two-thirds the income of non-indigenous people.

Poverty Profile

While poverty levels are high in Bolivia, social indicators give an even more dismal picture of the quality of life prevailing in the country.

Demographics

Ethnic inequality and poverty reflect distinct demographic patterns in urban Bolivia. As would be expected, geography plays an important role: some regions have a higher concentration of indigenous people and poverty than others. Furthermore, the age and sex distributions of language spoken indicate the evolving

Table 5.2: Distribution of Poverty Categories by Ethnicity
(percent)

Category	Indigenous		Non-indigenous	All	N
	Monolingual	Bilingual			
All	1.2	26.4	72.3	100.0	29,970
Not Poor	0.6	20.2	79.1	100.0	13,999
Poor	1.8	32.0	66.2	100.0	15,971
Extreme Poor	2.0	34.3	63.7	100.0	6,780

Source: EIH 1989.

Table 5.3: Mean Per Capita Income Levels
(bolivianos per person per month)

| Category | Indigenous | | Non-indigenous | All |
	Monolingual	Bilingual		
All	76.7	99.9	154.4	139.0
Not Poor	175.2	193.8	252.5	240.1
Poor	44.7	46.4	48.7	47.9
Extreme Poor	27.6	25.8	26.0	26.0

Source: EIH 1989.

demographics of ethnicity. Women and older individuals are disproportionately represented among those who speak no Spanish. This reflects the tendency for children and working males to learn Spanish either through school or in the workplace.

A profile of ethnicity and poverty in eight departments (Pando is not included in the survey) is given in Table 5.4. Overall, 27.7 percent of the urban population qualifies as indigenous. The Highland area includes the departments of Oruro, La Paz and Potosí. All have high concentrations of indigenous people. The Valley territory consists of Chuquisaca, Cochabamba and Tarija. Chuquisaca and Cochabamba have relatively high concentrations of indigenous people, while indigenous individuals make up a smaller minority in the cities of Tarija. The Lowlands region includes Beni and Santa Cruz; the indigenous population in these two departments is small relative to the national average.

According to the survey results, over half of all urban indigenous people can be found in the department of La Paz, and nearly one-quarter are located in Cochabamba. Oruro, Potosí and Chuquisaca follow with 8 percent, 7 percent and 5 percent of the urban indigenous population, respectively. The far right column of Table 5.4 gives the urban population distribution, along with the non-poor/poor/ extreme poor percentages in each department. In all departments except Beni and Oruro, the percentage of indigenous people who are poor exceeds the overall indigenous share of the total population. A disproportionately large share of urban poverty is concentrated among indigenous groups, particularly in the Highland departments of La Paz and Potosí.

It is clear from Table 5.5 that the age demographics are different for non-indigenous groups than for indigenous groups. The indigenous cohort is substantially older than its non-indigenous counterpart. This is particularly true for monolingual indigenous individuals. The strong correlation between age and knowledge of Spanish highlights the tendency for younger individuals to have learned Spanish at some point in their lives. At least within the urban context, the data suggest that a greater number of children with indigenous parents are learning only Spanish, and members of each generation are less likely to know an indigenous language than their parents. An important caveat raised by Table 5.5 is that

Table 5.4: Distribution of Urban Bolivian Population across Regions
(percent)

Region	Indigenous		Non-indigenous	Urban Population
	Monolingual	*Bilingual*		
National	1.2	26.4	72.3	100.0
La Paz (Highland)	1.6	37.6	60.8	38.1
Not Poor	1.1	29.0	70.0	41.6
Poor	2.0	43.7	54.3	58.4
Extreme Poor	1.9	45.0	53.1	26.8
Oruro (Highland)	1.3	24.0	74.7	8.7
Not Poor	1.1	24.6	74.3	29.1
Poor	1.4	23.7	74.9	70.9
Extreme Poor	1.4	23.7	74.9	36.5
Potosí (Highland)	4.1	34.8	61.1	4.8
Not Poor	1.2	25.4	73.5	27.2
Poor	5.2	38.3	56.5	72.8
Extreme Poor	6.2	42.8	51.1	39.0
Cochabamba (Valley)	0.1	36.0	63.0	17.0
Not Poor	0.7	33.6	65.7	51.6
Poor	1.3	38.6	60.1	48.4
Extreme Poor	1.0	36.6	62.4	18.0
Chuquisaca (Valley)	2.9	29.5	67.6	3.9
Not Poor	1.2	26.0	72.8	46.9
Poor	4.4	32.6	63.0	53.1
Extreme Poor	6.8	29.3	63.9	21.2
Tarija (Valley)	0.2	6.7	93.1	2.5
Not Poor	0.0	6.5	93.5	45.8
Poor	0.4	6.9	92.8	54.2
Extreme Poor	0.6	6.9	92.5	24.1
Beni (Lowland)	0.0	1.3	98.7	2.8
Not Poor	0.0	1.8	98.2	57.7
Poor	0.0	0.7	99.3	42.3
Extreme Poor	0.0	0.5	92.8	13.8
Santa Cruz (Lowland)	0.2	4.0	95.8	22.3
Not Poor	0.1	3.7	96.2	64.8
Poor	0.3	4.6	95.1	35.2
Extreme Poor	0.5	6.8	92.8	10.6

Source: EIH 1989.

the monolingual and bilingual indigenous populations are fundamentally different. The former is substantially older, and, as will be shown in the next section, predominantly female. It is important to keep these differences in mind when interpreting the analysis throughout this chapter.

While the gender distribution of the urban population is approximately equal for males and females in the bilingual indigenous and monolingual Spanish groups, the monolingual indigenous cohort is overwhelmingly female (Table 5.6). Furthermore, half of all households headed by a monolingual indigenous individual are headed by a female. Poorer households in each of the ethnic groupings are also more likely to be headed by a female.

Table 5.5: Mean Age of Individuals and Household Heads
(years)

Population Group	Indigenous		Non-indigenous	All
	Monolingual	*Bilingual*		
Individuals	50.5	33.9	24.4	27.2
Not Poor	49.2	35.7	26.3	28.3
Poor	50.9	32.9	22.4	26.3
Extreme Poor	50.3	33.0	22.4	26.6
Household Heads	55.9	44.0	42.2	43.2
Not Poor	52.9	43.7	42.0	42.6
Poor	56.7	44.2	42.6	43.7
Extreme Poor	57.5	45.3	44.6	45.3

Source: EIH 1989.

Table 5.6: Gender of Household Members and Household Heads
(percent female)

Population Group	Indigenous		Non-indigenous	All
	Monolingual	*Bilingual*		
Entire Population	79.1	52.8	51.1	51.9
Household Heads	49.9	15.1	15.9	16.1
Not Poor	47.6	14.0	13.4	13.8
Poor	51.1	15.8	19.5	18.5
Extreme Poor	53.0	18.2	24.0	21.8

Source: EIH 1989.

There is a distinct correlation between marital status and language spoken among individuals who are 15 years or older (Table 5.7). Whether for cultural, social or economic reasons, monolingual indigenous adults are most likely to be married, while the opposite is true for monolingual Spanish adults. For household heads, however, there is little difference between bilingual indigenous and monolingual Spanish individuals. The starkly lower tendency for monolingual indigenous household heads not to be married is partially due to the high number of widows in this category. For the population as a whole, there is a slight tendency for poorer persons not to be married.

Household size is greater for the indigenous cohort than for the non-indigenous group (Table 5.8). There is also a tendency for poorer households to be larger, though the difference between the size of poor and extremely poor households is negligible.

**Table 5.7: Marital Status of Individuals and Household Heads
Aged 15 Years and Over**

(percent married)

Population Group	Indigenous		Non-indigenous	All
	Monolingual	*Bilingual*		
Individuals	69.1	68.5	51.5	57.2
Not Poor	71.6	67.8	54.0	57.5
Poor	68.2	68.9	48.2	56.9
Extreme Poor	70.7	67.7	46.5	56.1
Household Heads	47.2	79.6	79.0	78.7
Not Poor	55.0	78.4	80.1	79.4
Poor	45.2	80.3	77.5	78.0
Extreme Poor	45.4	77.2	73.8	74.8

Source: EIH 1989.

Education

Educational attainment is an important factor affecting individuals' earnings and their ability to contribute to the overall income level of the household. While the relationship between education and earnings will be explored in greater detail later in the chapter, an overview of schooling levels across ethnic and income groups is presented here.

The mean years of schooling for individuals aged 18 years and over are presented in Table 5.9. Also included are figures for females and heads of household. There is a very strong correlation between schooling attainment and indigenous origin, and between schooling attainment and poverty category. This supports the well-documented tendency for people with less education to earn less than their more educated counterparts. Schooling levels of indigenous people are over three years less on average than for non-indigenous individuals. The difference is even greater for indigenous females, suggesting that they are the most disadvantaged in Bolivian society. Interestingly, the average number of years of schooling for household heads is slightly less than for all adults. This most likely reflects the higher mean age of household heads, who passed through their schooling years at

Table 5.8: Mean Household Size

(number of persons)

Household	Indigenous	Non-indigenous	All
All Households	4.9	4.7	4.8
Not Poor	4.3	4.4	4.4
Poor	5.3	5.2	5.2
Extreme Poor	5.4	5.1	5.2

Source: EIH 1989.

Table 5.9: Mean Years of Schooling

Population Aged 18 and Over	Indigenous		Non-indigenous	All
	Monolingual	*Bilingual*		
All Individuals	0.4	6.5.	9.7	8.4
Not Poor	0.6	7.5	10.2	9.4
Poor	0.3	5.8	8.9	7.3
Extreme Poor	0.3	5.5	8.7	7.0
Females	0.3	5.5	9.1	7.7
Not Poor	0.4	6.5	9.7	8.8
Poor	0.2	4.9	8.3	6.6
Extreme Poor	0.2	4.6	8.1	6.2
Household Heads	0.6	6.6	9.5	8.2
Not Poor	0.8	7.7	10.4	9.5
Poor	0.6	5.8	8.3	6.9
Extreme Poor	0.6	5.6	8.2	6.6

Source: EIH 1989.

a time when access to schooling and duration of enrollment were lower than for their younger counterparts.

Several factors feed into the indigenous/non-indigenous disparity in schooling levels. First, the high mean age of the monolingual indigenous cohort and the scarcity of bilingual education in Bolivia make it likely that this group spent little time in school precisely because they did not speak the language of instruction. Not a single individual in the monolingual indigenous group completed primary education. Second, individuals from poorer families often leave school earlier than their wealthier classmates in order to contribute to the household income. Third, though it is not discernible from the data, less access to education on the part of indigenous groups may be a factor in their lower schooling attainment. The determinants of educational attainment are examined in greater depth later in this chapter.

In general, individuals with no schooling are in a strongly disadvantageous position with respect to employment, earnings, health and welfare. Illiteracy among this group is often high, though illiteracy and no schooling are not synonymous. Table 5.10 shows the percentage of individuals and household heads who have received no schooling. The disparity between the indigenous and non-indigenous groups is startling. The bilingual indigenous cohort has a no-schooling rate which is more than three times higher than that of its non-indigenous counterpart. This discrepancy is a strong indication that basic education is not reaching different ethnic groups in an equitable manner. Furthermore, the very high no-schooling rate of monolingual indigenous individuals reflects the added barrier caused by language communication problems. Not surprisingly, the percentage of individuals with no schooling is higher for poorer groups than for wealthier ones. And as with mean years of schooling, the incidence of no schooling is about the

Table 5.10: Incidence of No Schooling
(percent)

Population Aged 15 and Over	Indigenous		Non-indigenous	All
	Monolingual	*Bilingual*		
All Individuals	77.9	11.0	2.8	6.6
Not Poor	68.3	7.9	2.3	4.2
Poor	81.0	12.9	3.5	9.1
Extreme Poor	81.3	14.2	3.9	10.5
Household Heads	67.7	10.5	2.8	6.9
Not Poor	56.5	7.7	2.0	4.1
Poor	70.5	12.3	3.4	9.7
Extreme Poor	74.0	13.1	2.9	10.2

Source: EIH 1989.

same for household heads as for all adults in both the bilingual indigenous and monolingual Spanish categories.

The distribution of educational level by gender and ethnicity is shown in Table 5.11. A greater percentage of females have incomplete primary schooling, while a higher percentage of males are likely to complete primary, secondary or university education. The majority of indigenous males and females have less than complete primary schooling, suggesting that illiteracy among these individuals may be high. A very high percentage of non-indigenous males have university education (11 percent), while a high proportion of non-indigenous females have completed primary and secondary education as compared with both indigenous males and females.

The relationship between years of schooling attained and indigenous origins by birth cohort is highlighted in Figure 5.1. The graph shows that the average schooling level of non-indigenous males increased until the 1949–53 cohort, after which

Table 5.11: Distribution of Schooling Attainment by Gender and Ethnicity
(percent)

Gender and Schooling	Indigenous	Non-indigenous	All
Males (Aged 15 and Over)	100.0	100.0	100.0
Incomplete Primary	51.3	23.2	32.5
Primary	23.7	30.6	28.3
Secondary	21.1	35.0	30.4
University	3.9	11.2	8.8
Females (Aged 15 and Over)	100.0	100.0	100.0
Incomplete Primary	69.2	32.1	44.3
Primary	14.8	29.6	24.5
Secondary	14.6	35.5	28.2
University	1.4	3.8	3.0

Source: EIH 1989.

the rate of increase slowed. For non-indigenous women, the schooling level increased for all cohorts born by 1959–63. The average schooling level of indigenous males increased continuously over time, with a sharp rise for those born in 1959 or later. For indigenous women, the increase is even more dramatic, particularly for the post-1952 Revolution cohorts born during 1949–53 and 1954–58, although the gap between the sexes is greater among indigenous people. This reflects the substantial increases in education investments and enrollment levels that were undertaken as part of the social reform goals of the 1952 Revolution (Kelley and Klein 1981).

The above data reflect the changing distribution of school attainment for successive age cohorts. A greater percentage of women and indigenous individuals are completing more school than in the past. Table 5.12 gives insight into the current schooling differentials across ethnic groups by comparing student enrollment levels. Non-indigenous children aged 6 to 18 years are still much more likely to be enrolled in school than indigenous children.

Employment

For most households, the primary source of income is labor market earnings. Examining employment characteristics across ethnic and income categories highlights important differences which underlie socioeconomic inequities. Because

Figure 5.1: Educational Attainment by Ethnicity and Birth Cohort

Years of Schooling

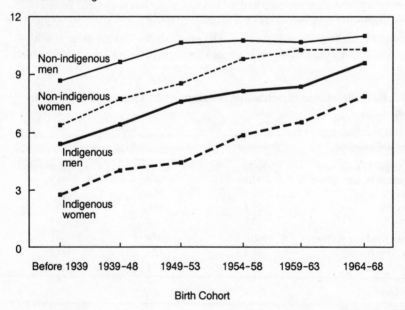

Birth Cohort

Source: EIH 1989.

Table 5.12: Student Enrollment Levels
(percent)

Students Aged 6–18	Indigenous	Non-indigenous	All
Enrolled in School	82.9	92.2	90.9
Not Poor	76.3	91.5	90.2
Poor	85.1	92.8	91.4
Extreme Poor	87.5	92.1	91.2

Source: EIH 1989.

the monolingual indigenous cohort is demographically quite different from the other two groups due to a heavy concentration of older women, it is not strictly comparable and should be analyzed with caution.

Table 5.13 presents an overview of employment status broken down by indigenous origins and income group. A greater percentage of all indigenous persons participate in the labor force, and a lower percentage of the indigenous cohort in the labor force is unemployed. Bilingual individuals are more likely to have a second job, and they spend more hours working per week than their non-indigenous counterparts. Yet the earnings of bilingual indigenous workers average less than two-thirds those of non-indigenous persons.

Not surprisingly, there is a strong correlation between poverty and employment status at the individual and head of household levels. By definition, the increased income from employment reduces the probability that household per capita income falls below the poverty line. In the same light, those with second jobs are less likely to fall in the poor and extreme poor categories than those who work only one job. However, less than 10 percent of the working population in any ethnic or income category works a second job. Interestingly, the number of hours worked is consistent across all income groups for those individuals who are employed. Given that 38 percent of poor individuals and 74 percent of poor household heads are working, there is a significant number of "working poor" who are unable to maintain their household per capita income above the poverty line despite active employment.

The distribution of workers across employment categories for indigenous and non-indigenous groups is shown in Table 5.14. Approximately one-half of indigenous people are self-employed, while the majority of non-indigenous individuals work as employees.

A relationship between indigenous origin, poverty and employment in the informal sector is indicated in Table 5.15.[1] Individuals working in the informal sector often lack the qualifications, such as sufficient education and training, to find employment in the formal sector. Given that these qualifications are less prevalent among indigenous and poor individuals, it is not surprising that these individuals comprise a relatively large share of the informal sector. However, heads of household have a lower likelihood of being employed in the informal sector than do other family members.

Table 5.13: Employment Status

	Indigenous		Non-indigenous	All
Population Group Status	*Monolingual*	*Bilingual*		
Individual Working (%)	45.3	57.9	41.2	46.1
Not Poor	61.3	71.3	49.6	54.5
Poor	40.0	49.9	31.4	38.1
Extreme Poor	36.5	41.4	24.2	31.0
Household Heads Working (%)	69.2	82.2	82.8	82.4
Not Poor	77.4	91.5	90.4	90.7
Poor	67.0	76.3	72.0	73.9
Extreme Poor	55.8	65.2	54.3	60.1
Individual Working Two Jobs (%)	5.3	7.3	6.9	7.0
Not Poor	6.5	8.9	8.4	8.5
Poor	4.7	5.8	4.1	4.9
Extreme Poor	4.1	3.5	4.7	2.4
Total Hours Worked per Week	46.2	49.0	48.4	48.6
Not Poor	45.3	49.4	48.4	48.6
Poor	46.7	48.7	48.3	48.5
Extreme Poor	48.0	49.1	47.3	48.2
Mean Labor Individual Income[a]	189.4	308.5	479.3	413.5
Not Poor	285.8	444.8	620.7	566.8
Poor	128.6	186.9	200.6	192.8
Extreme Poor	102.1	136.4	132.1	133.5
Unemployment Rate[b] (%)	4.5	7.6	9.0	8.4
Not Poor	5.7	3.1	5.3	4.6
Poor	3.8	11.1	15.2	13.1
Extreme Poor	6.1	17.9	22.0	19.6

Source: EIH 1989.
a. In *bolivianos* per month.
b. Not employed, but looking for work during the reference period.

Health

An overview of the general health of the urban population in Bolivia is provided in Table 5.16. On average, the indigenous groups are more likely to have been sick or injured in the previous month than the non-indigenous cohort. There is a higher tendency among indigenous individuals for their disabilities to be sufficiently severe to keep them out of work for more than a week. Furthermore, indigenous persons are less likely to seek medical help for their ailments. Both groups are equally likely to receive some form of medication for their health problems. Regarding an important preventative measure, the vaccination rate against yellow fever for non-indigenous individuals is double that for indigenous individuals.

Access to medical care for pregnant women is essential for the preservation of the mother's life and the healthy development of the newborn. Table 5.17 documents that indigenous women are in a substantially inferior position with respect

Table 5.14: Distribution of Employment Categories by Ethnicity and Poverty
(percent)

Employment Category	Indigenous		Non-indigenous	All
	Monolingual	*Bilingual*		
Employee	20.0	38.4	53.6	47.7
Self-employed	65.3	48.5	30.4	37.4
Employer	1.6	2.1	2.7	2.5
Other	13.1	11.0	13.3	12.5
Total	100.0	100.0	100.0	100.0

Source: EIH 1989.

to many important health inputs for a safe pregnancy cycle. Surprisingly, while the poor are less likely to receive professional attention at birth in a medical establishment, effectively targeted programs through public clinics have led to high provision rates of certain preventative health procedures for poor women. Still, outreach to indigenous women is considerably lower.

The strong correlation between being of indigenous origin and high rates of fertility/child mortality is highlighted in Table 5.18. Indigenous women give birth to more children, and suffer higher child mortality than do non-indigenous women. However, the monolingual indigenous sample is substantially older than the others, and therefore should be interpreted with caution since none of the three cohorts has been corrected for truncation bias. Poor women also have higher than average fertility and child mortality rates.

Knowledge and use of oral rehydration therapy (ORT) are principal means by which parents can prevent deaths of their young children, since diarrheal diseases

Table 5.15: Informal Sector Employment by Ethnicity and Income Group
(percent)

Population Group	Indigenous		Non-indigenous	All
	Monolingual	*Bilingual*		
All Individuals	84.8	66.7	52.2	57.9
Not Poor	89.1	65.9	49.0	54.2
Poor	82.5	67.5	58.1	62.9
Extreme Poor	76.8	68.0	61.3	65.1
Household Heads	75.0	56.7	43.2	49.0
Not Poor	72.9	56.1	39.5	44.7
Poor	75.7	57.2	50.0	54.2
Extreme Poor	61.9	57.0	51.1	54.7

Source: EIH 1989.

Table 5.16: General Health Conditions
(percent affected)

	Indigenous		Non-indigenous	All
Population Group	Monolingual	Bilingual		
Sick or Injured (in Past 30 Days)	38.8	20.5	14.3	16.2
Not Poor	40.1	17.9	13.7	14.7
Poor	38.4	21.9	15.0	17.6
Extreme Poor	44.5	22.8	16.0	18.9
Kept from Work over 7 Days	10.7	7.0	4.5	5.3
Not Poor	13.2	6.6	4.2	4.8
Poor	9.9	7.3	4.9	5.7
Extreme Poor	12.6	8.1	5.2	6.4
Received Medical Help If Sick	41.2	57.2	66.0	62.4
Not Poor	38.0	65.9	70.9	69.1
Poor	42.3	53.2	61.2	57.3
Extreme Poor	44.4	50.5	59.4	55.0
Received Medication If Sick	89.0	95.2	94.6	94.9
Not Poor	66.2	96.0	93.9	94.1
Poor	95.9	94.8	95.4	95.2
Extreme Poor	100.0	94.0	92.6	93.4
Vaccinated for Yellow Fever	8.4	18.9	36.3	31.4
Not Poor	7.9	21.5	43.0	38.4
Poor	8.5	17.5	29.1	25.0
Extreme Poor	6.6	14.9	25.8	21.7

Source: EIH 1989.

are one of the leading causes of death for young children. As Table 5.19 indicates, a greater percentage of non-indigenous adults are knowledgeable about the uses of ORT; non-poor adults are also better informed about ORT. This overlap is reflective of the educational attainment of these groups, since the know-how to provide ORT is often disseminated through community health programs and printed materials which may require some level of basic education to comprehend. However, among those who know ORT, the poorest bilingual indigenous adults have the highest actual usage of ORT with their children, which could be indicative of the health conditions in which that group lives.

Housing and Consumption

A breakdown of housing characteristics and home ownership is presented in Table 5.20. Given their higher household per capita income, it is not surprising that households headed by a monolingual Spanish speaker have a higher number of rooms and more rooms per capita than households headed by an indigenous speaker; the same is true of the non-poor relative to the poor. Interestingly, the indigenous group has a much higher level of home ownership. However, this says

Table 5.17: Indicators of Maternal Care

Indicator	Indigenous	Non-indigenous	All
Number of Prenatal Visits (mean)	4.0	4.7	4.5
Not Poor	3.7	5.0	4.7
Poor	4.2	4.4	4.3
Extreme Poor	4.0	4.0	4.0
Birth in Hospital/Clinic (%)	50.2	78.1	67.0
Not Poor	72.2	81.0	78.6
Poor	42.5	75.7	59.8
Extreme Poor	33.4	78.4	54.5
Birth with Doctor/Nurse/Midwife (%)	67.0	93.2	82.8
Not Poor	86.3	98.3	95.1
Poor	60.2	88.9	75.2
Extreme Poor	48.6	90.5	68.2
Took Iron during Pregnancy (%)	39.8	50.8	47.6
Not Poor	36.5	58.6	53.6
Poor	41.2	40.8	41.2
Extreme Poor	44.0	33.4	37.6
Tetanus Vaccination (1 or more) (%)	40.0	49.9	46.6
Not Poor	39.2	47.9	45.7
Poor	40.4	52.4	47.5
Extreme Poor	38.4	48.6	44.1

Source: EIH 1989.

Table 5.18: Mean Number of Children Born, Died and Currently Alive per Woman Aged 13 and Over

	Indigenous		Non-indigenous	All
	Monolingual	Bilingual		
Live Births	6.0	4.5	3.6	4.0
Not Poor	5.7	3.9	3.2	3.5
Poor	6.1	4.8	4.0	4.5
Extreme Poor	6.1	5.1	4.2	4.7
Children Died	1.7	0.9	0.4	0.7
Not Poor	1.6	0.8	0.3	0.5
Poor	1.7	0.9	0.6	0.8
Extreme Poor	1.6	1.0	0.5	0.8
Children Alive Today	4.3	3.6	3.1	3.3
Not Poor	4.1	3.1	2.9	3.0
Poor	4.4	3.8	3.5	3.7
Extreme Poor	4.5	4.1	3.6	3.9

Source: EIH 1989.

Table 5.19: Adult Knowledge of Oral Rehydration Therapy
(percent)

Adult Population	Indigenous	Non-indigenous	All
Know ORT (%)	51.7	65.8	61.9
Not Poor	56.0	71.3	68.2
Poor	50.0	61.1	57.4
Extreme Poor	48.8	60.3	56.1
Have Used ORT (%)	77.5	74.7	75.3
Not Poor	71.1	72.7	72.4
Poor	80.6	76.8	77.9
Extreme Poor	82.0	78.1	79.4

Source: EIH 1989.

little about quality of housing, which may be lower for the indigenous group. This possibility is reflected in the lower rate of sewage facility connections to indigenous households, and the lower prevalence of latrines for these households' use.

Table 5.20: Housing Characteristics and Ownership

Characteristic	Indigenous	Non-indigenous	All
Rooms per Household	2.9	3.2	3.1
Not Poor	3.3	3.5	3.4
Poor	2.7	2.8	2.7
Extreme Poor	2.5	2.8	2.7
Rooms per Capita	0.72	0.82	0.78
Not Poor	0.89	0.92	0.91
Poor	0.61	0.68	0.64
Extreme Poor	0.60	0.78	0.68
Percent of Homeowners	62.5	57.4	59.5
Not Poor	64.5	60.0	61.4
Poor	61.2	53.7	57.5
Extreme Poor	62.6	55.0	59.2
Percent of Landowners	26.7	19.0	22.1
Not Poor	28.4	21.7	23.8
Poor	25.6	15.0	20.4
Extreme Poor	21.5	16.3	19.2
Percent with Sewage/Water Drainoff	52.4	78.0	67.5
Not Poor	64.9	85.9	79.4
Poor	44.6	66.8	55.5
Extreme Poor	42.2	65.5	52.7
Percent with a Latrine	50.0	63.3	57.8
Not Poor	60.8	70.0	67.1
Poor	43.3	53.7	48.4
Extreme Poor	42.0	56.3	48.4

Source: EIH 1989.

An important finding is the substantially higher prevalence of land ownership among indigenous people. This could indicate that the urban indigenous population maintains ties to rural areas through the continued ownership of land.

Determinants of Poverty

The results of a model used to estimate the determinants of poverty are presented in Table 5.21. The model assigns a base probability of being poor equal to 45.8 percent. This is then modified according to the personal characteristics included in the model. For example, being healthy lowers the probability of being poor by 5.3 percent, while each additional child raises the probability of being poor by 6.3 percent.

Not surprisingly, the most substantial factor contributing to an increased probability of being poor is living in a household where the household head is unem-

Table 5.21: Determinants of Poverty for All Individuals

Independent Variable	Coefficient	Mean	Marginal Effect
Constant	1.8323		
Student Status	0.2706	0.445	0.0676
	(8.7)		
Schooling	–0.0282	7.032	–0.0070
	(7.6)		
Indigenous	0.6408	0.276	0.1602
	(18.8)		
Healthy (0,1 dummy)	–0.2130	0.843	–0.0532
(self-reported good health)	(5.4)		
Number of Children	0.2506	3.360	0.0626
	(28.2)		
Age of Household Head	–0.0204	42.571	–0.0051
	(13.6)		
Male Household Head	–0.5229	0.891	–0.1307
	(10.9)		
Schooling of Household Head	–0.0727	8.241	–0.0182
	(19.6)		
Household Head Unemployed	1.7928	0.050	0.4482
	(22.3)		
Rooms per Capita	–1.1620	0.645	–0.2905
	(26.8)		
Mean of Dependent Variable		0.458	
Chi-square	29819.2		

Source: EIH 1989.
Note: All coefficients are statistically significant at the 1 percent level or better. Numbers in parentheses are t-ratios. The sample consists of 25,986 individuals.

ployed—that is, not working but looking for work during the reference period. Given that poverty in this analysis is defined by household per capita income level, the employment status of the principal income earners will profoundly affect the welfare level of the household. The second most substantial factor associated with the probability of being poor is rooms per capita. This is also not surprising, given that additional housing space is often a function of wealth. But the third most relevant factor in the model is being indigenous. Indigenous individuals have a 16 percent greater probability of being poor than their non-indigenous counterparts. The probability of being poor is higher for students, and each additional child raises the chance of an individual being poor as well.

The schooling level of both the individual and the household head has a strong impact on *not* being poor. Also improving the chance of not being poor are good health, rooms per capita, and living in a household where the head is male or older. Table 5.22 gives the result of a similar model run solely on household heads. The results are very similar to the previous model.

Simulations of the probability that a household head is poor according to isolated characteristics are presented in Table 5.23. For all characteristics, the likeli-

Table 5.22: Determinants of Poverty for Household Heads

Independent Variable	Coefficient	Mean	Marginal Effect
Constant	2.9720		
Age	−0.0181 (7.5)	43.171	−0.0045
Male	−0.2313 (3.0)	0.837	−0.0578
Schooling	−0.0801 (12.9)	8.205	−0.0200
Indigenous	0.6709 (11.0)	0.412	0.1520
Member of Labor Force	−2.0172 (19.2)	0.876	−0.5043
Health (0,1 dummy) (self-reported good health)	−0.2783 (4.4)	0.769	−0.0696
Number of Children	0.2758 (16.1)	2.582	0.0689
Rooms per Capita	0.2758 (7.4)	0.773	−0.0967
Mean of Dependent Variable		0.743	
Chi-square	8560.9		

Source: EIH 1989.
Note: All coefficients are statistically significant at the 1 percent level or better. Numbers in parentheses are t-ratios. The sample consists of 6,991 individuals.

**Table 5.23: Probability of Household Head Being Poor
by Selected Characteristics**
(percent)

Characteristic	Overall	Indigenous	Non-indigenous
Household Head	50.0	58.8	43.8
Male	49.1	57.9	42.8
Female	54.8	63.4	68.6
Years of Schooling			
0	65.9	73.4	60.0
6	54.4	63.0	48.2
12	42.5	51.3	36.5
16	34.9	43.4	29.4
In Labor Force	43.8	52.7	37.7
Not in Labor Force	85.4	89.3	63.9
Healthy	48.4	57.3	42.2
Not Healthy	78.2	84.2	73.1

Source: Computed from Table 5.22.

hood of being poor is lower for non-indigenous household heads than for their indigenous counterparts. Human capital characteristics greatly influence the probability of being poor. Increased schooling leads to a rapid reduction in poverty. Being employed and being healthy are also associated with less poverty.

Effects of Gender and Ethnicity on Educational Attainment

Two subsamples were generated from the survey to assess the effects of gender and being indigenous on educational attainment. The first consisted of all individuals over 15 years of age and out of school. The second consisted of all youths, regardless of schooling participation, between the ages of 7 and 14. Schooling attainment was measured both by average years and by level of completion.

Adult Subsample

The results of an ordinary least squares (OLS) regression model, which estimates the determinants of years of schooling attained, and a logistic regression model, which estimates the probability of being a primary school dropout, are presented in Table 5.24. Both models are based on the adult subsample and use only three explanatory variables: age, gender and being indigenous. All three variables are statistically significant.

Years of schooling are adversely affected by age, indicating that younger adults have received more years of schooling than older adults. This is not surprising, given the expansion in access to education during the past several decades. Being male increases schooling attainment by 1.44 years on average after controlling for age and being indigenous. An almost three year schooling disadvantage is associated with being indigenous.

Table 5.24: Determinants of Schooling Attainment, Adult Subsample

		Dependent Variable	
Independent Variable	Independent Variable Mean	Years of Schooling (OLS)	Primary School Dropout (LOGIT)
Age	34.7	−0.071 (40.4)	0.011 (43.8)
Male	46.8	1.442 (26.7)	−0.148 (19.8)
Indigenous	33.9	−2.850 (49.0)	0.307 (40.4)
Constant		11.190	−0.559
Mean of Dependent Variable		8.5	0.388
N		22,348	22,348
R^2/Chi-square		0.205	5077.8

Source: EIH 1989.
Note: All coefficients are statistically significant at the 1 percent level or better. Numbers in parentheses are t-ratios.

The probability of being a primary school dropout is dichotomous: either one did or did not complete six years of schooling successfully. The factors associated with not completing primary school are similar to those related to years of schooling attained. Older individuals are more likely to have dropped out of school without completing six years. Males are more likely to have completed a primary level education, and being indigenous is strongly associated with not finishing primary school. After controlling for age and gender, indigenous individuals were 30 percent more likely to have not completed primary school than their non-indigenous counterparts.

Simulated estimates of the predicted probability of not completing primary school by age, gender and indigenous origin are presented in Table 5.25. The probability of having less than six years of schooling increases with age. As

Table 5.25: Probability of Not Completing Primary School Level, Adult Subsample
(percent)

	Males		Females	
Age	Indigenous	Non-indigenous	Indigenous	Non-indigenous
15	29.3	10.2	43.6	17.5
20	34.5	12.6	49.6	21.3
25	40.1	15.6	55.6	25.6
30	46.0	19.0	61.4	30.4
40	58.0	27.5	72.1	41.5
50	69.1	38.0	80.7	53.4

Source: Computed from Table 5.24.

expected, females have a higher probability of dropping out than do males, and indigenous individuals are less likely to complete primary school than their non-indigenous peers. Non-indigenous males at 15 years of age have the lowest probability of not completing primary school—10 percent. At the other end of the spectrum, indigenous females who are 50 years of age have more than an 80 percent chance of not finishing 6 years of school. Interestingly, the results show that non-indigenous females have a higher primary school completion rate than do indigenous males, indicating that the factors hindering school attainment are stronger for indigenous individuals than for females. The combination of these factors indicates that indigenous females are the most disadvantaged in urban Bolivia with respect to schooling attainment.

Youth Subsample

Parents' skills and educational attainment are expected to be reflected in the schooling and other human capital characteristics of their children. The youth subsample, aged 7 to 14 years, is analyzed to determine the most relevant factors associated with increased schooling attainment and schooling attendance of school-aged individuals.

The mean years of schooling by ethnicity and gender for all 7- to 14-year-olds who are currently enrolled in school are presented in Table 5.26. The sample shows that non-indigenous children receive more schooling than do indigenous children regardless of gender.

The results of an OLS regression analysis which assesses the determinants of schooling attainment for the in-school youth subsample are presented in Table 5.27. Age, as would be expected, has a very large effect on the schooling attainment of Bolivian children. But unlike the adult sample, gender is an insignificant factor in explaining the schooling attainment of Bolivian youngsters. Most noticeable, however, is the strong negative effect which ethnicity has on schooling attainment. This highlights the relatively greater importance of ethnicity over gender in explaining present levels of schooling attainment, at least for the "in-school" youth sample.

Other factors are also significant in explaining educational attainment. Geographic location can be important; youths living in the Valley *departamentos* of Cochabamba and Chuquisaca average more years of schooling relative to youths in

Table 5.26: Mean Years of Schooling by Ethnicity and Gender, In-school Youth Subsample

Youths Aged 7–14	Indigenous	Non-indigenous	All
All Enrolled	4.06	4.27	4.25
Male	4.01	4.32	4.29
Female	4.10	4.22	4.21

Source: EIH 1989.

Table 5.27: Determinants of Schooling Attainment, In-school Youth Subsample

Independent Variable	Variable Mean	Coefficient
Constant		−5.124
Age	10.240	0.859
		(151.9)
Male	0.508	0.003*
		(0.1)
Mother's Schooling	7.328	0.031
		(8.5)
Indigenous	0.101	−0.202
		(4.7)
Number of Siblings	4.003	−0.034
		(4.3)
Number of Rooms	3.125	0.047
		(6.8)
Running Water	0.467	0.090
		(3.3)
Kitchen	0.796	0.124
		(3.8)
Departamento		
Oruro	0.990	0.153
		(3.4)
Potosí	0.046	0.090*
		(1.5)
Cochabamba	0.166	0.234
		(6.4)
Chuquisaca	0.032	0.205
		(2.8)
Tarija	0.024	0.038*
		(0.5)
Beni	0.032	−0.242
		(3.3)
Santa Cruz	0.238	0.074
		(2.2)
Private School	0.245	0.155
		(4.4)
Family Income	708.477	0.000
		(0.4)
Male Head of Household	0.913	0.133
		(3.0)
R^2		0.813

Source: EIH 1989.
Note: The dependent variable is years of schooling attainment. All coefficients are statistically significant at the 5 percent level or better except where indicated by *. Numbers in parentheses are t-ratios. The sample consists of 5,616 individuals.

La Paz, while students in Beni average less. Family background, as determined by mother's schooling, has a positive and significant effect on the amount of education her children receive. Family income is an insignificant explanatory variable. However, other wealth indicators do show a significant impact on the schooling attainment of youths: the number of siblings has a negative effect, but the number of rooms in the household, the presence of running water and the presence of a kitchen all have positive effects on schooling attainment. A male head of household also has a positive effect on schooling attainment, as does private school attendance.

While the previous discussion assesses the characteristics and determinants of schooling for those youths actually enrolled in school, the following analysis examines those characteristics which differentiate youths who attend school from those who do not. Table 5.28 presents the overall characteristics of school attendance by ethnicity and gender for the entire 7- to 14-year-old subsample. Note the high overall participation rate, reflecting the fact that the sample is urban. In general, the participation rate is slightly higher among males, with a greater percentage of non-indigenous youths attending school than indigenous youths. Among non-indigenous youngsters, males and females participate equally. With respect to indigenous children, males attend school more frequently than do females.

The results of a logistic regression analysis which estimates the determinants of schooling participation for the entire youth subsample are presented in Table 5.29. Age has a strong negative effect on participation; this is to be expected, since older children are more likely to become involved in other activities, such as participation in the labor market. Unlike with schooling attainment, gender is significant regarding participation; males are more likely to be enrolled in school if all other variables are held constant. However the most important factor in determining participation in schooling is ethnicity; indigenous children are considerably less likely to be enrolled in school.

Simulated estimates of the predicted probability of *not* being enrolled in school by gender and ethnicity, based on the logit model presented in Table 5.29, are presented in Table 5.30. Non-indigenous males have a higher enrollment rate than any other group, with non-indigenous females close behind. Indigenous youths have a substantially lower participation rate. The lowest predicted probability of school enrollment is for indigenous girls, again reflecting the disadvantaged position which indigenous females occupy relative to all other groups in urban Bolivian society.

Table 5.28: Schooling Enrollment by Ethnicity and Gender, Entire Youth Subsample
(percent)

Youths Aged 7–14	Indigenous	Non-indigenous	All
All	90.4	97.2	96.2
Male	92.6	97.1	96.5
Female	88.5	97.2	95.9

Source: EIH 1989.

Table 5.29: Determinants of Schooling Participation, Entire Youth Subsample

Independent Variable	Variable Mean	Marginal Effect Coefficient
Constant		0.152
Age	10.353	−0.006
		(6.4)
Male	0.507	0.013
		(3.1)
Mother's Schooling	7.241	0.003
		(3.8)
Indigenous	0.110	−0.053
		(8.8)
Number of Siblings	3.858	0.002
		(1.9)
Number of Rooms	3.233	0.002*
		(1.5)
Running Water	0.475	0.007*
		(1.4)
Kitchen	0.796	0.032
		(6.5)
Departamento		
Oruro	0.094	−0.004*
		(0.4)
Potosí	0.046	0.014*
		(1.0)
Cochabamba	0.167	−0.007*
		(1.0)
Chuquisaca	0.032	0.008*
		(0.5)
Tarija	0.024	−0.033
		(2.2)
Beni	0.035	−0.040
		(3.6)
Santa Cruz	0.244	−0.032
		(7.5)
Family Income	1977.948	0.000*
		(1.2)
Male Head of Household	0.892	0.012
		(1.6)
Mean of Dependent Variable	0.969	
Chi-square		1626.3

Source: EIH 1989.
Note: The dependent variable is years of schooling attainment. All coefficients are statistically significant at the 5 percent level or better except where indicated by *. Numbers in parentheses are t-ratios. The sample consists of 6,924 individuals.

Education and Earnings: Males

In this section, an analysis of educational attainment and earnings differentials is performed for the subsample of males employed in the labor market. The differential rates of returns to schooling associated with specific characteristics are

Table 5.30: Predicted Probability of Being Enrolled in School, 7- to 14-Year-Olds
(percent)

	Indigenous	*Non-indigenous*	*All*
All	86.6	97.4	96.9
Male	89.0	97.9	97.5
Female	83.8	96.8	96.1

Source: Computed from Table 5.29.

then assessed. Differences in mean labor market earnings between indigenous and non-indigenous male workers are decomposed into "explained" and "unexplained" factors, controlling for differences in economic, social and demographic characteristics. The "explained" component refers to that portion of labor earnings differences attributable to variations in productivity-enhancing characteristics between ethnic groups, while the "unexplained" component is generally attributed to labor market discrimination and other unobserved factors.

The analysis excludes women who are employed in the labor market. This is because women are often subject to discrimination based on gender, and to include them would therefore bias an analysis which seeks to focus on discrimination due to being indigenous. The determinants of women's earnings in the Bolivian labor market are explored in a later section of this chapter.

A profile of relevant characteristics of the subsample according to ethnic category is presented in Table 5.31. Indigenous workers comprise 37 percent of the subsample population; over half of this group lives in La Paz, while an additional 22 percent lives in Cochabamba. Indigenous members of the labor force average 7.5 years of schooling, and almost half have a complete primary education.

Monolingual Spanish-speaking workers attain substantially more education. Over two-thirds have completed at least the primary level, and almost half have attended secondary school or beyond. A higher percentage of monolingual Spanish speakers have a university education (15 percent) compared with indigenous speakers (4 percent). Furthermore, monolingual Spanish speakers average 2.5 years more schooling, and earn almost two-thirds more than their indigenous counterparts.

Given that the indigenous workers are older and have fewer years of schooling, they have more years of potential labor market experience—calculated by subtracting 6 from the difference between age and years of schooling (age – schooling – 6). A large percentage of indigenous males in the labor force are self-employed relative to the non-indigenous population, while fewer indigenous workers are salaried employees, employers or professionals. Finally, the indigenous cohort is more likely to be married, while the non-indigenous cohort is slightly more healthy than the indigenous group of workers.

Table 5.31: Means of Sample Variables, Employed Males

Variable	Indigenous	Non-indigenous	All
Earnings (*bolivianos* per month)	359.44	591.37	505.40
Natural Log of Earnings	5.55	5.91	5.78
Experience (years)	25.12	19.90	21.84
Age (years)	38.54	36.04	36.96
Log of Hours Worked	3.93	3.90	3.91
Indigenous			0.37
Healthy (0,1 dummy) (self-reported good health)	0.81	0.84	0.83
Married	0.86	0.75	0.79
Schooling (years)	7.41	10.13	9.12
Education Level (%)			
Incomplete Primary	0.54	0.28	0.37
Primary	0.22	0.24	0.23
Secondary	0.20	0.34	0.29
University	0.04	0.15	0.11
Departamento (%)			
La Paz	0.54	0.29	0.38
Oruro	0.08	0.08	0.08
Potosí	0.06	0.03	0.04
Cochabamba	0.22	0.13	0.16
Chuquisaca	0.04	0.03	0.04
Tarija	0.01	0.04	0.03
Beni	0.00	0.04	0.03
Santa Cruz	0.05	0.35	0.24
Occupational Category (%)			
Laborer	0.20	0.18	0.18
Employee	0.35	0.47	0.43
Self-employed	0.40	0.28	0.32
Employer	0.04	0.06	0.06
Other	0.01	0.01	0.01

Source: EIH 1989.

Determinants of Labor Market Earnings for Males

The results of estimating earnings functions for both the indigenous and non-indigenous workers, as well as for the population as a whole, are presented in Table 5.32. The dependent variable is the natural logarithm of labor market earnings.

There is a significant negative effect on labor market earnings associated with being indigenous. Examining the determinants of earnings separately for indigenous and non-indigenous workers, the average returns to schooling are higher for non-indigenous males than for indigenous males by almost 3 percentage points. Similarly, non-indigenous workers receive higher returns to labor market experience. Good health is more highly rewarded among indigenous workers, while

Table 5.32: Determinants of Labor Earnings, Employed Males

Independent Variable	Indigenous	Non-indigenous	All
Constant	4.372	3.758	4.047
Schooling	0.057	0.086	0.075
	(14.1)	(23.7)	(27.8)
Experience	0.027	0.045	0.038
	(6.8)	(13.3)	(15.0)
Experience-squared	−0.0003	−0.0006	−0.0005
	(5.2)	(9.8)	(11.1)
Log of Hours Worked	0.154	0.238	0.208
	(3.5)	(6.5)	(7.3)
Indigenous			−0.129
			(5.8)
Healthy (0,1 dummy)	0.081	0.070	0.081
(self-reported good health)	(2.2)	(2.1)	(3.3)
Married	0.294	0.239	0.270
	(6.0)	(6.9)	(9.6)
Departamento			
Oruro	−0.079*	−0.269	−0.203
	(1.5)	(5.7)	(5.7)
Potosí	−0.156	−0.139	−0.149
	(2.6)	(2.0)	(3.2)
Cochabamba	0.141	0.120	0.121
	(3.9)	(3.0)	(4.4)
Chuquisaca	0.151	−0.020*	0.062*
	(2.2)	(0.3)	(1.2)
Tarija	−0.028*	−0.024*	−0.045*
	(0.2)	(0.4)	(0.8)
Beni	1.032	0.318	0.312
	(2.8)	(5.1)	(5.3)
Santa Cruz	0.392	0.402	0.384
	(5.7)	(13.0)	(14.7)
Occupational Category			
Laborer	−0.672	−0.788	−0.765
	(8.6)	(13.7)	(16.7)
Employee	−0.673	−0.628	−0.669
	(9.0)	(12.6)	(16.3)
Self-employed	−0.607	−0.499	−0.572
	(8.1)	(9.4)	(13.3)
Other	−1.196	−1.102	−1.153
	(8.5)	(6.9)	(11.0)
N	2,394	4,070	6,464
R^2	0.201	0.328	0.310
Adjusted R^2	0.195	0.325	0.308

Source: EIH 1989.

Note: Dependent variable is the natural logarithm of labor earnings. All coefficients are statistically significant at the 5 percent level or better, except where indicated by *. Numbers in parentheses are t-ratios.

number of hours worked per week has a higher payoff for non-indigenous workers by a margin of 8 percentage points.

Decomposition of Labor Market Earnings

Using the earnings functions estimated and presented in Table 5.32, the overall earnings differential between indigenous and non-indigenous male workers is decomposed using the technique outlined in Chapter 4.

The decomposition results are presented in Table 5.33. The portion of the overall earnings differential due to disparities in the productive characteristics of indigenous and non-indigenous working males is 71.7 percent. In other words, based on the variables included in Table 5.32, the earnings differential between indigenous and non-indigenous working males would narrow by 71.7 percent if each group were endowed with the same productive characteristics. The remaining 28.3 percent difference in earnings is "unexplained," and reflects both measurement error and unaccounted factors such as disparities in ability, quality of education, labor force participation, culture and labor market discrimination. Therefore, discrimination could account for as much as 28 percent of the overall earnings differential between indigenous and non-indigenous workers in the urban Bolivian labor market.

The contribution of individual variables to the overall earnings differential between indigenous and non-indigenous workers is shown in Table 5.34. A positive entry indicates an advantage in favor of non-indigenous workers while a negative entry indicates an advantage in favor of indigenous workers. With respect to the endowment of specific characteristics, much of the non-indigenous workers' earnings advantage can be explained by three factors: schooling attainment, residence in Santa Cruz and higher pay for self-employment.

Regarding the "unexplained" discrepancies in the pay structure, the returns to education, experience and hours worked are higher for non-indigenous workers. That is, for the same level of schooling, experience and hours worked, indigenous workers are always paid less than their non-indigenous counterparts. The only substantial advantage that indigenous workers have in terms of the pay structure is due to the very large entry for the constant term.

Table 5.33: Indigenous Workers' Earnings Disadvantage and Its Decomposition

Indigenous Worker's Earnings	Overall Differential	Amount Attributed to:	
		Endowments	Wage Structure
Gap (in current *bolivianos*)	232.0	166.0	66.0
As Percent of Overall Differential	100.0	71.7	28.3
As Percent of Non-indigenous Earnings	60.7	43.5	17.2

Source: Calculated from Table 5.32.

Table 5.34: Contribution of Each Variable to the Overall Differential

Variable	Contribution of Each Variable to (Log) Earnings Differential		Contribution as a Percentage of Total Earnings Differential	
	Endowments $b_n(X_n - X_i)$	Pay Structure $X_i(b_n - b_i)$	Endowments	Wage Structure
Constant	0.00000	−0.61412	0.00	−171.06
Schooling	0.23227	0.20954	64.70	58.37
Experience	−0.08092	0.66431	−22.54	61.38
Log of Hours Worked	−0.00618	0.33049	−1.72	92.06
Healthy	0.00231	−0.00893	0.64	−2.49
Married	−0.02457	−0.04783	−6.85	-13.32
Departamento				
Oruro	−0.00027	−0.01540	−0.08	−4.29
Potosí	0.00376	0.00103	1.05	0.29
Cochabamba	−0.01054	−0.00458	−2.94	−1.28
Chuquisaca	−0.00027	−0.00575	−0.07	−1.60
Tarija	−0.00067	0.00004	−0.19	0.01
Beni	0.01304	−0.00071	3.63	−0.20
Santa Cruz	0.12288	0.00040	34.23	0.11
Occupational Category				
Laborer	0.01734	−0.02299	4.83	−6.40
Employee	−0.07851	0.01591	−21.87	4.43
Self-employed	0.06041	0.04293	16.83	11.96
Other	0.00881	0.00131	2.46	0.37
Total	0.25887	0.10173	71.66	28.34
Overall	0.35900		100.0	

Source: Calculated from Table 5.32.

Education and Earnings: Females

As mentioned above, an analysis of discrimination in the labor market due to ethnicity would likely be biased if both sexes were included because discrimination often occurs on the basis of gender, independent of ethnicity. Furthermore, women face different issues than men in their decisions on whether to enter the labor market, and in what capacity. This occurs because childrearing, domestic housework and cultural factors are more likely to keep women out of the workforce than men. And when women do enter the workforce, they may be more inclined to work in the informal sector in order to have the flexibility to meet other responsibilities despite the lower pay which prevails there. On the other hand, they may be forced into the informal sector due to discrimination in the formal sector.

Because of the complexity of these issues, this section assesses the determinants of labor earnings for women separately from those of males. The analysis is based on the subsample of women aged 15 and older who were employed in the labor force at the time of the survey. Table 5.35 presents a profile of relevant characteristics of the subsample according to ethnic category.

Thirty-eight percent of working women in Bolivia are indigenous. On average, the indigenous women are almost four years older than their non-indigenous counterparts. Indigenous females employed in the labor force have 5.3 years of schooling, and less than 30 percent has completed primary school. In contrast, 65 percent of the non-indigenous group have completed primary education. Furthermore, non-indigenous females average almost 4 more years of schooling, and earn almost 50 percent more than their indigenous counterparts.

The higher average age and lower years of schooling for indigenous women mean that they have more potential years of labor market experience. A very high percentage of indigenous women are self-employed relative to the non-indigenous

Table 5.35: Means of Sample Variables, Employed Females

Variable	Indigenous	Non-indigenous	All
Earnings by Occupation[a]			
Overall	224.51	333.91	291.91
Laborer	169.06	246.47	221.22
Employee	225.56	333.73	312.29
Self-employed	243.77	375.07	307.00
Employer	435.07	933.57	831.08
Other	121.01	166.07	149.74
Natural Log of Earnings	5.02	5.39	5.25
Experience (years)	25.68	17.89	20.87
Age (years)	36.97	33.14	34.61
Log of Hours Worked	3.76	3.77	3.77
Indigenous (%)	100	0	38
Healthy (%)	76	81	79
Married (%)	72	59	64
Schooling (years)	5.31	9.26	7.74
Education Level (%)			
Incomplete Primary	71	35	49
Primary	12	20	17
Secondary	15	38	29
University	2	7	5
Occupational Category (%)			
Laborer	2	2	2
Employee	17	42	33
Self-employed	67	39	50
Employer	1	2	1
Other	13	15	14

Source: EIH 1989.
a. Earnings are reported in *bolivianos* per month.

group, while relatively few are salaried employees or employers. Lastly, the non-indigenous cohort is slightly more healthy, while employed indigenous females are more likely to be married relative to the non-indigenous group of workers.

Determinants of Labor Market Earnings for Females

Earnings function estimates are presented in Table 5.36. The effect of schooling, experience and hours worked on labor earnings is greater for non-indigenous

Table 5.36: Determinants of Labor Earnings, Employed Females

Variable	Indigenous	Non-indigenous	All (standard)	All (extended)
Constant	3.1664	2.7454	3.0214	3.4996
Schooling	0.0666	0.0843	0.0774	0.0751
	(12.6)	(20.6)	(24.1)	(20.0)
Experience	0.0342	0.0418	0.0398	0.0315
	(6.1)	(10.0)	(12.4)	(9.4)
Experience-squared	–0.0004	–0.0004	–0.0004	–0.0003
	(3.7)	(4.8)	(6.8)	(5.2)
Log of Hours Worked	0.2468	0.3493	0.3006	0.3208
	(5.7)	(9.1)	(10.5)	(11.5)
Indigenous				–0.1180
				(4.0)
Healthy (0,1 dummy) (self-reported good health)				0.1088
				(3.7)
Married				0.0402*
				(1.4)
Occupational Category				
Laborer				–0.8431
				(6.5)
Employee				–0.6827
				(6.6)
Self-employed				–0.5480
				(5.2)
Other				–0.9321
				(8.4)
Departamento				
Oruro				–0.2442
				(5.0)
Potosí				–0.2487
				(4.3)
Cochabamba				0.1128
				(3.4)
Chuquisaca				–0.0190*
				(0.3)
Tarija				–0.1113*
				(1.4)
Beni				0.2963
				(3.9)
Santa Cruz				0.3450
				(10.0)
R^2	0.100	0.165	0.173	0.238
N	1,661	2,675	4,336	4,336

Source: EIH 1989.
Note: All variables are significant at the 1 percent level or better, except where indicated by *.
Numbers in parentheses are t-ratios.

women. The extended model in the far right column shows that there is a strong, negative effect on earnings associated with being indigenous. Indigenous women earn much less than non-indigenous women, receive very low returns to productive characteristics, work effort and experience, and possess very low levels of human capital. All this evidence would suggest that indigenous women are the most disadvantaged portion of urban Bolivian society.

Fertility, Education and Female Labor Force Participation

In this final section, fertility and child mortality are examined within the context of female participation in the labor force. The role of ethnicity is included as a factor conditioning family size preferences and hence actual family size. After assessing the factors associated with the demand for children, the relationship between fertility, education and employment is explored.

The subsample for this analysis is all women in a union with a spouse present in the household at the time of the survey. Information on the woman and her spouse is included, as well as several household level variables. The fertility variable is simply the number of children ever born. Infant/child mortality is defined as the difference between the number of children ever born to a woman and the number of children alive at the time of the survey.

A profile of relevant subsample characteristics is presented in Table 5.37. These results differ somewhat from those presented in Table 5.18, since the earlier table is based on all women aged 13 or more regardless of the presence of a spouse. The average number of children ever born to a woman (all ages included) is 4.13, while the mean level of infant and/or child deaths per woman is 0.62. Three quarters of the women are under age 45. The average schooling attainment for all women is seven years. As seen in the table, 63 percent of the women are monolingual Spanish speakers, 34 percent are bilingual indigenous, and 3 percent are monolingual indigenous. In general, the husbands are 4 years older than their spouses, and have attained an additional 1.6 years of schooling.

Mean household income is 690 *bolivianos* per month. Husbands' earnings account for the majority of this, while working women contribute an average of 258 *bolivianos* through their earnings. While less than half of the women in a conjugal union are in the labor market, those who do work spend an average of 42 hours per week at their jobs. The unemployment rate among women labor force participants is 6 percent, and only one-third of working women are covered by social security.

Fertility and Child Mortality

One of the drawbacks of employing cumulative fertility is that it truncates the fertility history of women who are still in their reproductive years. The same is true with respect to child mortality. Furthermore, cumulative measures do not tell us much about the timing of births or deaths. Therefore, analyses have been con-

Table 5.37: Means and Standard Deviations of Sample Variables for Women in a Union with Spouse Present

Variable	Mean	Standard Deviation
All Women (N=6,043)		
Age (years)	37.9	12.1
45 or Under (%)	76.0	43.0
46 and Over (%)	24.0	43.0
Years of Schooling	7.0	4.7
Monolingual Indigenous (%)	3.0	17.0
Bilingual Indigenous (%)	34.0	47.0
Monolingual Spanish (%)	63.0	48.0
Fertility	4.13	2.6
Child Mortality	0.62	1.3
Labor Force Participation	0.48	50.0
Husband's Characteristics		
Age	41.9	13.0
Years of Schooling	8.6	4.6
Earnings (*bolivianos* per month)	465.4	953.0
Household Characteristics		
Household Income (*bolivianos* per month)	689.8	1154.7
Number of Persons	5.3	2.0
Number of Children	2.8	1.8
Working Women (N=2,740)		
Hours per Day	7.1	3.5
Days per Week	5.1	2.1
Hours per Week	41.9	25.2
Earnings (*bolivianos* per month)	258.1	333.0
Social Security Coverage (%)	33.0	46.0
Looking for Work (%)	6.0	26.0

Source: EIH 1989.

ducted separately for women 45 years and younger, and for women over 45 years of age, who are considered to have completed their reproductive cycle. Analyzing the two groups separately helps to disentangle some of the period and cohort effects. The ideal situation would be to have complete birth histories in order to analyze trends in fertility by cohort and time period. Alternatively, data from the older cohort could be employed to predict completed fertility for the younger cohort; however this would likely be biased given that the substantial increase in schooling for females during the last two decades has changed women's preferences for children. Due to these potential sources of error, the analysis of the younger cohort employs age controls (age and age-squared) to offset possible age differences in fertility patterns.

Mean fertility (children ever born) and mortality (child deaths) rates per woman for the two age groups according to ethnicity, educational level and place of residence are presented in Table 5.38. Of the 6,043 couples in the subsample, 76 percent of the women are in the childbearing ages of 15 through 45, while 24 percent of the women are past age 45 and therefore have completed their fertility at the time of the survey.

Women over age 45 at the time of interview gave birth to an average of 5.7 children during their reproductive years; on average 1.1 children died per woman in this group. The mean number of children ever born to women aged 45 or under was 3.6, with an average of 0.5 child deaths per woman.

It is evident that indigenous respondents have substantially higher fertility levels than non-indigenous interviewees. For women with complete fertility histories, the indigenous cohort has given birth to an average of almost one child more than the non-indigenous group. This difference increases to almost two children per woman for those in their childbearing years; however the disparity between the two groups is partially due to the fact that women of indigenous origin tend to marry at a younger age. Child mortality levels show a pattern similar to fertility

Table 5.38: Mean Fertility and Child Mortality by Socioeconomic Characteristics for Women in a Union with Spouse Present

Characteristic		Aged 15 through 45		Aged Over 45	
		Fertility	Mortality	Fertility	Mortality
Ethnic Group					
Monolingual Spanish		3.3	0.3	5.3	0.7
Bilingual Indigenous		4.1	0.6	6.0	1.4
Monolingual Indigenous		5.5	1.1	6.5	1.8
Educational Level					
No Schooling		5.5	1.3	6.4	1.7
Primary Dropout		4.6	0.8	6.5	1.5
Primary Completed		4.0	0.5	5.9	0.9
Secondary Dropout		3.4	0.3	5.1	0.6
Secondary Completed		2.5	0.1	4.1	0.4
University Dropout		2.6	0.1	4.3	0.4
University Completed		2.4	0.1	4.2	0.2
Department and Mean Household Income per month[a]					
La Paz	619	3.5	0.4	5.1	0.9
Oruro	552	4.3	0.8	6.8	1.8
Potosí	496	4.5	0.9	6.8	2.1
Cochabamba	713	3.3	0.3	6.0	1.1
Chuquisaca	602	3.6	0.4	5.9	0.9
Tarija	564	3.6	0.3	5.9	1.0
Beni	1,034	4.2	0.5	7.1	1.3
Santa Cruz	876	3.5	0.4	5.9	1.0
Overall		3.6	0.5	5.7	1.1

Source: EIH 1989.
a. In *bolivianos*.

levels, being substantially higher among indigenous women. This is not surprising since women with higher fertility levels are more likely to see a greater absolute number of their children die; in fact, high child mortality levels are often a primary factor resulting in high fertility levels as couples seek to ensure that an adequate number of children lives to adulthood. Figure 5.2 depicts the variation of fertility and child mortality by ethnicity and level of education.

For women of all ages, there is a strong correlation between level of education and both fertility and child mortality levels. Fertility is higher among the older cohort for two principal reasons. First, as discussed earlier, this group has completed their reproductive cycle while the younger group may still have children in the future. Second, knowledge and availability of contraception were probably less widespread when the older cohort was in its prime reproductive years, although use of modern contraceptive methods is still low in Bolivia in comparison to the rest of Latin America. Third, reductions in infant mortality may have impacted the fertility rate of women, as couples feel more assured that a greater number of children will survive to adulthood.

Many of the factors presented in Table 5.38 are interrelated and jointly determine the observed fertility behavior. Table 5.39 presents the results of a simple logistic regression model which assesses the factors associated with fertility. Separate regressions are reported for younger and older women in order to take into account the truncated fertility histories of the former. The dependent variable is the total number of live births per woman. The independent variables serve the following purposes: educational levels of the woman and her husband capture differential fertility preferences; age and its square reflect biological differences; income assesses the income effect on fertility behavior; and ethnicity captures possible cultural differences regarding preferred family size. Monolingual indigenous and bilingual indigenous status are assessed using non-indigenous women as the comparison group.

Education demonstrates the strongest effect in reducing fertility for both age groups. However the husband's educational level, though highly significant, has less than half of the impact on lowering fertility as does the educational level of the woman. Importantly, ethnicity and household income levels are not significantly associated with fertility once education is controlled for in the regression. This implies that fertility behavior is not an insurmountable cultural datum, but rather is susceptible to change through policy-based interventions such as increased access to education. Table 5.40 presents the results of a similar model regarding the determinants of child mortality.

Fertility, Schooling and Female Labor Force Participation

Mean characteristics for working versus non-working women in the subsample are presented in Table 5.41. Working women have barely a one year educational advantage over non-working women. Interestingly, women who work average the same number of children as those who do not. The mean income from the husband's employment is about the same for each group; therefore, as a result of

Figure 5.2: Fertility and Child Mortality for Women Over Age 45 by Ethnicity and Education

Children Ever Born

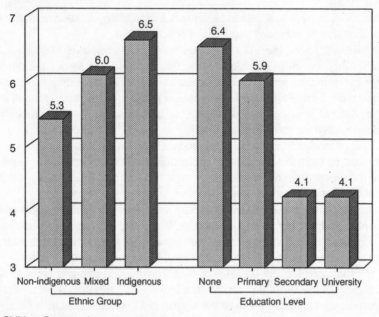

Children Deceased

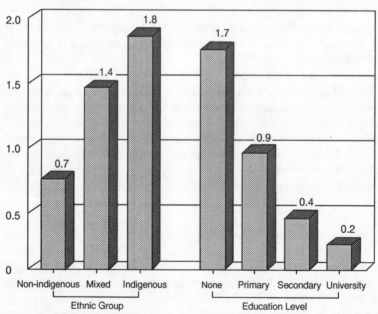

Source: EIH 1989

Table 5.39: Determinants of Fertility for Women in a Union with Spouse Present

Variable	Aged 45 or Under	Aged 46 and Over
Constant	−1.758	6.691
Woman's Education	−0.135	−0.146
	(14.3)	(5.5)
Husband's Education	−0.055	−0.050
	(5.8)	(2.0)
Age	0.289	
	(8.2)	
Age-squared	−0.002	
	(4.2)	
Monolingual Indigenous	0.015*	−0.043*
	(0.1)	(0.1)
Bilingual Indigenous	−0.080*	0.203*
	(1.3)	(1.2)
Household Income (thousands of *bolivianos*)	0.005*	0.058*
	(0.2)	(0.6)
R^2	0.370	0.089
N	4,370	1,400

Source: EIH 1989.
Note: Dependent variable is number of live births ever born to a woman. Numbers in parentheses are t-ratios. All variables are significant at the 1 percent level or better, except where indicated by *.

their own earnings, women who work belong to households with significantly higher incomes. Finally, the incidence of indigenous women among those working is half of those not working. Figure 5.3 depicts female labor force participation and earnings by ethnicity and level of education.

The results of a logit model that attempts to capture the major determinants of female labor force participation are presented in Table 5.42. The independent variables include years of schooling, age, number of children, ethnicity, student status and household income. The analysis has been restricted to women between the ages of 20 and 60; women younger than this group may not yet have been in a position to enter the labor force, while women older than 60 may show employment inactivity simply because they have retired.

The base probability that a woman is a labor force participant is 51 percent. This is then modified according to her endowment of the isolated characteristics. Every extra year of schooling increases the probability of participating in the labor force by 0.60 percentage points, while each additional child lowers this probability by 2.02 percentage points. However, an important finding is that, after controlling for education and household income, being bilingual indigenous is strongly and significantly associated with a higher labor force

Table 5.40: Determinants of Child Mortality for Women in a Union with Spouse Present

Variable	Aged 45 or Under	Aged 46 and Over
Constant	0.078	1.832
Woman's Education	−0.045 (9.0)	−0.056 (3.7)
Husband's Education	−0.021 (4.1)	−0.045 (3.2)
Age	0.027 (12.7)	−0.005* (0.8)
Monolingual Indigenous	0.152* (1.3)	0.340 (1.8)
Bilingual Indigenous	0.093 (2.9)	0.362 (3.7)
Household Income (thousands of *bolivianos*)	0.004* (0.3)	−0.007* (1.1)
R^2	0.137	0.106
N	4,370	1,400

Source: EIH 1989.
Note: Dependent variable is number of children who have died per woman. The subsample is women in a union with spouse present. Numbers in parentheses are t-ratios. All variables are significant at the 1 percent level or better, except where indicated by *.

participation rate for women. Yet indigenous women have been shown to receive less education than any other group. This disadvantaged position with respect to educational attainment by urban indigenous women represents a clear inefficiency in the development of the productive potential within Bolivian society.

Table 5.41: Characteristics of Working versus Non-working Women in a Union with Spouse Present

Characteristic	Working	Non-working
Mean Age	37.6	38.3
Mean Schooling (years)	7.4	6.7
Number of Children in Household	2.8	2.8
Mean Husband's Income (*bolivianos* per month)	469.5	461.7
Mean Household Income (*bolivianos* per month)	807.5	582.8
Indigenous (%)	2.0	4.0
Non-indigenous (%)	56.0	60.0
Sample Size	2,878	3,165

Source: EIH 1989.

Figure 5.3: Female Labor Force Participation and Earnings by Ethnicity and Education

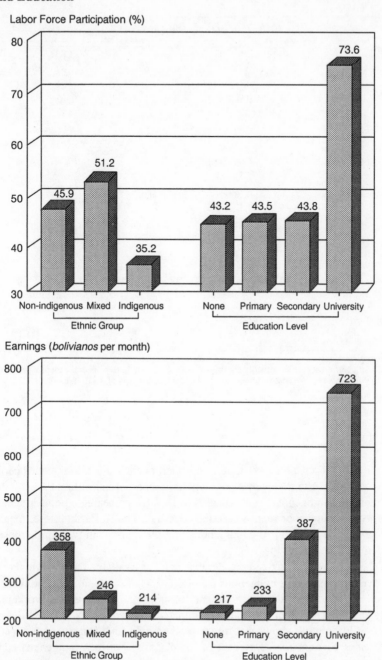

Labor Force Participation (%)

Earnings (*bolivianos* per month)

Source: EIH 1989

Table 5.42: Female Labor Force Participation among Women Aged 20–60 Years

Variable	Logit Coefficient	Variable Mean	Marginal Effect
Constant	−5.913		
Schooling (years)	0.024 (3.3)	7.1	0.60
Age	0.303 (12.0)	37.1	7.57
Age-squared	−0.0038 (11.3)	1442.5	−0.09
Number of Children	−0.081 (5.5)	3.1	−2.02
Monolingual Indigenous	−0.283* (1.3)	0.026	−7.07
Bilingual Indigenous	0.378 (5.9)	0.396	9.44
Student	0.438 (2.1)	0.024	10.94
Household Income	0.0002 (5.6)	722.5	0.00
Chi-square	194.3		
Mean Probability		0.513	

Source: EIH 1989.
Note: All coefficients are statistically significant at the 5 percent level or better, except where indicated by *. Numbers in parentheses are t-ratios. The sample consists of 4,813 individuals.

Conclusion

The findings in this chapter show that a disproportionate share of indigenous people are poor relative to the overall population. Even after controlling for schooling attainment, indigenous individuals have a 16 percentage point greater probability of being poor than non-indigenous individuals. Furthermore, mean per capita income levels for the indigenous group are less than two-thirds those of the non-indigenous group.

This chapter also shows that considerable scope is available for policymakers to improve the situation of indigenous people. This is because human capital factors such as education are so important for improving indigenous workers' incomes and reducing inequalities. For example, detailed decomposition analysis of earnings differentials shows that for the male sample, endowments of assessed characteristics account for 72 percent of the disparity between indigenous and non-indigenous earnings. "Unexplained" factors such as variations in ability, quality of education, labor force participation, culture and labor market discrimination are responsible for the remaining 28 percent of the earnings gap. Thus much of the earnings differential between ethnic groups can be reduced by reducing the education gap between indigenous and non-indigenous people.

Of the measured personal characteristics in this analysis, higher schooling attainment is the strongest factor in the greater earnings of non-indigenous males, accounting for nearly two-thirds of the total differential. Non-indigenous males in the labor force average almost three more years of schooling than their indigenous counterparts, while the disparity between indigenous and non-indigenous females is almost four years. Furthermore, the returns to schooling are substantially higher for both sexes of the non-indigenous population.

These findings indicate that raising the schooling levels of the indigenous population is an important step towards increasing their incomes, which in turn will lower the high incidence of poverty which affects them. Kelley (1988), using a rural Bolivian sample from the mid-1960s, finds that most, if not all, of the disadvantages faced by indigenous males would disappear if human capital and family background differences were equalized. The results here show that while the gains for modern-day urban areas would not be as substantial as those found by Kelley, a very large share of the earnings differential would disappear if indigenous workers possessed equal levels of human capital and other attributes.

But investigation into the determinants of schooling attainment shows that being indigenous is strongly associated with lower schooling levels even after controlling for family income and maternal education level. This is true for both adults and youths currently in school. With respect to indigenous individuals in the labor force, over half of the males and over two-thirds of the females never completed primary school. This compares with about one-third of non-indigenous individuals who did not finish primary school. In fact, the negative association between being indigenous and schooling attainment is stronger than between gender and schooling attainment. Indigenous females are the most disadvantaged group with respect to schooling, and subsequently earnings as well. Interestingly, though, bilingual indigenous women are more likely to participate in the labor force than non-indigenous women.

Thus there is a need for educational programs to raise the participation and completion rates of indigenous persons, particularly females. Bilingual education is a possible method for achieving this goal. This could be an effective means not only for raising enrollment levels, but also for increasing the rate of returns to education for indigenous groups by improving the quality of the learning which they receive.

However, increased education affects more than earnings. Fertility and child mortality levels decline significantly in response to greater education for both the mother and the father. Lower fertility, in turn, is associated with higher participation in the labor force for women, thereby reflecting one indirect effect of education on earnings. Education demonstrates the strongest effect in reducing fertility for both age groups. More importantly, ethnicity and household income levels are not significantly associated with fertility once education is controlled for. This implies that fertility behavior is not an insurmountable cultural datum, but rather is susceptible to change through policy-based interventions such as increased access to education.

Increasing the educational attainment of indigenous persons is not the only means by which to improve the conditions in which this group lives. Equally important are improvements in their access to health care and family planning, as well as assessments for improving demand in the labor market for indigenous and non-indigenous poor alike. However, as this analysis has shown, education is a highly relevant policy variable for reducing the disparities which exist between the indigenous and non-indigenous populations. In the case of fertility and family size preference, the effect of education is strong enough to attenuate and even nullify the effects of cultural differences between indigenous and non-indigenous people.

Note

1. For the purposes of this analysis, a worker is classified as being in the informal sector if the conditions of his/her employment meet one of the following four criteria: (i) if one owns his/her business and hires less than five employees, (ii) if one is self-employed and not a professional, (iii) if one is an employee of a small-scale private enterprise which employs less than five workers or, (iv) if one is a part of a miscellaneous category such as a domestic service, family and other unremunerated work.

6

Guatemala

Diane Steele

The way of life for Guatemala's indigenous people has not changed considerably since the Spanish conquest over 400 years ago. In the Mayan tradition, a person is expected to produce enough food and sustenance to support the family and to meet community obligations. Accumulation of goods is not admired; excess is perceived as having been gained through theft, greed or witchcraft. Hard work, especially working on the land, is highly valued, and is seen as leading to a life where basic needs are satisfied and any surplus is given to communal activities. Land represents a major link to the earth, a key element of Mayan cosmology, and working the land is associated with a sense of community (Goldin 1992).

Prior to the arrival of the Spanish, indigenous people did not "own" land in the Western sense; at least part of all farm land was communal. Families worked plots to provide for their needs and for the needs of the community as a whole. After the Spanish domination, the indigenous people resisted proving ownership of their land and often failed to register titles. This made it easy for outsiders to gain possession and push the indigenous people from their lands. While some efforts were made to fight back, the usual response was to retreat further into the higher elevations. Even in the 1980s, many indigenous people had no legal title to the land they farmed (Nyrop 1983).

Occupational change resulted as the indigenous people were forced to resort to wage labor when unable to provide for their needs on increasingly smaller farm plots. The economy of Guatemala has long been based on the labor provided by the indigenous people. Legal methods for coercing labor began with the sixteenth century *encomienda*, which transferred the Crown's right to tribute to an individual. Indigenous people were included in the grant and the *encomendero* enjoyed total dominion over the indigenous people (Handy 1984). Various additional measures were used continuing into the twentieth century when vagrancy laws were written requiring landless peasants to work as many as 100 days per year on the plantations. Today, few indigenous families could survive without the income from seasonal migrant work. In addition, as the indigenous people were pushed entirely from the land, they took on new occupations: as wage laborers, as teachers, in trade, in tourism.

This chapter uses data from a recent national household survey of Guatemala, the *Encuesta Nacional Socio-Demografica* (ENSD 1989), to examine poverty, education, child labor, occupation and earnings. The analyses compare and contrast the situations for indigenous and non-indigenous people. It is shown that human capital variables such as schooling are important factors that can be used to increase earnings and reduce the gap between indigenous and non-indigenous workers.

Population Distribution

The population of Guatemala is approximately 36 percent indigenous and 64 percent non-indigenous (ENSD 1989). In this case, identification as indigenous does not include reference to observance of historical cultural traditions, speaking a native language or wearing traditional clothing. Instead, respondents were asked "Are you indigenous?" The indigenous portion of the population has been decreasing over time. According to the 1981 census, the population was 42 percent indigenous and 58 percent *ladino*; the 1950 census reported that 54 percent of the population was indigenous; in 1940 the census reported indigenous people as 55.7 percent of the population; and in 1921 the percentage was 64.8 percent (PAHO 1990; Whetten 1961).

For the most part, indigenous people live in rural areas; 80 percent of all indigenous people live in such regions (ENSD 1989). While rural is not synonymous with agricultural, the main economic activity is agricultural. In addition, indigenous people tend to live in the least accessible, mountainous regions of Guatemala. These factors play a large part in determining the level of education, the income level and the accessibility to health care of indigenous people.

According to ENSD 1989, the Guatemalan indigenous and non-indigenous populations are similar in their distributions by gender (see Table 6.1). The indigenous population is also similar in age to the non-indigenous population. Indigenous people live primarily in rural locations while non-indigenous people are as likely to live in urban areas as rural areas.

Table 6.1: Demographic Distribution of the Sample

Characteristic	Indigenous	Non-indigenous
Male (%)	48.0	48.2
Average Age (years)	30.1	30.6
Urban (%)	19.6	47.0

Source: ENSD 1989.

Table 6.2: Distribution by Marital Status, Individuals Aged 15 and Over
(percent)

	Indigenous			Non-indigenous		
Marital Status	Total	Male	Female	Total	Male	Female
Single	23.2	26.5	20.2	29.7	34.3	25.4
Married/Union	68.6	70.9	66.7	60.4	61.5	59.4
Separated/ Divorced	2.0	0.8	3.0	4.7	1.9	7.2
Widow/er	6.2	1.9	10.1	5.3	2.3	8.0

Source: ENSD 1989.

Among people aged 15 and older, the majority of Guatemalans are married or in a union (see Table 6.2). Non-indigenous women are the most likely to be separated or divorced, and indigenous women are the most likely to be widowed.

Households in Guatemala are usually headed by married couples; over 80 percent of both indigenous and non-indigenous households are headed by such couples (see Table 6.3). Non-indigenous households are slightly more likely to have single-parent household heads, whether male or female.

Poverty Incidence

In general, the population of Guatemala is poor. In 1989, the Gini coefficient measuring income inequality was 0.60 and the share of income for the bottom 20 percent of the population was only 2.1 percent. Income inequality increased during the 1980s overall and among indigenous people in particular (Psacharopoulos et al. 1992). In fact, the probability of an indigenous worker belonging to the bottom 20 percent of the income distribution increased from 10.1 to 14.4 percent between 1986 and 1989. Thus inequality and poverty affect indigenous people more than they affect non-indigenous people.

Table 6.3: Marital Status of Household Head
(percent)

	Married Couple	Female, Spouse Absent	Male, Spouse Absent
Indigenous	85.3	10.7	4.0
Non-indigenous	80.3	13.8	5.9

Source: ENSD 1989.
Note: "Married" refers to household heads, whether male or female, who reported themselves as married or in a union. "Spouse absent" includes the possibility that the spouse is dead.

Interethnic Distribution of Income

Income distribution in Guatemala is extremely uneven and is believed to have worsened through the 1980s. The indigenous people in Guatemala are primarily found in the lowest income quintiles. Half of all indigenous people are in the lowest two quintiles compared to half of all non-indigenous people who appear in the top two quintiles (Psacharopoulos et al. 1992).

Within quintile, average incomes are lower for indigenous people than non-indigenous people. In the lowest quintile, the average income for indigenous people is 89 percent of the non-indigenous while in the top quintile, the average income for indigenous people is only 68 percent of that for non-indigenous people. It is noteworthy that the differences between ethnic groups in the bottom three quintiles are very small (Psacharopoulos et al. 1992).

Poverty Incidence by Ethnicity

The poverty line used in this chapter is consistent with the US$60 per person per month in 1985 purchasing power parity (PPP) and is applied throughout this book. The extreme poverty line is US$30 PPP per person per month. The majority of the population of Guatemala is poor; 66 percent of all households are below the poverty line and 38 percent of all households are below the extreme poverty line (ENSD 1989). Indigenous people are, however, disproportionately poor. Table 6.4 shows that 87 percent of all indigenous households are below the poverty line and 61 percent of all indigenous households are below the extreme poverty line. The average household per capita income is calculated by dividing the total household income by the number of people in the house (excluding domestic servants). For indigenous households, it is one-third of that for non-indigenous households.

Families with incomes below the poverty line receive more of their total income from sources other than their primary job than do non-poor families. Income from the primary job is supplemented by income from additional jobs, transfers and in-

Table 6.4: Households below Poverty Line and Other Poverty Indices

	Indigenous	*Non-indigenous*	*Total*
Below Poverty Line (%)	86.6	53.9	65.6
Below Extreme Poverty Line (%)	61.0	25.3	38.1
Average Household per Capita Income (*quetzales* per month)	34.35	111.34	83.78
Aggregate Poverty Gap Index	55.7	26.9	37.4
FGT P_2 Index	40.9	16.8	25.5

Source: ENSD 1989.
Note: In 1989, at the time of the survey, 34.35 *quetzales* equaled approximately US$12.36.

Table 6.5: Sources of Family Income
(percent of total)

Income Type	Below Extreme Poverty Line	Below Poverty Line	Non-poor	Total
Indigenous				
Primary Job	62.6	67.6	82.5	69.6
Secondary Job	10.7	9.4	5.7	8.9
Pension	0.4	0.4	1.1	0.5
Transfer	2.1	2.1	3.1	2.2
In-kind	24.2	20.5	7.6	18.8
Non-indigenous				
Primary Job	72.0	79.5	86.4	82.6
Secondary Job	7.2	4.4	1.9	3.3
Pension	2.0	1.8	2.2	2.0
Transfer	5.2	5.1	5.7	5.4
In-kind	13.7	9.2	3.8	6.8

Source: ENSD 1989.

kind payments. Indigenous families below the poverty line rely on in-kind payments for up to one-quarter of their total monthly income (see Table 6.5). In addition, they rely on secondary jobs for up to 10 percent of their monthly income.

Non-indigenous families, regardless of the level of poverty, receive a larger proportion of their monthly income from their primary job. Reliance on in-kind payments is greatest for families below the extreme poverty line, but the percentage of total income from in-kind payments for non-indigenous families is only half of that for indigenous families.

Income from transfers is more important as a portion of non-indigenous family income than of indigenous family income. Between 5 and 6 percent of non-indigenous total income is derived from transfers. If the income derived from transfers were to be eliminated from monthly income, an additional 5 percent of those currently defined as non-poor would fall below the poverty line. This would have only a small effect on the overall classification of families by poverty level. The classification of indigenous families by poverty level changes by only 1 percent with the removal of transfer income; the classification of non-indigenous families changes by almost 3 percent at both the poverty and extreme poverty lines.

Distribution of Public Services

In Guatemala, the majority of the population does not have access to such public services as water, sanitation and electricity, although urban areas are not as limited in services as rural areas. Table 6.6 shows the presence of services for all households. Less than one-third of all indigenous households have water piped to their homes for their exclusive use compared to almost half of non-indigenous households. Half of indigenous households have no sanitary services, and three-fourths have no electricity.

Table 6.6: Presence of Public Services, All Households
(percent)

Service	Indigenous			Non-indigenous		
	Total	*Urban*	*Rural*	*Total*	*Urban*	*Rural*
Water						
Exclusive Use	30.9	44.4	27.4	48.2	61.4	36.1
Shared Use	4.4	14.7	1.8	13.7	22.4	5.7
Public Source	19.3	22.9	18.5	7.2	4.6	9.5
Well	16.1	5.8	18.7	15.5	4.1	25.9
River, Lake or Spring	25.8	4.5	31.2	9.9	0.8	18.2
Other	3.5	7.7	2.4	5.6	6.6	4.6
Sanitary Services						
Private Facilities	4.7	17.8	1.3	27.1	48.9	7.2
Shared Facilities	2.5	9.5	0.8	10.1	17.9	2.8
Public Washroom	3.1	13.0	0.6	6.3	9.6	3.3
Well	23.3	28.4	22.0	23.6	16.4	30.2
Latrine	20.9	14.3	22.5	11.4	3.9	18.2
None	45.6	17.0	52.8	21.6	3.3	38.2
Electricity						
Yes	25.4	65.6	15.1	63.4	91.8	37.5
No	74.6	34.4	84.9	36.6	8.2	62.5

Source: ENSD 1989.

Because the majority of indigenous households are below the poverty line, the presence of public services in poor indigenous households is virtually identical to that in all indigenous households (see Table 6.7). Non-indigenous poor households do show differences from all non-indigenous households, with fewer households having services.

More indigenous households own their homes than non-indigenous households; 84 percent of all indigenous households own their homes, compared to only 66 percent of non-indigenous households (see Table 6.8). In urban areas the indigenous advantage is maintained; 74 percent of indigenous urban households own their homes compared to 58 percent of non-indigenous urban households. The advantage is also maintained among poor households. For example, 84 percent of poor indigenous households own their homes, while only 69 percent of poor non-indigenous households own their homes.

Although more indigenous households own the homes in which they live, those homes are smaller than the homes in which non-indigenous households live. The

Table 6.7: Presence of Public Services for Households below Poverty Line
(percent)

	Indigenous			*Non-indigenous*		
Service	*Total*	*Urban*	*Rural*	*Total*	*Urban*	*Rural*
Water						
Exclusive Use	29.0	41.0	26.2	38.5	51.3	30.7
Shared Use	4.2	13.8	1.9	11.5	22.7	4.6
Public Source	20.4	26.1	19.0	9.6	7.7	10.8
Well	16.2	6.0	18.6	18.8	6.4	26.4
River, Lake or Spring	27.0	5.2	32.2	14.8	1.5	23.0
Other	3.2	7.7	2.1	6.8	10.5	4.5
Sanitary Services						
Private Facilities	3.2	13.2	0.7	13.0	30.4	2.4
Shared Facilities	2.1	7.7	0.7	8.5	18.8	2.2
Public Washroom	2.9	13.2	0.4	5.8	12.2	1.8
Well	22.9	30.9	21.0	28.2	25.6	29.7
Latrine	21.2	15.9	22.5	13.3	6.5	17.5
None	47.8	19.2	54.6	31.3	6.6	46.4
Electricity						
Yes	22.2	60.7	12.9	50.0	85.4	28.3
No	77.8	39.3	87.1	50.0	14.6	71.7

Source: ENSD 1989.

average number of rooms in an indigenous household is 2.2 compared to 2.8 for a non-indigenous household. Information on the quality of homes is lacking.

The *Encuesta Nacional Socio-Demografica* contains information on two more measures which can be used to describe the level of basic services in households: the presence of a kitchen in the household and type of fuel used for cooking. Overall and in rural areas, indigenous households are as likely to have a room inside the household in which cooking is done as non-indigenous households (see Table 6.9). However, indigenous households are overwhelmingly dependent on firewood as the main fuel for cooking. Non-indigenous households also use firewood as cooking fuel, but have much greater access to propane.

Poor indigenous households do not show large differences from all indigenous households. This is because the majority of indigenous households are poor. Non-indigenous poor households are also similar to all non-indigenous households except in the use of propane as a cooking fuel (see Table 6.9).

Table 6.8: Home Ownership

| | | Average Number of Rooms | |
	Homes Owned (%)	Total	Bedrooms
All Households			
Indigenous			
Total	83.6	2.2	1.3
Urban	73.9	2.5	1.5
Rural	86.1	2.1	1.3
Non-indigenous			
Total	65.9	2.8	1.6
Urban	57.7	3.3	1.8
Rural	73.5	2.4	1.4
Households Below Poverty Line			
Indigenous			
Total	84.4	2.1	1.3
Urban	75.6	2.3	1.4
Rural	86.5	2.0	1.2
Non-indigenous			
Total	69.1	2.4	1.4
Urban	55.9	2.6	1.5
Rural	77.1	2.2	1.3

Source: ENSD 1989.

Education

One of Guatemala's greatest challenges is to overcome the low educational attainment levels of its economically active population. This results in low productivity and a high concentration of workers in low-skilled occupations. The situation for indigenous people is especially grave. Inherent problems in the Guatemalan education system are compounded for indigenous people by their potential inability to speak Spanish and by their inability to afford the direct (clothes, shoes, books, tuition and transportation) or indirect (foregone earnings of the child) costs necessary to send their children to school.

Level of Education

Figure 6.1 presents the level of education of people in Guatemala. Indigenous people have lower educational levels than non-indigenous people; 60 percent of

Table 6.9: Kitchens and Cooking Fuel
(percent)

	Location of Kitchen		Cooking Fuel	
	Inside House	Outside House	Firewood	Propane
All Households				
Indigenous				
Total	69.3	30.7	96.6	2.2
Urban	69.5	30.5	87.0	9.3
Rural	69.1	30.9	99.0	0.5
Non-indigenous				
Total	74.4	25.6	62.8	31.7
Urban	85.2	14.8	34.5	56.5
Rural	64.6	35.4	88.7	8.9
Households Below Poverty Line				
Indigenous				
Total	69.4	30.6	98.4	1.0
Urban	66.6	33.4	94.1	3.8
Rural	70.1	29.9	99.4	0.3
Non-indigenous				
Total	68.4	31.6	81.2	15.4
Urban	78.5	21.5	56.8	35.8
Rural	62.1	37.9	96.2	2.8

Source: ENSD 1989.

all indigenous people have no education. For those who do have education, the vast majority never go beyond primary school. Among indigenous people, males attain higher education levels than females. Although half of all indigenous males have no education, three-fourths of indigenous females have no education (see Figure 6.2). The levels of education are higher for non-indigenous people than for indigenous people and the profiles for non-indigenous males and females are more similar (see Figure 6.3).

Years of Schooling

On average, indigenous people have only 1.3 years of schooling compared to 4.2 years for non-indigenous people. The average number of years of schooling for indigenous males is 1.8 years and for indigenous females 0.9 years. Non-indigenous males have 4.5 years of schooling on average and non-indigenous females have 4.0 years. Table 6.10 details the average number of years of schooling by

Figure 6.1: Educational Distribution by Ethnicity
Percent

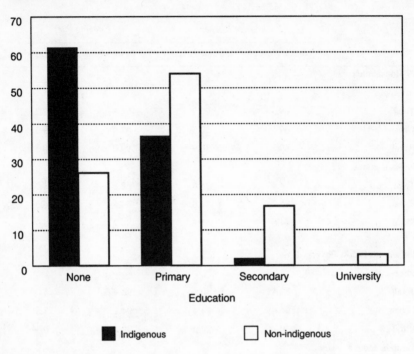

Source: ENSD 1989.

gender and ethnicity. For both indigenous and non-indigenous people, males have more education than females, but non-indigenous females have more education, on average, than indigenous males. Average years of schooling peaks in the 14- to 19-year age group for indigenous people and in the 20- to 24-year age group for non-indigenous people.

Ordinary least squares regression analyses run separately on the school age population (ages 10 to 18) and the adult population (ages 19 and older) show the effects of gender, age and ethnicity on years of schooling (see Table 6.11). Being male increases average schooling for both age groups, with the average increasing by almost one year for the adult group. Being indigenous decreases average years of schooling by two years for school-aged children and by over three years for adults. Age is a positive characteristic for the school-aged group and a negative characteristic for the adult group. These results indicate an improvement in access to schooling over time for younger cohorts, especially indigenous people.

A more detailed analysis was performed on children aged 10 to 14 who were in school at the time of the survey and who had at least one year of schooling. This analysis includes more personal characteristics that can influence children's edu-

Figure 6.2: Indigenous Educational Distribution

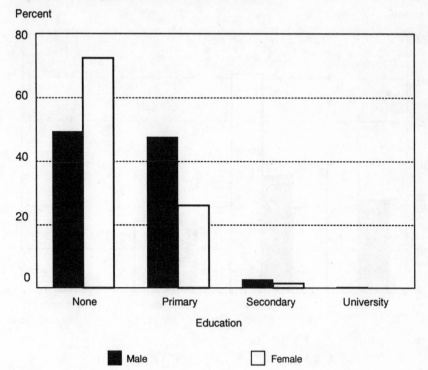

Percent

Source: ENSD 1989.

cation. These additional influences include those which indicate the economic condition of the household, parental employment and mother's education level (see Table 6.12).

As in the previous analyses, age is a positive characteristic and being indigenous is a negative characteristic in determining how many years a student attends school. The number of siblings is also negative: the larger the number, the less likely a student will remain in school. The three variables representing the father's occupation and the variable denoting a male head of household are all negative characteristics. Mother's schooling is a positive characteristic, which is consistent with various studies showing that more schooling for women has wide-ranging effects on the health and well-being of their families.

School Attendance

The data from the *Encuesta Nacional Socio-Demografica* are limited to those aged ten and above, but show that indigenous children are attending school at lower rates than non-indigenous children. In the Guatemalan education system,

Figure 6.3: Non-indigenous Educational Distribution

Percent

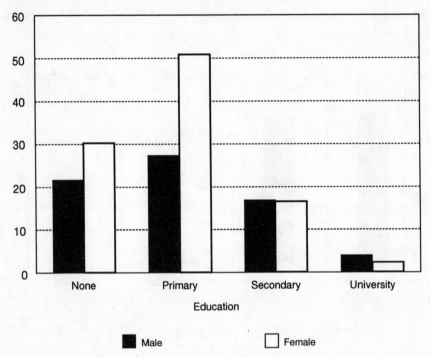

Education

■ Male   □ Female

Source: ENSD 1989.

Table 6.10: Average Years of Schooling

	Indigenous			Non-indigenous		
Age Group	Total	Male	Female	Total	Male	Female
Overall	1.3	1.8	0.9	4.2	4.5	4.0
10–13	1.4	1.6	1.2	2.8	2.9	2.8
14–19	2.4	2.9	1.8	5.1	5.2	4.9
20-24	1.9	2.7	1.3	5.7	6.2	5.4
25–29	1.5	2.3	0.9	5.3	5.7	5.2
30–34	1.2	1.9	0.6	5.1	5.5	4.7
35–39	0.9	1.5	0.4	4.1	4.5	3.9
40–44	0.7	1.0	0.4	3.7	4.4	3.2
45–49	0.6	0.9	0.3	3.2	3.6	2.8
50–54	0.4	0.7	0.2	3.0	3.2	2.7
55–59	0.4	0.8	0.2	2.9	3.3	2.5
60 and Older	0.3	0.5	0.1	2.1	2.4	2.0

Source: ENSD 1989.

Table 6.11: Determinants of Years of Schooling

	School Age (10–18)	Adults (19 and Over)
Constant	−1.264	6.354
Male	0.413	0.865
	(9.1)	(17.7)
Indigenous	−2.002	−3.213
	(42.6)	(62.8)
Age	0.362	−0.064
	(40.7)	(40.8)
R^2	0.25	0.21
N	10,888	22,373

Source: ENSD 1989.
Note: Numbers in parentheses are t-ratios. All coefficients are significant at the .01 level.

children ideally attend primary school between the ages of 7 and 12 years, and secondary school between the ages of 13 and 18 years. Secondary school is divided into three years of basic and three years of diversified education. Education is compulsory for ages 5 through 15. Among survey respondents in the ages for primary school (ages 10–12 years), 57 percent of indigenous children and 75 percent of non-indigenous children are students. For children above the age of 15, only 8 percent of indigenous children are students while 32 percent of non-indigenous children are students (see Table 6.13).

For survey respondents of school age, 10 to 18 years, it is possible to calculate the probability that they are students using logistic regression analysis. The purpose of this analysis is to identify the factors associated with the probability of attending school. Table 6.14 reports the results of an analysis looking at characteristics including gender, ethnicity and age. Once again, being male increases the probability of attendance. Age has a negative effect and being indigenous has a strong negative effect.

The partial derivatives in the last column of Table 6.14 indicate the effect each variable has on an individual's probability of attending school. For example, being male increases the probability that an individual will attend school by 4.8 percent and being indigenous decreases an individual's probability of attending school by 27 percent.

It is possible to use the results of the logit analysis to predict the probability of attending school for each selected characteristic. The probabilities are calculated by varying one characteristic at a time, while holding the other variables constant at their mean levels (see Table 6.15).

Probability of school attendance is always lower for indigenous students than for non-indigenous students and is always lower for females than for males. The probabilities of attendance show large increases for 18-year-old indigenous males, and 17- and 18-year-old indigenous females.

Table 6.12: Determinants of Years of Schooling, Ages 10 to 14 Only

	Coefficient
Constant	–3.478
Male	0.016*
	(0.4)
Indigenous	–0.264
	(5.3)
Age	0.556
	(34.4)
Number of Siblings	–0.105
	(6.9)
Male Household Head	–0.082*
	(1.3)
Kitchen in House	–0.019*
	(0.4)
Rural	–0.393
	(8.4)
Mother's Schooling	0.174
	(19.6)
Total Household Income	0.000
	(2.1)
Number of Rooms in House	0.120
	(6.8)
Father's Occupation	
Employer	–0.292
	(2.2)
Private Sector	–0.142
	(2.3)
Self-Employed	–0.233
	(3.8)
R^2	0.50

Source: ENSD 1989.
Note: Numbers in parentheses are t-ratios. All coefficients are significant at the .01 level, except where indicated by *. The sample size is 2,892.

Probability of Primary School Dropout

As shown, the highest level of educational attainment for the majority of the population is primary. Far more non-indigenous people have secondary and university education than indigenous, but they make up only a small percentage of the non-indigenous population.

Using logistic regression analysis, it is possible to examine the probability of an individual dropping out of primary school as a function of characteristics including gender, ethnicity and age. Table 6.16 presents the results of an analysis on

Table 6.13: Children Attending School as a Percentage of the Age Group

Age Group	Indigenous	Non-indigenous
10–12 (Primary)	56.5	75.0
13–15 (Secondary-basic)	28.7	51.4
16–18 (Secondary-diversified)	6.8	26.3
19–24 (University)	1.5	5.6

Source: ENSD 1989.
Note: Although the age groups in the table represent the ages at which students should be in the school level indicated, because of the high repetition rates in Guatemala, it is likely that those who are students are not at the level indicated by their age.

individuals aged 19 and older. School-aged children, 10 to 18 years, who theoretically could still complete their education, and adults with no education were eliminated from the analyses. Individuals are considered primary school dropouts if they reported primary school as their highest attained education level and if they reported completing less than six years at that level. Being male slightly decreases the probability of dropping out and age has a slight positive effect. These results are in keeping with earlier results which show males to have more education, on average, and for education to increase with age up to a certain point. Being indigenous strongly increases the probability of an individual dropping out of primary school at the mean age of the whole population for each gender.

Illiteracy

The low levels of education are also reflected in the illiteracy rates for indigenous people. Overall, 60 percent of all indigenous people are illiterate compared to 24

Table 6.14: Probability of School Attendance

	Coefficient	Partial Derivative
Constant	5.683	
Male	0.192 (4.4)	0.048
Indigenous	−1.090 (23.2)	−0.270
Age	−0.411 (42.4)	−0.101
Chi-square	2691.9	

Source: ENSD 1989.
Note: School-aged population only, aged 10 to 18. The dependent variable is 1 if student. Numbers in parentheses are t-ratios. All coefficients are significant at the .01 level. The sample size is 10,889.

Table 6.15: Predicted Probability of School Attendance
(percent)

| | Indigenous | | Non-indigenous | |
Age	Male	Female	Male	Female
10	67.8	63.4	86.2	83.8
11	58.2	53.4	80.6	77.3
12	48.0	43.2	76.3	69.4
13	38.0	33.6	64.6	60.1
14	28.9	25.1	54.7	49.9
15	21.2	18.2	44.4	39.8
16	15.2	12.8	34.7	30.5
17	10.6	89.0	26.1	22.5
18	72.8	60.8	18.9	16.2

Source: ENSD 1989.

percent of all non-indigenous people. Illiteracy is defined as those who answered no to the question "Do you know how to read and write a paper, a story or a message?" There are large differences between the illiteracy rates by place of residence. For both indigenous and non-indigenous people, the rural illiteracy rate is well above the urban illiteracy rate. Figure 6.4 shows illiteracy rates by area of residence.

Illiteracy rates for indigenous people are lowest among the young, probably representing increased access to schooling. However, even among the young, illiteracy rates for indigenous people are higher than the rates for non-indigenous people. Table 6.17 details the illiteracy rate by age group for indigenous and non-indigenous people.

A logistic regression was run on the adult population aged 19 and older to examine the effect of characteristics on the probability of being illiterate. Table 6.18

Table 6.16: Probability of Dropping Out of Primary School

	Coefficient	Partial Derivative
Constant	−1.035	
Male	−0.086 (2.3)	−0.034
Indigenous	1.531 (28.0)	0.608
Age	0.026 (18.7)	0.010
Chi-square	1178.4	

Source: ENSD 1989.
Note: Adult population only, aged 19 and older. The dependent variable is 1 if dropped out. Numbers in parentheses are t-ratios. All coefficients are significant at the .01 level. The sample size is 22,373.

Figure 6.4: Illiteracy by Area of Residence

Percent

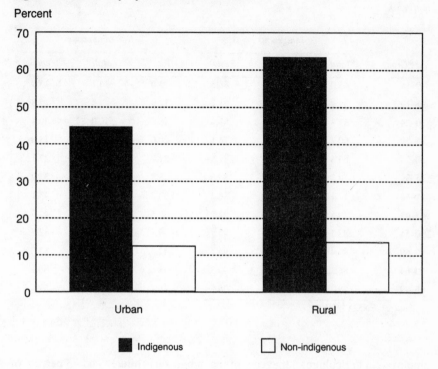

Source: ENSD 1989.

presents the results. Being male has a strong negative effect. Age has a slight positive effect and being indigenous has a strong positive effect.

Child Labor

As shown in Table 6.13, only 57 percent of indigenous children aged 10 to 12 years and 29 percent of indigenous children aged 13 to 15 years are attending school. Though the labor force in Guatemala will be analyzed below using all individuals aged 14 to 65 years, it is also possible to look at the working status of children aged 10 to 13. Some of these children are reported as being employed in the *Encuesta Nacional Socio-Demografica*.

This survey reports 9 percent of non-indigenous children and 21 percent of indigenous children as being employed. The majority of these children are

Table 6.17: Illiteracy Rates by Age Group
(percent)

	Indigenous			Non-indigenous		
Age Group	Total	Male	Female	Total	Male	Female
10–14	43.0	37.7	48.5	15.0	14.1	15.9
15–19	39.9	27.9	51.2	12.9	9.8	15.8
20–24	53.4	35.2	68.4	15.6	10.0	20.4
25–29	60.4	41.5	76.1	20.0	15.8	23.8
30–34	63.4	44.0	81.5	21.2	14.7	27.1
35–39	70.3	53.1	86.5	28.8	21.5	33.9
40–44	77.1	64.6	88.2	33.3	22.0	43.1
45–49	79.8	65.3	92.2	37.4	29.4	44.9
50–54	83.1	69.5	95.1	39.1	30.3	47.5
55–59	81.4	67.3	94.4	42.9	33.3	53.0
60–64	86.1	76.7	95.3	48.6	36.2	60.1
65–99	89.2	81.1	96.8	46.7	46.2	59.8

Source: ENSD 1989.

employed in agriculture; 82 percent of the indigenous children and 73 percent of the non-indigenous children are in this sector (ENSD 1989).

Table 6.19 shows the characteristics of the working children. They are most often male and live in rural areas. The average age of both indigenous and non-indigenous working children is 12.

Table 6.18: Probability of Illiteracy

	Coefficient	Partial Derivative
Constant	–2.116	
Male	–1.028 (31.9)	–0.248
Indigenous	1.951 (58.0)	0.471
Age	0.041 (39.0)	0.010
Chi-square	6094.2	

Source: ENSD 1989.
Note: Adult population only, aged 19 and older. The dependent variable is 1 if illiterate. Numbers in parentheses are t-ratios. All coefficients are significant at the .01 level. The sample size is 22,373.

Table 6.19: Characteristics of Working Children

Characteristic	Indigenous	Non-indigenous
Male (%)	87.0	70.4
Rural (%)	89.8	76.9
Average Age (years)	12.0	12.0
Education Level (%)		
None	57.3	48.2
Primary	42.7	51.8
Average Years of Schooling	1.1	1.6
Female Head of Household (%)	22.3	15.3
Mother's Years of Schooling	0.6	1.4
Father's Years of Schooling	1.1	1.8

Source: ENSD 1989.
Note: Children aged 10 to 13 only.

Non-indigenous working children are evenly split between having no education and having primary education. One-third more indigenous working children have no education than primary education. Non-indigenous working children have slightly more years of schooling than indigenous working children.

Working children, whether indigenous or non-indigenous, are far more likely to live in a female headed household than the population as a whole (see Table 6.3). This is especially true for indigenous working children. Parents of working children also have fewer years of schooling than the population as a whole (see Table 6.10).

Using logistic regression, the probability that a child will be employed is calculated. The results of an analysis looking at characteristics of both children and their parents are presented in Table 6.20. Being indigenous, male, living in a rural area and living in a female headed household increase the probability that a child will be working. The partial derivatives indicate that being male increases the probability by 24 percent. The results also indicate that the more education the parents have, the less likely a child is to work. The results also imply that female children are less likely to be working, thus allowing them the opportunity to attend school. Also, the effect of being indigenous upon the probability that a child will be working is small, at 4.5 percent.

The results of this logistic regression analysis are used to predict the probability of a child working at each age by gender and ethnicity. Only the age, gender and ethnicity values are manipulated in these calculations. All other variables are held constant at their mean values. Table 6.21 presents the results.

The predicted probabilities are higher for indigenous children than non-indigenous children, and the gaps increase with every year of age. Both indigenous and non-indigenous girls show large increases in probability from ages 12 to 13 years. Indigenous boys have a 57 percent probability of working at age 13.

Table 6.20: Probability of a Child Working

	Coefficient	Partial Derivative
Constant	–9.936	
Indigenous	0.375	0.045
	(2.4)	
Male	1.958	0.236
	(11.3)	
Age	0.610	0.074
	(8.5)	
Years of Schooling	–0.254	–0.031
	(3.7)	
Rural	0.315	0.038
	(1.5)	
Female Head of Household	0.476	0.057
	(2.6)	
Mother's Years of Schooling	–0.149	–0.018
	(3.3)	
Father's Years of Schooling	–0.061	–0.007
	(1.0)	
Chi-square	385.6	

Source: ENSD 1989.
Note: Children aged 10 to 13 only. The dependent variable is 1 if employed. Numbers in parentheses are t-ratios. All coefficients are significant at the .01 level. The sample size is 2,106.

Occupational Attainment

The workforce in Guatemala is made up primarily of males among both indigenous and non-indigenous workers. Indigenous workers, overall, (i) are more likely than non-indigenous workers to be self-employed, (ii) are more likely than non-indigenous workers to work more than one job and, (iii) earn less than non-indigenous workers. Indigenous women laborers work the least number of hours per week on average, over 6 hours less a week than non-indigenous women (see Table 6.22).

Table 6.21: Predicted Probability of a Child Working
(percent)

	Indigenous		Non-indigenous	
Age	Male	Female	Male	Female
10	17.7	3.0	12.9	2.0
11	28.4	5.3	21.4	3.7
12	42.2	9.3	33.4	6.6
13	57.4	15.9	48.0	11.5

Source: ENSD 1989.

Table 6.22: Selected Characteristics of Working People

Characteristic	Indigenous	Non-indigenous
Total Employed (%)	49.7	49.2
Males		
Portion of Total Workforce (%)	79.5	71.4
Working More than 1 Job (%)	4.1	2.8
Self-employed (%)	46.7	25.8
Average Income - All Workers (*quetzales* per month)	87.30	250.56
Average Income - Formal Sector (*quetzales* per month)	88.26	253.85
Average Hours per Week	46.9	46.2
Females		
Portion of Total Workforce (%)	20.4	28.6
Working More than 1 Job (%)	2.2	1.6
Self-employed (%)	47.1	28.4
Average Income - All Workers (*quetzales* per month)	51.54	206.81
Average Income - Formal Sector (*quetzales* per month)	51.53	207.25
Average Hours per Week	35.8	42.1

Source: ENSD 1989.
Note: Includes respondents aged 14 to 65.

Interethnic Occupational Differences

Differential poverty experiences are reflected in the occupational distribution (Table 6.23). The most prevalent occupation for both indigenous and non-indigenous people is agricultural worker, but almost twice as many indigenous people as non-indigenous people are employed in agriculture. Artisan—which includes craftspeople and other qualified workers—represents the second most common occupation, and vendor the third. Because the workforce is predominantly male, the distribution of males by principal occupation mirrors the overall distribution. For females, both indigenous and non-indigenous, however, the distribution is different. Among female indigenous workers, the most common occupation is artisan, followed by agricultural worker and vendor. The two most common occupations for non-indigenous females are personal servicer and vendor, with artisan being third.

Earnings

There are many factors that determine an individual's earnings: one's occupation, the area in which the one lives, one's level of education, the amount of training one receives, and years of one's experience, among others. Indigenous people in

Table 6.23: Principal Occupation
(percent)

Occupation	Indigenous			Non-indigenous		
	Total	Male	Female	Total	Male	Female
Professionals	1.3	1.3	1.5	7.9	5.9	13.1
Administrators	0.7	0.6	1.1	3.9	3.8	4.4
Office Workers	0.5	0.4	0.6	5.1	3.7	8.6
Vendors	7.9	5.3	18.1	11.1	6.3	23.1
Agriculture	67.6	78.0	26.9	35.2	45.7	9.1
Miners	0.2	0.2	n.a.	0.2	0.2	n.a.
Transport	0.7	0.8	n.a.	3.3	4.5	0.2
Artisans	14.7	8.9	37.6	18.2	19.3	15.4
Manual Laborers	2.7	3.3	0.5	5.7	7.0	2.4
Personal Service	3.8	1.2	13.6	9.4	3.7	23.7

Source: ENSD 1989.
Note: Includes respondents aged 14 to 65.
n.a. Not applicable.

Guatemala are often far less endowed in such factors, especially education, yet often have more experience than their non-indigenous counterparts.

Average Income Levels

As shown above, the principal occupational category for indigenous workers is agriculture; 68 percent of all indigenous workers are employed in agriculture (ENSD 1989). An analysis of data from the Guatemalan Institute of Social Security shows that wages for agricultural workers steadily declined during the 1980s; the average agricultural wage stood at only 50 percent of the average wage of the overall economy. This low level wage is reflected in the average incomes reported in the ENSD (see Table 6.24). On average, indigenous workers' income is less than half of non-indigenous workers' income. From their principal occupation, the monthly income of indigenous workers is 34 percent of non-indigenous income. From all sources of income, indigenous workers earn 38 percent of non-indigenous workers' income.

Formal sector workers fare only slightly better than all workers combined. Those in the formal sector represent different proportions among indigenous and non-indigenous workers; 16 percent of indigenous workers are in the formal sector compared with 46 percent of non-indigenous workers (ENSD 1989). Among both indigenous and non-indigenous workers, the average income for formal sector workers is only 1 percent higher than for all workers.

Table 6.24: Average Incomes
(quetzales per month)

	Indigenous	*Non-indigenous*
Income From Principal Occupation		
All Workers	79.97	238.03
Formal Sector Only	80.69	240.40
Total Income		
All Workers	99.24	259.32
Formal Sector Only	100.04	261.88

Source: ENSD 1989.
Note: Total income includes income from principal occupation, other jobs, retirement, other transfers and payment in-kind. The sample consists of respondents aged 14 to 65.

Differences in Income by Education

As expected, average income increases as education level increases. As shown in Table 6.25, average monthly income for individuals with no education or only primary education (0 to 6 years) is the lowest. At all education levels, indigenous people earn less than non-indigenous people.

Differences in Income by Age

By age group, the average monthly income of indigenous males is similar to that of non-indigenous females, although the income for non-indigenous females falls sharply after ages 50 to 54 (see Figure 6.5). Indigenous females' average incomes remain fairly constant regardless of age. Average incomes for non-indigenous males peak at ages 40 to 44, after which they steadily decrease, with the exception of a rebound at ages 55 to 59.

Differences in Occupational Earnings

Within any profession, there are large differences in the hourly wages, years of schooling, weekly hours and potential experience of indigenous and non-indigenous workers (see Table 6.26). Hourly wages for indigenous workers are always

Table 6.25: Average Monthly Income by Education Level, Ages 14 and Older
(quetzales)

Years of Education	*Indigenous*	*Non-indigenous*
0–6	42.06	94.41
7–11	109.35	147.78
12	232.61	316.44
13 and Over	409.51	661.38

Source: ENSD 1989.

Figure 6.5: Average Monthly Income by Age Group

Quetzales

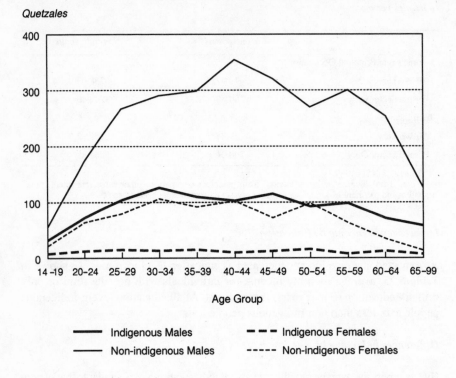

Age Group

——— Indigenous Males   − − − Indigenous Females

——— Non-indigenous Males   - - - - - Non-indigenous Females

Source: ENSD 1989.

lower than for non-indigenous workers with the exception of those in the transportation occupations where the indigenous hourly wage is 25 percent higher than the non-indigenous wage. In all other occupations, the indigenous hourly wage ranges from 38 to 72 percent of the non-indigenous hourly wage and averages 54 percent of the non-indigenous hourly wage.

Among males in all professions, the hourly wage for indigenous workers averages 63 percent of the non-indigenous hourly wage. Indigenous female hourly wages are, on average, 53 percent of non-indigenous female hourly wages. Indigenous females in office worker occupations receive slightly higher hourly wages than indigenous males in these occupations. This could be a result of the small number of women in these occupations. Although the percentages of indigenous males and females in this area are similar (see Table 6.23), the overall percentage of indigenous female workers is small. Only 20 percent of all indigenous workers are female (see Table 6.22). Non-indigenous females in the office worker occupations also have higher hourly wages than non-indigenous males in these occupations. In addition, hourly wages in the professional and manual labor occupations are essentially equal for non-indigenous males and females.

Table 6.26: Wages, Schooling, Weekly Hours and Potential Experience by Occupation

	Indigenous				Non-indigenous			
Occupation	Hourly Wage (quetzales)	Years of Schooling	Weekly Hours	Years of Experience	Hourly Wage (quetzales)	Years of Schooling	Weekly Hours	Years of Experience
Overall								
Professionals	2.37	8.7	33.1	17.5	3.52	12.2	35.3	15.7
Administrators	1.34	3.3	46.9	27.9	3.55	9.3	46.9	23.1
Office Workers	1.29	6.9	44.2	19.5	1.93	10.2	42.7	12.7
Vendors	0.64	1.8	47.0	27.7	1.40	5.6	48.2	23.6
Agriculture	0.29	1.4	45.7	25.3	0.68	2.3	44.9	24.6
Miners	0.39	1.1	45.6	18.4	0.90	2.2	42.1	31.2
Transport	1.93	3.4	51.8	24.2	1.54	4.8	51.2	26.4
Artisans	0.54	1.9	37.1	23.2	1.15	4.9	43.8	21.5
Manual Laborers	0.78	2.3	45.4	23.0	1.08	3.8	46.2	20.2
Personal Service	0.44	1.9	52.3	22.2	0.71	3.7	49.9	22.4
Males								
Professionals	2.36	9.2	34.9	17.8	3.54	12.2	40.0	15.7
Administrators	1.61	4.3	50.3	27.1	4.03	10.3	46.8	22.1
Office Workers	1.14	5.6	44.7	24.7	1.80	9.4	44.6	14.5
Vendors	0.76	2.2	50.5	26.9	1.92	6.6	50.4	22.3
Agriculture	0.30	1.4	46.7	25.3	0.70	2.4	45.3	24.8
Miners	0.39	1.1	45.6	18.4	0.90	2.2	42.1	31.2
Transport	2.00	3.3	53.0	24.9	1.56	4.9	51.5	26.4
Artisans	0.78	2.8	46.5	22.9	1.26	5.3	46.4	20.8
Manual Laborers	0.79	2.3	45.4	23.3	1.08	3.7	46.2	20.4
Personal Service	0.78	2.9	57.3	27.8	1.12	5.1	53.7	24.4
Females								
Professionals	2.38	7.2	27.3	16.3	3.49	12.1	30.1	15.6
Administrators	0.83	1.4	40.2	29.5	2.55	7.3	47.1	25.3
Office Workers	1.69	10.3	42.9	5.2	2.07	11.2	40.7	10.7
Vendors	0.50	1.4	43.2	28.6	1.05	4.9	46.6	24.4
Agriculture	0.18	0.7	33.8	25.8	0.41	1.8	40.0	21.8
Miners	n.a.	n.a.	n.a.	n.a.	n.a.	n.a.	n.a.	n.a.
Transport	n.a.	n.a.	n.a.	n.a.	0.74	3.1	36.4	27.7
Artisans	0.33	1.1	28.4	23.5	0.80	3.8	35.5	23.5
Manual Laborers	0.51	2.8	45.7	16.6	1.05	4.5	45.9	18.4
Personal Service	0.32	1.5	50.5	20.3	0.55	3.1	48.4	21.7

Source: ENSD 1989.
Note: Includes only respondents aged 14 to 65.
n.a. Not applicable.

Indigenous workers have fewer years of schooling than non-indigenous workers in all occupations. Even in the transportation occupations where they receive higher hourly wages, indigenous workers have fewer years of schooling.

As shown in Table 6.22, overall both indigenous and non-indigenous male labor-ers work approximately the same number of hours per week. However, in five of the occupations, indigenous male workers actually work more hours than non-indigenous male workers. Although, female indigenous workers overall average fewer hours per week than female non-indigenous workers, in two occupations (office work and personal service) they average more hours (see Table 6.26).

With a few exceptions, indigenous workers have more potential experience in all occupations than non-indigenous workers. This potential experience is calcu-lated by subtracting the number of years of schooling plus 6 (the age at which chil-dren are supposed to begin school) from age (age–schooling–6); actual experience was not included in the data set. In the mining occupations, indigenous workers have 13 years less experience than non-indigenous workers. Female indigenous office workers have only half as much potential experience as non-indigenous female office workers.

Earnings Differentials

Prior to the current study, an analysis of the effects of ethnicity and education on earnings in Guatemala was done using the ENSD 1989. If indigenous people had the same educational level as non-indigenous people, but retained their present structure of experience, occupation and residence, they would still earn about half that of non-indigenous people. Other factors beyond education, experience and hours worked determined the earnings of indigenous workers relative to non-indigenous workers. While education did boost earnings for indigenous workers, it was not to the extent shown for non-indigenous workers (Psacharopoulos 1993). Here the exercise is repeated, but includes additional explanatory vari-ables, such as marital status, rural location and self-employment.

In order to analyze earnings it is necessary to select a sample from the ENSD. For these analyses, only those individuals between the ages of 14 and 65 are included giv-ing a sample of 26,286 individuals. Those people who reported positive hours and positive income are classified as working. In this sample, 13 percent of the indige-nous people and 31 percent of non-indigenous people are classified as working.

These percentages are smaller than the percentages of those who self-report being employed. Fifty percent of both indigenous and non-indigenous respondents report that they are employed (ENSD 1989). Of the indigenous respondents who report they are employed, but report either no hours or no wages, 87 percent are employed in agricul-tural occupations, presumably as family workers or self-employed subsistence farmers. Sixty-seven percent of the non-indigenous respondents who report they are employed but report no positive hours or positive wages are in agricultural occupations.

Table 6.27 presents the means and standard deviations of the variables used in the following analyses. As with the full sample, indigenous people have less edu-cation, more potential experience, are more likely to be self-employed, are more likely to live in rural areas and are more likely to own their homes. Indigenous workers are most heavily represented in agricultural occupations.

Table 6.27: Labor Market Participation Analysis Variables (Workers Only)
(means and standard deviations)

Variable	Indigenous			Non-indigenous		
	Total	Male	Female	Total	Male	Female
Years of Schooling	1.70	1.81	1.30	5.13	4.89	5.68
	(2.57)	(2.58)	(2.50)	(4.60)	(4.44)	(4.88)
No Education	0.56	0.52	0.69	0.22	0.22	0.23
	(0.50)	(0.50)	(0.46)	(0.41)	(0.41)	(0.42)
Some Primary Education	0.33	0.37	0.22	0.33	0.35	0.27
	(0.47)	(0.48)	(0.41)	(0.47)	(0.48)	(0.44)
Complete Primary Education	0.07	0.08	0.05	0.19	0.19	0.17
	(0.26)	(0.27)	(0.22)	(0.39)	(0.40)	(0.38)
Some Secondary Education	0.02	0.02	0.03	0.12	0.12	0.13
	(0.15)	(0.15)	(0.17)	(0.33)	(0.32)	(0.34)
Complete Secondary Education	0.01	0.01	0.12	0.08	0.06	0.13
	(0.10)	(0.09)	(0.11)	(0.27)	(0.24)	(0.33)
University	0.00	0.01	0.00	0.06	0.06	0.07
	(0.07)	(0.08)	(0.03)	(0.24)	(0.23)	(0.26)
Potential Experience	27.73	28.35	25.51	22.87	23.61	21.14
	(14.50)	(14.38)	(14.73)	(14.51)	(14.57)	(14.22)
Self-employed	0.55	0.52	0.63	0.27	0.25	0.30
	(0.50)	(0.50)	(0.48)	(0.44)	(0.43)	(0.46)
Rural	0.72	0.76	0.58	0.46	0.53	0.30
	(0.45)	(0.43)	(0.49)	(0.50)	(0.50)	(0.46)
Own Home	0.52	0.62	0.15	0.29	0.38	0.08
	(0.50)	(0.49)	(0.36)	(0.46)	(0.49)	(0.28)
Total Household Monthly Earnings (*quetzales*)	265.36	238.64	361.18	658.26	573.75	856.03
	(345.92)	(271.00)	(523.49)	(851.68)	(735.48)	(1049.50)
Income from Principal Occupation (*quetzales*)	119.72	132.65	73.34	269.11	289.76	220.79
	(170.77)	(185.74)	(85.34)	(366.39)	(388.19)	(304.04)
Weekly Hours	45.91	48.09	38.10	46.93	48.25	43.83
	(12.68)	(9.64)	(18.07)	(14.14)	(12.21)	(17.46)
Hourly Wage (*quetzales*)	0.64	0.67	0.51	1.49	1.52	1.42
	(0.93)	(1.00)	(0.58)	(2.74)	(2.89)	(2.36)
Age	35.42	36.16	32.80	34.00	34.51	32.82
	(13.53)	(13.38)	(13.78)	(12.93)	(13.08)	(12.49)
N	3,180	2,459	721	8,597	6,029	2,568

Source: ENSD 1989.
Note: Standard deviations in parentheses. Includes respondents aged 14 to 65.

In terms of principal occupation, indigenous workers earn 44 percent of non-indigenous worker earnings overall (see Table 6.27). Male indigenous workers earn 46 percent of male non-indigenous earnings and female indigenous workers earn only 33 percent of the female non-indigenous earnings. Both indigenous and non-indigenous workers reported approximately the same number of hours worked per week although, when broken down by gender, indigenous female workers reported almost six hours a week less than non-indigenous female workers.

Earnings Functions

The results of earnings regressions for indigenous and non-indigenous workers using ordinary least squares regression are presented in Table 6.28. Overall, the rate of returns to schooling is 11 percent for indigenous workers and 12 percent for non-indigenous workers. The rate of returns to schooling is higher for female workers, both indigenous and non-indigenous. Log earnings increase with experience, but as expected in a normal age-earnings profile, they decrease with age. Living in a rural area is always negative regardless of ethnicity or gender.

Table 6.28: Earnings Functions

Variable	Indigenous			Non-indigenous		
	Total	Male	Female	Total	Male	Female
Constant	2.229	3.630	1.638	2.082	2.525	3.576
Years of Schooling	0.106	0.091	0.121	0.120	0.105	0.144
	(14.6)	(10.7)	(8.7)	(53.9)	(38.6)	(40.0)
Log of Weekly Hours	0.411	0.170	0.433	0.432	0.309	0.378
	(9.0)	(2.1)	(7.5)	(19.6)	(9.2)	(13.0)
Experience	0.030	0.029	0.040	0.038	0.043	0.041
	(5.5)	(4.4)	(4.4)	(16.4)	(15.2)	(10.4)
Experience-squared	−0.000	−0.000	−0.001	−0.000	−0.001	−0.001
	(4.8)	(4.0)	(3.7)	(12.2)	(12.2)	(7.7)
Self-employed	−0.336*	−0.572*	0.127*	−0.028*	0.236*	−1.528
	(1.1)	(1.5)	(0.3)	(0.1)	(0.9)	(2.4)
Rural	−0.190	−0.239	−0.310	−0.157	−0.267	−0.179
	(5.3)	(5.5)	(5.1)	(8.9)	(12.8)	(5.5)
Formal Sector Worker	0.273*	0.073*	0.307*	0.316*	0.558	−1.302
	(0.9)	(0.2)	(0.8)	(1.3)	(2.2)	(2.1)
Married	0.170	0.038*	0.053*	0.232	0.162	0.081
	(4.1)	(0.7)	(0.8)	(12.2)	(6.6)	(2.6)
R^2	0.21	0.18	0.25	0.40	0.37	0.50
N	3,180	2,459	721	8,597	6,029	2,567

Source: ENSD 1989.
Note: Numbers in parentheses are t-ratios. The dependent variable is the log of earnings. All coefficients are significant at the .01 level, except where indicated by *.

Table 6.29: Decomposition of the Earnings Differential

Specification	Percentage of Earnings Differential Due to Differences in	
	Endowments	*Wage Structure*
Males		
Evaluated at Indigenous Means	48	52
Evaluated at Non-indigenous Means	57	43
Females		
Evaluated at Indigenous Means	76	24
Evaluated at Non-indigenous Means	69	31

Source: ENSD 1989.
Note: For males, $W_n/W_i = 218$ percent, and for females, $W_n/W_i = 301$ percent.

The earnings function for indigenous workers has far less explanatory power than the function for the non-indigenous group, whether that equation is calculated overall or by gender. This means there are other factors beyond the human capital variables included that determine the earnings of the indigenous group relative to the non-indigenous group. This is especially true for indigenous males for whom the earnings function has the least explanatory power.

Decomposition

Using the Oaxaca (1973) method, described in Chapter 4, it is possible to decompose the earnings differential into a component attributable to differences in human capital endowments, and a component which is largely attributable to wage discrimination. Theoretically, there is no advantage to estimating the results using indigenous means or non-indigenous means, so both are presented.

Table 6.29 presents the results separately for males and females. For males, approximately one-half of the earnings differential can be attributed to differences in endowments. For females, as much as three-fourths of the differential is due to differences in human capital. These represent the upper bounds on discrimination. Non-indigenous workers may have endowments superior to indigenous workers which are not measured. This lack of information will cause an upward bias of the estimate of the component due to wage discrimination.

Conclusion

Guatemala is a country where the income distribution is highly unequal and the majority of the population is poor. The indigenous people in Guatemala are the poorest of the poor. They have the lowest education levels, the least access to health services, the least access to basic services such as water and sanitation, and income levels half that of non-indigenous people. Most indigenous people work in the agricultural sector where wages are lower than any other sector with the exception of personal services. Overall, indigenous wages average only 55 percent of non-indigenous wages.

Indigenous people lag far behind non-indigenous people in all of the indicators for poverty that can be defined using the present data set. For example, 39 percent of the indigenous population is in the lowest income quintile; 87 percent of all indigenous households are below the poverty line. In terms of living conditions, 65 percent of indigenous households do not have a safe water supply, 46 percent have no sanitary services and 75 percent have no electricity. The majority of indigenous people have no formal education and of those who do, the majority have only primary education. On average, indigenous people have only 1.3 years of schooling and 60 percent indicate that they are illiterate.

Still, education can go a long way towards improving the welfare of Guatemala's indigenous people. The returns to schooling are high in Guatemala, for indigenous and non-indigenous workers alike. Especially high returns to schooling are estimated for females. Indigenous females would increase their earnings substantially with increased investments in schooling, and a considerable reduction in the earnings gap would result. Increasing the human capital attainment of Guatemalan indigenous males would lead to a substantial reduction in the gap in earnings between ethnic groups. Equalizing income-generating characteristics between ethnic groups, especially policy-relevant variables such as education, would reduce the wage gap by about 50 percent.

7

Mexico

Alexis Panagides

According to the 1990 Mexican census, 7.5 percent or 5.3 million of Mexico's population speaks an indigenous language. In absolute numbers, no other country in the Americas has an indigenous population as large as Mexico's. One researcher examining the state of indigenous people in Mexico states that "because of the great diversity of languages, habitats, and world-views, relatively little can be said to characterize the Indian population as a whole, except that it is overwhelmingly rural and poverty stricken" (Modiano 1988: 315). Though indigenous people in Mexico have been commonly associated with poverty, the degree and dynamics of poverty in indigenous communities have yet to be fully explored. Much of the difficulty in studying the indigenous population stems largely from the paucity of information. Other than census information, relevant data are rare and limited in scope, and often very difficult to access. Through a technique described in Chapter 4, this chapter attempts to bypass obstacles presented by data insufficiency and will examine the socioeconomic condition of indigenous people in Mexico.

This study combines information from the literature on indigenous peoples and new analyses of a 1989 household survey. It examines such topics as income, earnings, education and child labor. The earnings differential between indigenous and non-indigenous workers is decomposed into its "explained" and "unexplained" components. Additionally, the determinants of poverty are estimated and policy simulations are conducted. The results show that increasing schooling would reduce overall poverty and decrease the gap in earnings between workers in indigenous areas and workers in non-indigenous areas.

Sample Characteristics

Though some general discussion of the data upon which this chapter is based is presented in Chapter 4, what follows are some important details concerning the

Figure 7.1: Distribution of Observations by Indigenous Concentration of *Municipios*

Number of Observations

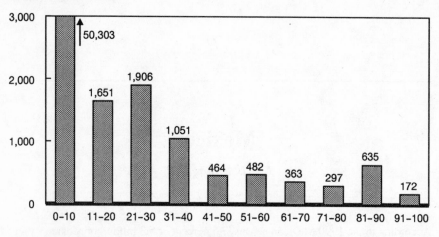

Source: INEGI 1989.   *Municipio* Indigenous Percent

data's distribution and how the results will be interpreted using the aforementioned geographical signature for ethnicity: namely, the comparison of socio-economic differences between *municipios* of varying indigenous percentages. Figure 7.1 illustrates the distribution of observations by the concentration of indigenous inhabitants per *municipio*. *Municipios* with indigenous populations representing 0 to 10 percent of their total population contain the vast majority of observations within the sample (over 50,000). All other *municipios* (10 percent indigenous population and above) represent the remaining cases at just over 7,000 observations. Generally, as the indigenous percentage of *municipios* increases, the number of observations decreases.

Figure 7.2 illustrates the predominance of indigenous people in the southeastern states of Mexico. States with the highest indigenous percentages include Chiapas, Oaxaca, Quintana Roo and Yucatán.

Table 7.1 lists mean values for several key individual and household variables for three levels of indigenous concentration in *municipios*. Number of children, number of household members, and household income illustrate household characteristics. It is interesting to note that average household sizes increase and average total household incomes decrease as indigenous percentages of *municipios* increase. This observed interaction between household size and household income is concurrent with the commonly noted correlation between larger family size and poverty. Individual characteristic averages reveal an increasingly younger sample as indigenous percentage increases. Less schooling and consequently illiteracy are also observed in *municipios* with greater indigenous populations. Employment characteristics reveal that employment, as measured by a question asking whether

Figure 7.2: Percentage of Indigenous Population by Mexican State

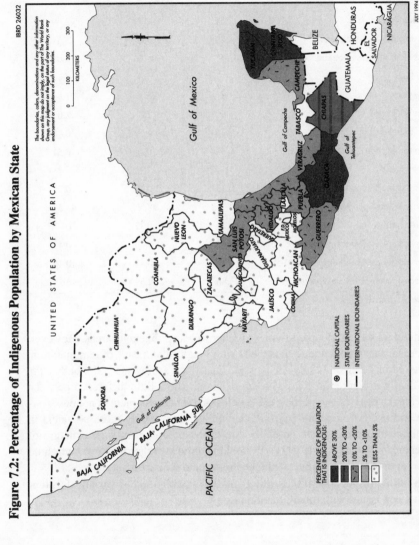

Source: INEGI 1989.

129

Table 7.1: Sample Characteristics of Population of *Municipios*

Variable	*Indigenous Concentration*		
	Non-indigenous (0–30%)	*Medium-indigenous (30–70%)*	*High-indigenous (70–100%)*
Household			
Children (mean)	2.59	2.79	3.09
Household Members (mean)	4.89	5.42	5.51
Household Income (thousands of *pesos*)	1863.63	390.66	375.07
Individual			
Age (years)	24.8	23.3	21.4
Years of School	4.9	2.8	2.0
Able to Read (proportion)	0.76	0.59	0.48
Male (proportion)	0.49	0.49	0.51
Employment			
Has Income (proportion)	0.35	0.29	0.25
Hours Worked per Week	42.3	38.3	43.5
Union (proportion)	0.21	0.12	0.07
Worked in Last Week (proportion)	0.47	0.48	0.45
Worked in Last Month (proportion)	0.46	0.49	0.46
Personal Income (thousands of *pesos*)	323.86	112.39	90.5

Source: INEGI 1989.

an individual has an income or not, is higher in less indigenous areas. However, this measure may not capture those jobs with less formal means of remuneration, such as farm labor or family businesses. Questions asking instead whether the individual has worked in the last week or month show little difference between *municipio* categories, supporting the conclusion that employment is not necessarily determined by monetary payment. Unionization is clearly more prevalent in less indigenous areas, most probably due to the predominantly rural nature of indigenous *municipios* (INI 1991). Personal income averages reaffirm household income averages, decreasing as indigenous population increases.

The following sections discuss the empirical examination of various development related issues with regard to ethnicity.

Income and Poverty Incidence

This section examines average income levels and potential determinants of poverty. Prior studies have provided strong evidence of a correlation between average income levels and ethnicity. Further empirical analysis examines the incidence of poverty by ethnicity and tests various determinants on the probability of being poor.

It should be noted that since the method of analysis in this chapter is really based on the probability of being indigenous instead of its actuality, some estimates may be biased. Income estimates may underestimate the incidence of poverty among indigenous people since it is inevitable that in a 70 percent and over *municipio*, for example, some individuals will not be indigenous people and thus probably raise the estimated mean income.

Income

Previous research on indigenous issues in Mexico has often relied on the methodology employed in this chapter. Comparing regional socioeconomic conditions to regional indigenous population levels has been a popular analytical method for overcoming the difficulties of attaining timely and adequate data on indigenous populations in Mexico. Following the discussion of prior studies, the research presented here aims to contribute to the small but existing body of literature by adding analyses of recent survey data (1989), and by exploring some previously unexamined issues concerning the indigenous population.

In a 1985 study, researchers examined the geographic distribution of individual socioeconomic conditions in Mexico. To conduct the study, a single measure of socioeconomic well-being was created and named the "marginalization" index, a composite of 19 indicators related to income, economic activity, nutrition, health, housing and services. The higher the value of the "marginalization" index, the worse an individual's socioeconomic condition. Once determined, the index was examined at the *municipio*, state and regional level, by serving as a dependent variable for assorted geographic determinants. Analyses revealed that rural residence, agricultural activity, and regions with ineffective means of communications had a strong positive impact on the index, indicating poorer socioeconomic conditions. On the other hand, non-agricultural activity and *municipios* located in the north had a weak impact on the index, indicating better conditions. Most of the *municipios* with the greatest positive effect on the index were located in the rural areas of the "highly indigenous" states of Oaxaca, Chiapas, Guerrero, Hidalgo, Puebla and Yucatán. According to the study, 84 percent of the indigenous population was living in *municipios* and regions with a "very high" index of marginalization. People living in these areas had the worst social conditions. Seventy-seven percent of the economically active population earned less than the minimum salary (Ovalle and Cantu 1982).

The Instituto Nacional Indigenista (INI) in Mexico has been collecting information on the indigenous population in an effort to build a pool of data that includes geographic distribution, poverty, economic and social indicators, as well as cultural activities. Recent examination of this data in terms of poverty analysis, employing an index of "marginalization" similar to that used by Ovalle and Cantu (1982), reveals a direct relationship between density of indigenous population and socioeconomic conditions, especially in the rural *municipios*. In 1980, 97 percent of indigenous people of 5 years and over were living in *municipios* classified as having "high" and "very high" levels of marginalization. In highly-marginalized rural *municipios*, 65 percent of the marginalized population was indigenous, while only 19 percent was non-indigenous. None of the rural *municipios* with more than a 70 percent indigenous population fit into the categories of "medium" or "low" levels of marginalization. Only two *municipios* with a range of indigenous population from 31 to 59 percent fit into the category of "medium" marginalization level (Warnam 1992).

In another publication, the INI states that 70 percent of indigenous people base their economy on primary and subsistence economic activities. Most indigenous economic activity is agricultural and little production is market oriented (INI 1991).

The findings of both Ovalle and Cantu (1982) and the INI (1991) are consistent with the findings of the research conducted in this chapter. As this chapter will illustrate, individuals in more indigenous *municipios* are on average in a poorer socioeconomic condition than individuals in less indigenous *municipios*. Also, in a simple model, a positive correlation exists between the indigenous concentration of a *municipio* and incidence of poverty.

Municipio analysis conducted on three different categories of indigenous concentration, under 10 percent, 10 to 40 percent and above 40 percent, shows a consistent inverse relationship between household and personal income, and the percentage of indigenous people within each *municipio*. Higher income levels, whether individual labor earnings or household per capita income, for *municipios* with lower percentages of indigenous population persist in every tested category. Table 7.2 illustrates the average income differences across various categories by *municipio* grouping.

Table 7.2: Average Monthly Income per Person by *Municipio* Indigenous Group
(thousands of pesos)

Category	Indigenous Concentration of Municipios (percent)		
	Under 10	*10–40*	*Above 40*
Age			
20–29	483.4	322.9	214.2
30–39	661.4	450.3	259.2
40–50	729.8	328.3	242.3
Education			
None	283.8	154.9	102.7
Primary Completed	441.3	294.3	171.2
Secondary Completed	484.4	358.9	273.7
Employment			
Agricultural Worker	257.8	161.4	114.5
Non-agricultural Worker	579.5	393.5	353.6
Total	548.2	317.1	196.5

Source: INEGI 1989.

The correlation between average incomes and the indigenous percentage of a *municipio* can be clearly seen in a scatter plot. In Figure 7.3, each point represents a *municipio* and is plotted by the average household income per capita (vertical axis) and the indigenous percentage of the *municipio* (horizontal axis). The great majority of observations form a vertical scatter on or near the vertical axis. Nevertheless, there is a trend of falling household average per capita incomes as *municipios* become increasingly indigenous. This trend is confirmed by the imposition of a downward sloping linear regression line.

Poverty

To examine the incidence of poverty among populations of varying indigenous concentration a poverty line is used. As described above in Chapter 4, the poverty line is US$60 PPP. Extreme poverty is one-half of the poverty line. As Figure 7.4 illustrates, *municipios* of increasing indigenous concentration experience higher percentages of poverty and extreme poverty. *Municipios* with 40 percent and

Figure 7.3: Average Household Income per Capita and Indigenous Concentration

Income per Capita (thousands of *pesos*)

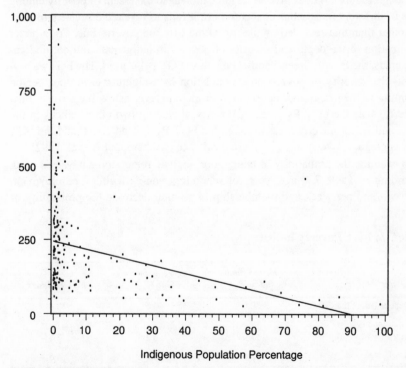

Indigenous Population Percentage

Source: INEGI 1989.

Figure 7.4: Poverty Incidence by *Municipio* Type

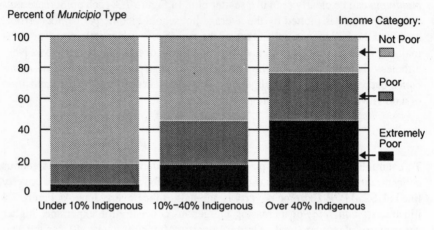

Source: INEGI 1989.

above indigenous population have a much higher incidence of extreme poverty than do *municipios* below 10 percent indigenous.

Though Figure 7.4 does give some indication as to the extent of poverty among areas of different indigenous concentration, it fails to reveal the severity of poverty other than that revealed by the use of the extreme poverty line. For a better examination of the depth and severity of poverty in indigenous and non-indigenous areas, the Foster-Greer-Thorbecke index (FGT P_2) is used. The FGT P_2 represents the severity of poverty in a population by weighting each poor person according to their degree of deprivation or income level below the poverty line. Table 7.3 lists the FGT P_2 index of poverty, including two other indices in the FGT "family" of poverty measurement: the FGT P_0 or head count, and the FGT P_1 or aggregate poverty gap (for more detail, see Psacharopoulos et al. 1992).

To examine the probability of being poor, logistic regression analysis is used. According to Table 7.4, age, years of schooling, non-agricultural employment, hours worked per week and membership in a union decrease the probability of

Table 7.3: FGT Poverty Indices

Subsample	Head Count Index (P_0)	Aggregate Poverty Gap (P_1)	FGT P_2 Index
Indigenous (more than 70%)	80.6	44.5	28.4
Non-indigenous (less than 10%)	17.9	6.2	3.1
Total	22.6	8.6	4.6

Source: INEGI 1989.

Table 7.4: Determinants of Poverty
(logit)

Variable	Heads of Household	18 Years and Older
Age	−0.0048	−0.0045
	(118.4)	(17.2)
Male	0.0556	0.0921
	(3.1)	(10.8)
Years of Schooling	−0.0344	−0.0346
	(19.2)	(29.4)
Employment		
Agricultural Worker	0.0449	0.0103*
	(3.3)	(1.0)
Non-agricultural Worker	−0.1788	−0.1698
	(15.4)	(21.3)
Employer	−0.1935	−0.1604
	(7.0)	(6.9)
Hours Worked per Week	−0.0017	−0.0015
	(5.9)	(7.8)
Union	−0.075	−0.0713
	(5.2)	(6.4)
Municipio Indigenous	0.0049	0.0045
	(17.4)	(22.2)
Children	0.0406	
	(18.6)	
Constant	0.536	1.235
N	9,660	17,274
Model χ^2	2,869	4,361
Mean of Dependent Variable	0.1826	0.1626

Source: INEGI 1989.
Note: Values for variables indicate marginal effects. Numbers in parentheses are t-ratios. * Insignificant at the 5 percent level. The omitted category of employment variables includes informal sector and domestic workers.

being poor in both samples. Variables with the greatest negative marginal impact for both samples are non-agricultural worker and employer. Being an employer in the head of household subsample decreases the probability of poverty by nearly 20 percent relative to the 18.3 percent mean of the dependent variable, at the mean values of all other variables.

Years of schooling are very influential on the probability of poverty. Within the subsamples, schooling ranged from 0 to 17 years with about a 6.5 year average overall. The estimated coefficient of −3.46 percent in the 18 year and older subsample indicates, all other factors being constant, that 6.5 years of education would decrease an individual's probability of being poor by 22.5 percent relative to the 16.3 percent average of the dependent variable. This represents a greater marginal reduction in the probability than possible with any other variable. Educational attainment, therefore, is a critical determinant of the incidence of poverty and should be considered closely in implementing poverty alleviation programs. Of course, an overall increase in the level of education of the population may reduce the returns to schooling. However, if this scenario were to occur, it would take a very long time, and in the meantime, macroeconomic and other changes could occur to alter the basic demand-supply relationship. Also, an increase in the schooling of one individual not only has an impact on that individual's productivity and, hence, earnings, but may also influence the productivity and earnings of others with whom that individual interacts. In other words, the returns to schooling may be higher for indigenous people if the average level of schooling of the indigenous population is increased.

The positive *municipio* indigenous variable indicates that as the probability that a surveyed individual is indigenous rises, so does the individual's probability of being poor by approximately 0.49 and 0.45 percent, depending on the respective equation, all other determinants held constant. This variable has considerable impact considering the potential range of percentage concentration, 0 to 100. Living in a 50 percent indigenous *municipio* increases the probability of a household head being poor by a substantial 24.5 percent, marking a greater potential *increase* in the marginal probability of being poor than possible with any other variable.

Services such as piped water, electricity and telephone service are also more common in less indigenous areas (Figure 7.5). In contrast, home ownership shows greater incidence in more indigenous areas. However, closer examination reveals a clear disparity in the physical composition of homes between more and less indigenous *municipios* (Figure 7.6). Homes in less indigenous areas are built from higher quality materials: 71 percent are constructed with concrete and brick, while in more indigenous areas only 29 percent are concrete and brick. A larger percent of homes in indigenous areas are built with wood than in less indigenous areas, 21 to 6 percent, respectively.

Measuring access to health care is an important element in the examination of individual socioeconomic welfare. Unfortunately, the survey upon which this study is based does not provide extensive health information. Nevertheless, one of the few variables available is health insurance coverage. Of those sampled, 47 percent of individuals in less indigenous *municipios* (under 30 percent indigenous) have some form of health insurance as opposed to 34 percent of those in more indigenous *municipios* (30 percent and over indigenous). Food welfare does not show great dissimilarity between the two groups. Of those sampled, 1.6 percent in less indigenous areas and 1.4 percent in more indigenous areas are receiving some sort of food assistance. Though a lower incidence of food assistance in usually more impoverished indigenous *municipios* may seem counterintuitive, it may reflect the rural and agricultural nature of indigenous areas. The distribution of food alleviation programs may be hindered by the remoteness of rural populations (which make up the bulk of the indigenous subsample), as opposed to urban areas (most of the non-indigenous subsample) where knowledge of and access to such services may be less obstructed. And perhaps more importantly, reliance on sub-

Figure 7.5: Living Assets in Indigenous and Non-indigenous Areas

Material Property

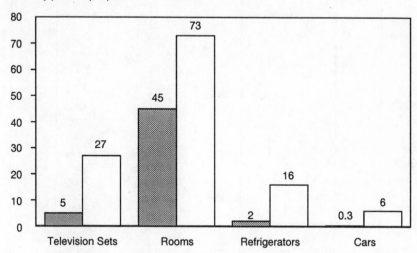

Quantity per 100 people

Household Assets

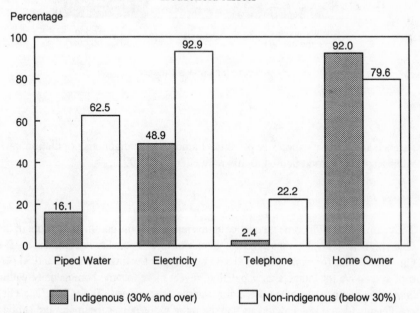

Percentage

Source: INEGI 1989.

Figure 7.6: Material Composition of Walls of Homes

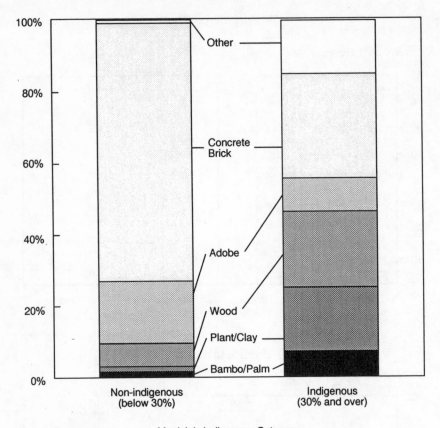

Source: INEGI 1989.

sistence agriculture, especially prominent among the indigenous population, provides a source of food denied to urban dwellers (INI 1991).

Income Inequality

The examination of income inequality in this report uses the common measure of the Gini coefficient, a value that indicates greater income inequality as it increases. The Gini coefficients for *municipios*, divided into groups of below 30 percent and 30 percent and above for indigenous population, reveal more income homogeneity within *municipio* groups than when the entire sample is examined (Table 7.5). The Gini coefficients for the less indigenous and the more indigenous subsamples are similar, at 0.539 and 0.533. When both subsamples are put together, the coefficient rises to 0.550, indicating greater income inequality. Closer examination of average incomes

Table 7.5: Income and Inequality

Municipio Sample	Mean Household per Capita Income (thousands of pesos)	Income Inequality (Gini coefficient)
Below 30% Indigenous	256.133	0.539
30% and Above Indigenous	72.309	0.533
All	245.020	0.550

Source: INEGI 1989.

between the two groups exposes large differences, explaining the Gini result for the entire sample. According to the 30 percent division, those in non-indigenous areas earn about 3.5 times more on average than those in indigenous areas.

Educational Characteristics

Because of the strong correlation between educational attainment and poverty (see Figure 7.7), this section examines educational characteristics among the indigenous and non-indigenous populations.

Figure 7.7: Income and Educational Attainment

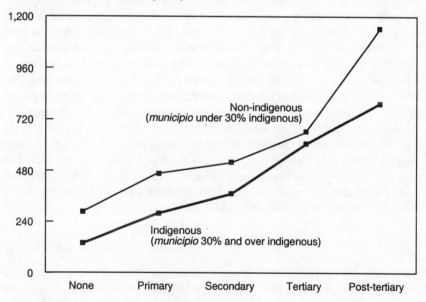

Source: INEGI 1989.

Figure 7.7 illustrates the high correlation between education and income among indigenous and non-indigenous areas for those older than 18 years and earning positive income. It is interesting to note that the returns to education are slightly higher in indigenous areas than in non-indigenous areas until tertiary education. Post-tertiary education experiences a dramatic increase in returns to education (slope of line) in non-indigenous areaș. This phenomenon could have several explanations. It may indicate that there exist greater non-market returns at higher educational levels in non-indigenous areas than in indigenous areas. These may include, for example, the use of connections in the workforce within non-indigenous areas or labor market discrimination against those in indigenous areas. The gap in returns to education may also be reflecting geographic disparities; highly indigenous areas tend to be rural. Figure 7.7 may be showing lower demand for higher education in these areas as opposed to more urban areas which are typically less indigenous. These issues are examined in greater detail below.

Access to Formal Education

Access to formal education has grown in recent years. According to the 1990 census, illiteracy has decreased from 25.8 percent in 1970, to 12.4 percent in 1990. In addition, the percentage of the population with incomplete primary schooling has decreased from 38.9 percent in 1970, to 22.8 percent in 1990 (INEGI 1992b). The findings of this study corroborate those of the census and add that improvements also occurred in indigenous areas, though educational levels still remain lower here than in non-indigenous areas.

Figure 7.8 illustrates the improvement in access to schooling over the last several decades. Figure 7.8, however, also reveals the vast inequities that still exist between those who live in indigenous and non-indigenous areas, and between genders. Despite an improving trend, those in indigenous areas still have the lowest schooling averages, and of this group, women have less schooling than men. The 1960–1969 cohort shows a situation wherein male/female disparities have narrowed while indigenous/non-indigenous area disparities have remained large.

It is interesting to note that between the 1950–59 and 1960–69 age cohorts, the growth rate of female average educational attainment experiences a sharp increase. From 1950 to 1960, federal government expenditures on education increased by 220 percent in real terms (UNESCO 1964). From 1965 to 1969 there was a 61 percent increase in expenditures, marking a rate of increase that was faster than the rate of enrollment (USAID 1977).

Illiteracy

Despite the improving trends in access to education, illiteracy continues to be an important problem for some states, especially in predominantly indigenous states. In 1980, Oaxaca had the highest level of illiteracy at 46 percent. In 1990, this percentage had decreased to 28 percent but still remained more than twice the 1990 national average of 12 percent. In 1990, the relatively indigenous state

Figure 7.8: Average Educational Attainment by Age Cohort

Years of Schooling

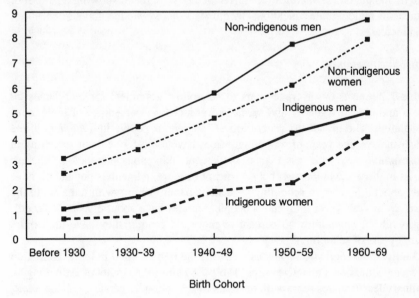

Birth Cohort

Source: INEGI 1989.

of Chiapas had the greatest incidence of illiteracy at 30 percent of the population aged 5 years and older (INEGI 1992b).

Table 7.6 reports illiteracy rates by gender and type of *municipio*: those with less than 10 percent, 10 to 40 percent, and those with more than 40 percent of an indigenous population. Illiteracy increases for both males and females as the indigenous percentage of *municipios* rises. The ethnic disparity is greatest in the female subsample where the illiteracy rate is more than four times greater in the "high" indigenous *municipio* category than the "low" indigenous *municipio* category. In addition, it is interesting to note that the gender disparity in the illiteracy

Table 7.6: Illiteracy by Gender and *Municipio* Category
(percent)

Municipio Category	Male	Female
Less than 10% Indigenous (low)	7	10
10–39% Indigenous (medium)	17	25
40% and Over Indigenous (high)	23	43

Source: INEGI 1989.
Note: Sample restricted to those individuals aged 14 and older.

rate increases as the indigenous percentage of *municipios* increases. For the least indigenous *municipios*, the male/female difference is only 2 percent; but for the "high" indigenous *municipios*, the difference is 16 percent, showing a pattern of increasing male/female educational inequities as *municipio* indigenous concentration increases.

Schooling Attainment

Table 7.7 reports the average years of schooling attainment for individuals 20 years and older by gender and *municipio* grouped by percentage of indigenous population. The higher the proportion of indigenous people in a *municipio*, the lower the average years of schooling. Males have almost 7 years of schooling in those *municipios* with less than a 10 percent indigenous population, whereas males in those *municipios* with a 40 percent or more indigenous population have only about 3.5 years of schooling. The same pattern occurs with females. In the *municipios* with fewer indigenous people, females have about 6 years of schooling, while in *municipios* 40 percent or more indigenous, they have little more than 2 years of schooling.

Multivariate regression analysis confirms the trends found in the examination of mean educational characteristics. Table 7.8 shows the results of estimating an ordinary least squares regression on years of schooling by gender, age and *municipio* percentage. As indicated by the coefficient, being male increases average schooling by nearly a year. Age is negatively related, showing an improvement in access to schooling over the last few decades. The coefficient on *municipio* percentage is negative indicating that for every percentage point of indigenous population in a *municipio*, there is a 0.06 drop in average years of schooling. The regression reveals that young, non-indigenous men have the highest average levels of education, while elderly, indigenous woman have the lowest average levels of education.

Primary School Completion

Table 7.9 reports the proportion of people (14 years and older) by gender that have failed to complete primary school. In non-indigenous *municipios*, 34 percent of the total population 14 years and older has not completed primary school,

Table 7.7: Average Schooling Years by Gender and *Municipio* Category

Municipio Category	Males	Females
Less than 10% Indigenous (low)	6.8	5.8
10%–39% Indigenous (medium)	4.4	3.6
40% and Over Indigenous (high)	3.4	2.2

Source: INEGI 1989.
Note: Sample restricted to those individuals aged 20 and older.

Table 7.8: Determinants of Schooling Years

Variable	Coefficient	Mean Value
Male	0.99 (21.0)	0.47
Age	−0.12 (80.9)	39.87
Municipio Indigenous	−0.06 (33.3)	5.41
Constant	10.53	
R^2	0.224	

Source: Computed from INEGI 1989.
Note: All coefficients are significant at the 99 percent level. Numbers in parentheses are t-ratios. Sample restricted to those aged 20 and older. The sample consists of 28,355 individuals.

while in the more indigenous *municipios* this value increases to 71 percent. Disparities continue between genders, especially in more indigenous *municipios*. In non-indigenous *municipios*, the disparity between men and women with regards to primary school completion is only 2 percent. In indigenous *municipios*, this disparity increases to 8 percent, where 75 percent of women as opposed to 67 percent of men fail to complete primary school. This pattern of increasing gender inequality with higher concentrations of indigenous people compares to the same pattern found in illiteracy rates.

Because primary school completion represents a dichotomous or binary variable, to examine the probability of completing primary school, logistic regression analysis is used. Table 7.10 shows the results of a logistic regression on a binary response variable for primary education, in this case, not completing primary school (1) or completing primary school (0). The logit model expresses the probability of someone completing primary school as a function of various characteristics, such as age, gender and *municipio* indigenous percentage (see above for details).

Table 7.9: Primary School Dropout Rates by Gender and
***Municipio* Category**
(percent)

Municipio Group	Male	Female	Total
Below 10% Indigenous	32	36	34
10–39% Indigenous	53	59	56
40% and Above Indigenous	67	75	71

Source: INEGI 1989.
Note: Sample restricted to those aged 14 and older.

Table 7.10: Determinants of Primary School Dropout
(logit)

Variable	Logit Coefficient	Variable Mean	Marginal Effect
Gender	−0.183 (7.4)	0.48	−0.0428
Age	0.062 (78.0)	34.50	0.0146
Municipio Indigenous	0.030 (33.0)	5.42	0.007
Constant	−2.818		
Model χ^2	9030.15		
Mean of Dependent Variable	0.3727		

Source: Computed from INEGI 1989.
Note: All coefficients are significant at the 99 percent level. Sample restricted to those aged 20 and older. Numbers in parentheses are t-ratios. The sample consists of 28,355 individuals.

The reported coefficients in the last column of Table 7.10 are partial derivatives indicating the change in the probability of completing primary school relative to a unit change in the corresponding independent variable. For example, every extra percentage of indigenous population in a *municipio* increases the probability that an individual has not completed primary school by 0.7 percentage points, relative to an average dropout rate of 37.3 percent. A *municipio* with a 50 percent indigenous population would increase an individual's chance of being a primary school dropout by 35 percent.

The results of the logit analysis are used to estimate probabilities of primary school completion against selected sample characteristics. Probabilities of completion are simulated by varying one characteristic at a time, while holding other variables constant at their mean levels. The results of the simulations are presented in Table 7.11.

Table 7.11: Simulated Probability of Primary School Dropout
(percent)

	Indigenous Concentration of Municipios					
	0 percent		40 percent		80 percent	
Age	Male	Female	Male	Female	Male	Female
20	15.6	18.3	38.3	42.7	67.4	71.3
30	25.7	29.4	53.6	58.1	79.4	82.2
40	39.2	43.7	68.3	72.1	87.8	89.6
50	54.7	59.2	80.0	82.8	93.1	94.1

Source: Based on results presented in Table 7.10.

The results of the logit regression and simulation further confirm prior findings. Table 7.11 illustrates trends in the probability of primary school dropout as different values for the independent variables are adjusted. As age and the percentage of indigenous people in a *municipio* rise, the percentage chance of completing primary school falls. In addition, being male possesses a distinct advantage over being female with regards to the probability of primary school completion. A good illustration of the pattern of probability for primary school dropout is the disparity between a 20-year-old male in a non-indigenous *municipio* and a 50-year-old woman in an 80 percent indigenous *municipio*. The predicted probability for the former of not having completed primary school is only 15.6 percent, while for the latter the probability is 94.1 percent.

A recent report, concurring with the poorer performance of those in indigenous areas found in this study, cites that only 1 percent of first graders in indigenous areas will successfully complete their sixth year of study (Modiano 1988). However, where a bilingual program has been put into effect in the first grade, substantially lower rates of desertion and grade repetition have been observed. The report further notes that the major problem facing bilingual education is the lack of funds to accomplish what is needed, especially in regards to the production of curriculum materials. Since this funding depends on the economic health of the nation, which has been precarious, this problem may not be solved for many years (Modiano 1988).

Regarding the apparent gender disparities in access to education, in past years the educational system has largely serviced the male population, and though *de facto* single sex (male) schools are no longer as widespread, greater demand for male education still exists. The persistence of this gender bias largely stems from cultural values that induce women to fulfill traditional domestic roles; roles that generally do not require much formal education (Bensusan 1988). In a recent study examining student performance in Mexico, it was found that though girls and boys were equally represented among the school population (49 to 51 percent of the sample, respectively), boys scored better than girls in all tested categories (Palafox et al. 1993).

Determinants of Earnings

The examinations of poverty and education above clearly illustrate a disparity in per capita income and human capital endowment levels between indigenous and non-indigenous areas. However, average income and educational attainment comparisons and logistic regressions leave room for further in-depth analyses of earnings determination and variation. This section examines potential determinants of labor earnings and tests for ethnic discrimination in the wage structure.

Indicative of potential labor market discrimination is the more detailed intra-sector examination of average earnings levels illustrated in Table 7.12. Even within sectors of employment, large disparities in earnings levels between indigenous and non-indigenous areas still persist. As Table 7.12 illustrates, those

Table 7.12: Average Monthly Wages for Selected Sectors by
Municipio **Category**

Description	Sector	Non-indigenous (thousands of pesos)	Indigenous (thousands of pesos)
		Municipio Category	
Agriculture	1111	126.58	73.57
Forestry	1112	116.15	58.36
Construction	5011	407.31	274.25
Food and Beverage	6210	113.58	53.66
Public Education	9212	641.47	413.84
Domestic Services	9540	197.29	77.13

Source: INEGI 1989.
Note: All sector codes are from the *Clasificación Mexicana de Actividades Económicas y Productos (CMAP)*. "Non-indigenous" refers to *municipios* below 30 percent indigenous. "Indigenous" refers to *municipios* 30 percent and above indigenous.

employed in non-indigenous *municipios* often earn more than twice what their counterparts in indigenous *municipios* earn.

Earnings Attainment

The apparent differences in earnings between those in indigenous areas and those in non-indigenous areas are examined using the decomposition technique described in Chapter 4.

The variation in earnings in the sample due to differences in human capital characteristics (endowments) will first be examined by using earnings functions. Years of schooling, years of potential labor market experience (age – schooling – 6) and its transformation (experience-squared), hours worked per week and several additional variables with potential significance to earnings levels, such as gender and unionization, are the independent variables. The dependent variable is the log of monthly earnings.

The first column of estimated coefficients in Table 7.13 is based on the full sample of employed adults. Regression analyses on this sample allow the inclusion of a *municipio* indigenous variable, representing the probability of being indigenous. The estimated negative coefficient for this variable indicates that for each percent of indigenous population within a *municipio* (increasing probability of an individual being indigenous), the log of earnings of the individual in the *municipio* decreases. However, though this indicates a tendency of lower earnings in more indigenous areas, it does not reveal what portion of the decrease between more and less indigenous areas is due to differences in income generating personal characteristics or "unexplained" causes such as discrimination. To answer this question a decomposition technique is employed.

Table 7.13: Sample Characteristics of Male Workers

Characteristic	Total Sample	Indigenous Concentration of Municipios	
		Below 30% (less indigenous)	30% and Above (more indigenous)
Natural Log of Earnings	12.83	12.89	11.70
Years of Schooling	7.15	7.34	3.83
Experience (years)	20.51	20.27	24.66
Natural Log of Work Hours	3.78	3.78	3.73
Married (proportion)	0.61	0.61	0.62
Employment (proportion)			
Non-agricultural Worker	0.80	0.83	0.26
Agricultural Worker	0.16	0.14	0.54
Employer	0.004	0.003	0.01
Informal Sector (proportion)	0.04	0.03	0.19
Unionization (proportion)	0.23	0.23	0.13

Source: INEGI 1989.
Note: Sample restricted to men earning positive income and aged 14 and older only.

Table 7.13 lists the means of earnings function characteristics between the two *municipio* indigenous categories. *Municipios* with a greater percentage of indigenous people experience not only lower mean earnings but also less of those characteristics expected to influence earnings positively, with the exception of experience. Average years of schooling are 91 percent higher in less indigenous *municipios*. Experience levels are higher for the indigenous areas largely reflecting the lower levels of schooling due to the construction of the experience variable. Non-agricultural laborers formed 87 percent and agricultural laborers only 10 percent of the "less" indigenous group. In the "more" indigenous subsample, agricultural laborers outnumbered non-agricultural laborers, 48 to 34 percent, respectively. These differences are indicative of the predominance of indigenous people in the rural areas of Mexico. Furthermore, the percentage of employers in indigenous areas is substantially greater. Regarding organized labor, unions are nearly two times more prevalent in less indigenous *municipios* than in more indigenous *municipios*, largely reflecting the greater tendency of unionization to occur in urban areas (Hirsch 1980).

The last 2 columns of Table 7.14 present the results of the expanded earnings function estimated separately for both "less" and "more" indigenous *municipios*. With the exception of coefficients on dummy variables, all other coefficients can be interpreted as the percentage change in earnings caused by a unit change in the corresponding characteristic. The coefficients on dummy variables can be converted to percentage values by following the equation as described in Halvorsen and Palmquist (1980).

Table 7.14: Earnings Functions by *Municipio* Category

		Indigenous Concentration of Municipios	
Variable	Total	Below 30% (low)	30% and Above (high)
Years of Schooling	0.092 (47.9)	0.093 (47.6)	0.087 (7.4)
Experience	0.036 (22.0)	0.037 (22.0)	0.020 (2.5)
Experience-squared	−0.0005 (−19.0)	−0.0005 (−18.9)	−0.0002 (−2.1)
Log of Hours Worked per Week	0.300 (16.1)	0.297 (15.5)	0.286 (3.3)
Married (1,0)	0.261 (15.6)	0.262 (15.2)	0.192 (2.5)
Employment (1,0)			
Non-agricultural Worker	0.925 (26.2)	0.892 (22.5)	1.203 (12.4)
Agricultural Worker	0.465 (12.6)	0.439 (10.4)	0.492 (5.9)
Employer	0.448 (4.0)	0.409 (3.2)	0.575 (2.2)
Union (1,0)	0.028* (1.8)	0.023* (1.4)	0.190* (1.9)
Municipio Indigenous (%)	−0.010 (−20.6)		
Constant	9.68	9.68	9.28
N	8,820	8,343	476
R^2	0.502	0.443	0.465

Source: INEGI 1989.
Note: * Insignificant, otherwise all parameter estimates are significant at the 95 percent level. Numbers in parentheses are t-ratios. Sample restricted to men earning positive income and aged 14 and older. The omitted category of employment variables is the informal sector.

For the first 4 variables listed, Table 7.14 reveals few substantial differences in coefficients between the indigenous and non-indigenous earnings functions. The average return for years of schooling for those in highly indigenous *municipios* is nearly 9 percent per additional year and only slightly higher in less indigenous *municipios*. Those living in less indigenous areas receive higher returns for labor market experience than do those in more indigenous areas, 3.7 to 2.0 percent, respectively. This disparity may be explained in part by the higher level of experience in indigenous areas. The premium for hours worked per week is nearly the same for the two areas.

Table 7.15: Male Unionization and Earnings by *Municipio* Category

Municipio Category & Union Status	Income housands of pesos)	Percentage of Individuals in Uni
Nonindigenous (under 30%)		
Majority in a Union	520.1	76.3
Minority in a Union	651.2	23.7
Indigenous (30% and above)		
Majority in a Union	146.6	86.3
Minority in a Union	397.5	13.7

Source: INEGI 1989.
Note: Numbers in parentheses are percentages of individuals in a union.

Type of employment has the greatest impact on earnings. In non-indigenous areas, a non-agricultural worker earns 144 percent more than those in the residual category (informal sector work); agricultural workers earn 59.2 percent more. Even more dramatic is the impact of non-agricultural employment in indigenous areas. Non-agricultural workers earn 232 percent more, on average, than do workers in the residual category. This figure is considerably reduced, though still a high 63.6 percent increase in earnings, for agricultural workers in indigenous areas. However, the non-agricultural and agricultural worker variables might be capturing much of the urban/rural differences not controlled for because of a missing variable identifying urban/rural residence.

Table 7.15 shows the mean incomes of unionized and non-unionized male workers in indigenous and non-indigenous areas. A greater percentage of workers in less indigenous areas are members of unions than those in more indigenous areas. According to the earnings functions listed in Table 7.14, the union estimates are insignificant at the 95 percent level, possibly indicating the long-run inability of unions to maintain long-run, above-market wage rates (Hirsch and Addison 1986). However, evidence suggests that unions provide additional, non-monetary remuneration. Within the sample, the percentage of unionized workers with health insurance is nearly twice that of non-unionized workers, approximately 40 to 80 percent, respectively.

Table 7.16 lists the results of a decomposition performed on the two earnings functions detailed in Table 7.14. By putting the two earnings functions together in the method described in Chapter 4, a decomposition identifies the "explained" and "unexplained" portions of the difference in earnings between non-indigenous and indigenous areas.

For the first specification, the portion of the differential that is due to the productive characteristics or endowments of individuals is equivalent to 52 percent of the differential in log of wages between workers in indigenous and non-indigenous areas. In other words, if those in indigenous areas were endowed with the same amounts of productive characteristics as those in non-indigenous areas, the difference in earnings between them would narrow by 52 percent. However, the remaining 48 percent difference in earnings is "unexplained." For the second

Table 7.16: Decomposition of Ethnic Earnings Differential

Specification	Percentage of the Differential Due to Differences in	
	Endowments	Wage Structure
$\hat{b}_n(\bar{X}_n - \bar{X}_i) + X_i(\hat{b}_n - \hat{b}_i)$	52	48
$\hat{b}_i(\bar{X}_n - \bar{X}_i) + X_n(\hat{b}_n - \hat{b}_i)$	66	34

Source: Computed from Table 7.14.
Note: $Wage_n$ / $Wage_i$ is the ratio of the non-indigenous to indigenous mean monthly earnings. It is 328 percent.

specification, 66 percent of the wage differential is "explained," and 34 percent is "unexplained." The "unexplained" portion is comprised of the unmeasured difference in earnings between indigenous and non-indigenous areas and may include differences in ability, health, quality of education, labor force attachment, culture as well as wage discrimination. Therefore, depending on the specification, discrimination against those in indigenous areas may explain up to 48 or 34 percent of the wage differential, thus forming the "upper bound" of discrimination. The actual figure would be much lower if the unexamined factors just mentioned could be controlled for in the analysis. But it should be kept in mind that these values in themselves may reflect discrimination (Oaxaca and Ransom 1989).

As Table 7.16 indicates, regardless of which decomposition specification is used, part of the indigenous/non-indigenous wage differential comes from "unexplained" sources other than an individual's initial endowments. In other words, discrimination against those in indigenous areas appears to exist in the Mexican labor market.

Table 7.17 shows the contribution of each variable to the earnings differential between non-indigenous and indigenous areas. A positive value indicates an earnings advantage in favor of workers in non-indigenous areas, whereas a negative value indicates an earnings advantage in favor of workers in indigenous areas. For the differential in earnings due to "explained" factors or endowments, higher educational attainment plays a large role in explaining the non-indigenous earnings advantage. However, the largest contribution to the non-indigenous advantage stems from non-agricultural employment, reflecting the predominance of non-agricultural workers in non-indigenous areas. As previously mentioned, non-agricultural workers have higher salaries on average than most other employment categories examined. The negative value of the agricultural worker variable indicates the predominant percentage of agricultural workers in indigenous areas. Greater labor market experience among the indigenous subsample also further reduces the earnings differential. The contribution of endowment differences in the remaining determinants is not very large.

The last column of Table 7.17 lists each variable's percentage contribution to the "unexplained" differential in earnings. Higher labor market returns for experience in non-indigenous areas are the greatest "unexplained" contributor to the

Table 7.17: Variable Contribution to Earnings Differential

Variable	Contribution of Each Variable to (log) Earnings Differential		Contribution as a Percentage of Total Earnings Differential	
	Endowments $b_n(X_n-X_i)$	Pay Structure $X_i(b_n-b_i)$	Endowments "Explained"	Pay Structure "Unexplained"
Years of Schooling	0.32545	0.02352	27.42	1.98
Experience	–0.16332	0.42399	–13.76	35.72
Experience-squared	0.10954	–0.22681	9.23	–19.11
Log of Hours Worked per Week	0.01650	0.03979	1.39	3.35
Married	–0.00276	0.04337	–0.23	3.65
Non-agricultural Worker	0.50822	–0.08146	42.82	–6.86
Agricultural Worker	–0.17888	–0.02857	–15.07	–2.41
Employer	–0.00482	–0.00244	–0.41	–0.21
Union (1,0)	0.00235	–0.02199	0.20	–1.85
Constant	0	0.40518	0	34.14
Subtotal	0.61228	0.57459	51.6	48.4
Total	1.18686		100	

Source: Computed from Table 7.14.

earnings differential. Employment categories all play a relatively small role towards detracting from the differential. Slightly higher returns in indigenous areas among the three employment categories may be reflecting greater unemployment in those areas. The high value for the constant term in the "unexplained" column means that regardless of education, experience and all the other tested factors, those in indigenous areas are paid less than those in non-indigenous ones, possibly for the simple fact that they are indigenous.

Women's Earnings

The above examination of earnings differentials is based on a male only sample in an attempt to isolate wage differences due to ethnic discrimination without interference from possible gender biases within the wage structure. To examine earnings determination and earnings differentials among indigenous and non-indigenous women and between women and men, three additional earnings functions are estimated and the results listed in Table 7.18.

The women's earnings functions are similar to those of men but differ with respect to the inclusion of a gender variable in the first two listed functions, and a variable controlling for the number of children in all three. The first two functions examine non-indigenous and indigenous areas as a whole and control for gender.

Table 7.18: Earnings Functions by Gender

Variable	Non-indigenous Men and Women	Indigenous Men and Women	Indigenous and Non-indigenous Women
Years of Schooling	0.098 (58.0)	0.099 (8.6)	0.110 (32.4)
Experience	0.038 (25.9)	0.021 (2.6)	0.045 (16.4)
Experience-squared	−0.0005 21.6	−0.0002 (2.0)	0.0007 (13.3)
Log of Hours Worked per Week	0.421 (27.9)	0.447 (6.2)	0.540 (22.0)
Male	0.185 (13.8)	0.473 (4.4)	
Married (1,0)	0.185 (11.5)	0.165* (1.9)	0.116 (3.1)
Non-agricultural Worker	0.812 (21.3)	1.120 (11.0)	0.532 (4.4)
Agricultural Worker	0.390 (9.5)	0.470 (5.3)	0.219* (1.5)
Employer	0.330 (2.8)	0.510* (1.8)	−0.086* (0.3)
Union (1,0)	0.061 (4.4)	0.322 (3.3)	0.124 (4.8)
Municipio Indigenous			−0.009 (7.0)
Children	−0.0009* (0.2)	−0.010* (0.5)	−0.048 (4.1)
Constant	9.083	8.181	8.848
N	11,743	544	3,467
R^2	0.425	0.455	0.420

Source: INEGI 1989.
Note: * Insignificant. Otherwise all parameter estimates are significant at the 99 percent level. Numbers in parentheses are t-ratios. Sample restricted to those earning positive income and aged 14 and older. "Non-indigenous" refers to *municipios* below 30 percent indigenous. "Indigenous" refers to *municipios* 30 percent and above indigenous.

Comparisons of the estimated coefficients on the male dummy variable between the two equations reveal that men in indigenous areas earn 60.5 percent more than their female counterparts, as opposed to 20.3 percent in non-indigenous areas. This disparity may indicate greater income inequities between genders in indigenous areas than in non-indigenous areas.

The last column lists the results of an earnings function on a female only subsample. Education, log hours worked per week, non-agricultural labor, unionization and children play significant roles in earnings determination. Education has a very strong impact on female earnings. The estimated coefficient on education indicates that for each year of a woman's education, her earnings increase by 11 percent. This is a very significant determinant considering female education in the subsample can range from 0 to 17 years. All other determinants equal, a woman who has completed primary school (6 years) earns 66 percent more than a woman without education. Another variable of significant impact is the log hours of work. Each one point of increase in the log hours of work increases a woman's earnings by 54 percent. Non-agricultural labor increases a woman's income by 70 percent. Interestingly, the number of children becomes statistically significant in the women only subsample, indicative of the greater impact of children on female rather than male earnings in a traditional society.

The negative value on the *municipio* indigenous percent variable confirms the trend of lower earnings in indigenous areas than in non-indigenous areas. The −0.009 value listed for the female subsample is nearly the same as the −0.01 value seen in the male only earnings functions. This finding reveals that individual earnings, regardless of gender, fall by 1 percent for each percent of indigenous concentration within a *municipio*, all other factors constant.

Child Labor and Education

This section attempts to empirically examine the determinants of schooling and non-schooling activities for children in non-indigenous and indigenous areas. Household and demographic determinants of schooling participation, years of schooling attainment and child employment will be analyzed for *municipios* of varying indigenous population percentages.

Figure 7.9 schematically describes the sample and the school/non-school activities of Mexican children and youths (those 12–18 years of age) for "more" and "less" indigenous areas. The subsamples to be used in the analysis are also shown. The "in school" population includes 6,071 and 295 observations for the less and more indigenous *municipios*, respectively. The "not in school" population com-

Figure 7.9: Sample and Subsample Distribution

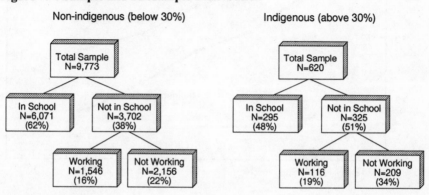

Source: INEGI 1989.

prises the remainder, or 3,702 non-indigenous and 325 indigenous observations. The "not in school" sample is further divided into "working" (those working 30 or more hours per week) and "not working" subsamples. Due to the nature of the survey, schooling and non-schooling decisions are mutually exclusive. That is, either a child is in school or is not; a child cannot be classified as working and be enrolled in school at the same time. This represents a limitation since it is known from other sources that working children often attend school (Myers 1989).

Figures 7.10 and 7.11 describe the activities and educational performance of Mexican children by age. In general, the younger the child, the greater the "in school" population of the age group; the older the child, the greater the likelihood of employment. Figure 7.10 shows non-indigenous areas have greater percentage enrollments per age group than indigenous areas. The gap between the percentage enrollments of the two areas widens, reaching its greatest difference at 17 years of age where non-indigenous percentage enrollment is more than twice indigenous. Figure 7.11 shows labor force participation percentages per age group. Indigenous areas experience greater child participation in the labor force than non-indigenous areas. This can be partially explained by the predominantly rural geography of indigenous populations. Though child labor is found to some extent in all sectors of economic activity, it is in the agricultural sector that child labor is most pervasive. In this sector children from about the age of 6 years onward begin by carrying out light tasks on the family plot and eventually aid in the sowing and harvesting

Figure 7.10: "In School" Distribution by *Municipio* Group

Percent of *Municipio* Group in School

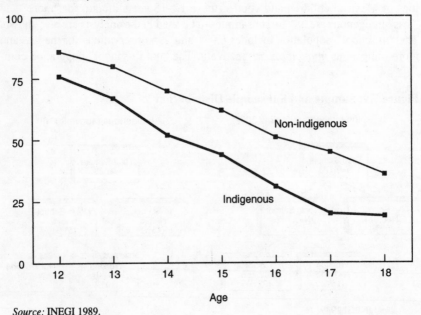

Source: INEGI 1989.

Figure 7.11: "Working" Distribution by *Municipio* Group

Percent of *Municipio* Group Working

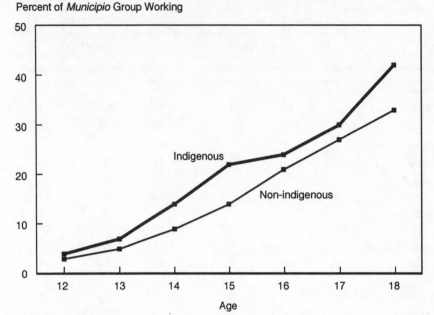

Source: INEGI 1989.

of crops (Bensusan 1988). Furthermore, the difference in child labor percentages between indigenous and non-indigenous areas fluctuates with a noticeable extreme occurring at 15 years of age. This may be reflecting increased entry into the labor force at age 15 that is prevented at earlier ages due to the 14 year minimum age labor restriction (Sinclair and Trah 1991).

Table 7.19 presents mean educational attainment and its correlates broken down into the "in school" and "not in school" subsamples for non-indigenous and indigenous areas. The "not in school" sample is further broken down into "working" and "not working" subsamples.

Examination of average years of schooling for the indigenous and non-indigenous subsamples reveals much higher educational attainment averages among the non-indigenous (Figure 7.12). Within indigenous and non-indigenous groups, the "in school" subsamples have the highest average schooling followed by those "not in school" and "working." Children not in school and unemployed have the lowest average schooling attainment.

Average years of schooling between genders are mixed. Consistent differences favoring one gender over the other do not appear. The largest difference in average years between genders appears among employed children in non-indigenous areas, where females experience an average of 1.1 more years of education than do males.

Table 7.20 expands the examination of gender educational differences within the youth population by listing average educational attainment levels by gender,

Table 7.19: Mean Years of Schooling by Selected Sample Characteristics

| | *Non-indigenous Municipios* | | | *Indigenous Municipios* | | |
| | | *Not in School* | | | *Not in School* | |
Characteristic	*In School*	*Working*	*Not Working*	*In School*	*Working*	*Not Working*
Gender						
Male	7.1	6.0	5.7	5.3	4.7	4.6
Female	7.4	7.1	5.7	5.8	4.6*	4.0
Mother's Education						
None	5.9	5.0	4.3	4.6	4.1	3.6
Primary and Below	7.3	6.7	6.3	6.2	6.1*	4.9
Secondary and Above	8.3	9.4	8.3*	8.5*	0.0	0.0
Father's Education						
None	5.7	5.1	4.5	4.4	4.1	3.4
Primary and Below	7.2	6.6	6.1	5.6	5.2	4.6
Secondary and Above	8.2	8.7	7.5	7.3	0.0	0.0
Household Head Employment						
Non-agricultural Worker	7.6	7.1	6.3	7.5	5.1*	4.1*
Agricultural Worker	5.6	4.8	5.3	4.6	4.2*	4.4
Other	7.1	5.9	5.7	5.1	4.4	3.9

Source: INEGI 1989.
Note: Sample for children aged 12 to 18. * Mean computed with less than 30 observations. Working is defined by 30 plus hours of labor per week. "Non-indigenous" refers to *municipios* below 30 percent indigenous. "Indigenous" refers to *municipios* 30 percent and above indigenous.

age and *municipio* indigenous concentration. The educational averages listed indicate a pattern of decreasing levels of educational attainment as *municipio* indigenous concentration increases, regardless of gender. In addition, the differences in educational attainment between greater and lesser indigenous areas become larger as age increases. However, this increasing difference due to age is more pronounced within the female subsample. Furthermore, as *municipio* indigenous concentration increases, so does the gender disparity favoring greater male educational attainment.

Parental education seems to play an important role in average educational levels among children. The average increase in educational achievement for a child with a mother with secondary or greater education, as opposed to a mother with no edu-

Figure 7.12: Average Educational Attainment by Ethnicity

Years of Schooling

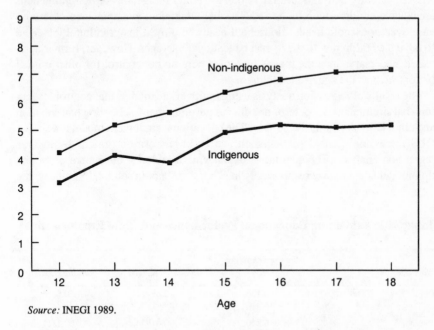

Source: INEGI 1989.

cation, is 3.5 years in non-indigenous areas. For fathers the impact is only slightly diminished to a 3.0 year difference. Similar differences exist in indigenous areas, but due to the lack of mothers with education above the primary level in the subsample, this could not be fully examined. However, where comparisons are available between areas, the impact of parental education is greatest in indigenous areas.

The employment conditions of the head of the household have a clear impact on a child's average educational achievement. Educational means are computed for

Table 7.20: Average Years of Schooling by Gender, Age and *Municipio* Category

(percent)

Municipio Category	Male Ages			Female Ages		
	6–12	*13–17*	*18–24*	*6–12*	*13–17*	*18–24*
Less than 10% Indigenous	3.1	6.9	8.7	3.2	7.2	8.4
10%–39% Indigenous	2.7	6.0	6.7	2.8	5.8	6.6
40% and Over Indigenous	2.4	5.2	5.3	2.4	4.9	4.4

Source: INEGI 1989.

non-agricultural, agricultural and "other" categories. The "other" employment category contains the self-employed including the informal sector. Households whose heads are non-agricultural workers in either indigenous or non-indigenous areas have children with higher educational attainment averages than otherwise employed household heads. Household heads employed in agricultural jobs tend to have the children with the lowest educational averages. However, further analysis is necessary since the means presented here do not control for other critical factors such as the age of the children.

The results of regression analysis using multivariate models that control for factors that simultaneously determine educational attainment, schooling participation and child labor appear in Table 7.21. The educational attainment model is a simple OLS regression. School participation and child labor are estimated by logistic regression analysis. The qualitative dependent variable for the school participation model is the binary response of "in school" or "not in school." Similarly, the

Table 7.21: Explaining Educational Performance and Child Employment

Variable	Years of Schooling (OLS)	In School (Logit)	Working (Logit)
Age	0.136	−0.099	0.0689
	(8.5)	(29.6)	(26.2)
Male	0.850	0.0197*	0.1111
	(12.2)	(1.3)	(10.4)
Municipio Indigenous	−0.010	0.0004*	0.0*
	(4.5)	(1.1)	(0.1)
Siblings	0.100	−0.0271	0.0055
	(5.9)	(9.0)	(2.6)
Male Household Head	0.100*	0.0723	−0.0403
	(1.0)	(3.8)	(3.1)
Mother's Schooling	0.586	0.0494	−0.0221
	(64.1)	(20.6)	(13.1)
Household Income Per Capita	0.000*	0.0002	0.0*
	(1.5)	(5.3)	(0.6)
Household Head Occupation			
Non-agricultural Worker	0.192	0.1587	-0.0514
	(3.1)	(12.3)	(5.5)
Agricultural Worker	−0.423	−0.0783	0.0034*
	(3.3)	(3.9)	(0.2)
Constant	0.460	5.988	−9.038
R^2/Chi-square	0.501	2,350	1,238
N	5,684	8,893	8,893

Source: INEGI 1989.

Note: * Insignificant. All other values are significant at the 99 percent level. Numbers in parentheses represent t-ratios. Years of schooling estimated for in-school sample. The omitted category of household head occupations includes self-employed and the informal sector. Logit results report marginal effects.

child labor dependent variable assumes a binary response as the child is either "working" or "not working."

The first column of Table 7.21 reports the results from the OLS regression on years of schooling. Determinants such as number of siblings, household income per capita and head of household occupation show positive and significant correlations with a child's educational attainment. However, the most significant contributor to a child's educational attainment is mother's education. The estimated coefficient of 0.586 suggests that, on average, other determinants held constant, a child's educational attainment is increased 58.6 percent or 7 months for each year of her/his mother's educational attainment.

The only negative coefficient in the school attainment model is the *municipio's* indigenous concentration. Though this coefficient is significant, it is not very large. A child living in a 70 percent indigenous *municipio* will, on average, all else held constant, have about 8 months less schooling than a child in a completely non-indigenous *municipio*. The small impact of the indigenous variable indicates differences in school attainment are better explained by the other determinants. Table 7.22 lists the significant determinants found in the regressions and their average values for areas of different indigenous concentration.

As Table 7.22 illustrates, most determinant averages drop as indigenous concentrations increase. Most notable is the fall in mother's education, the determinant with the most pronounced impact on child schooling attainment. It is clear that the poorer scholastic achievement of children in indigenous areas is due largely to poor levels in these significant determinants and any significance

Table 7.22: Means of Significant Determinants of Schooling Attainment

	Indigenous Concentration of Municipios		
Variable	*Below 10%*	*10–50%*	*Above 70%*
Male	0.25	0.25	0.27
Siblings	3.6	3.6	4.1
Mother's Education	4.4	2.6	1.0
Household Income per Capita	228.2	98.7	44.9
Household Head as Laborer	0.54	0.46	0.33
Dependent Variables			
School Attainment in Years	5.4	3.8	2.2
Student	0.64	0.59	0.44
Worker	0.16	0.16	0.24

Source: INEGI 1989.

Note: The dependent variables "student" and "worker" are dummy variables, therefore mean values are equivalent to rates. For example, 64 percent of the below 10 percent indigenous subsample is students.

remaining to the indigenous percent variable is captured in relevant determinants not included in the model.

The second column of Table 7.21 presents the results of a model attempting to explain participation in schooling. The qualitative dependent variable is school attendance. Positive coefficients indicate increased probability of school attendance. Male headed households and households headed by laborers tend to substantially increase the probability of school attendance. Again mother's education has a significant and large impact on a child's enrollment probability. For every year of a mother's educational attainment, the marginal probability of her child's enrollment increases by nearly 5 percent, all else held constant. A mother with incomplete primary school education, representing 3 years, increases her child's probabilities of enrollment by nearly 15 percent. If a mother has completed primary school, the probability increases to 30 percent. Number of siblings and age have negative coefficients, reducing enrollment probabilities as their values rise. It is interesting to note that the *municipio* indigenous percentage coefficient is not statistically significant, though it is negative. This lack of significance is discussed below.

The last column of Table 7.21 shows the results of a logit regression on the probability of employment among the child population. Among those determinants with the greatest positive impact on the probability of employment are age, gender, and number of siblings. Gender has a strong positive impact; being male increases a child's chances for employment by nearly 8 percent. Those determinants detracting from child employment are male head of household, a laborer as the head of household and mother's education. The coefficient of household income per capita is insignificant. This does not indicate that the probability of child labor is not partly determined by household income, but instead may represent bias introduced by a simultaneity condition since household income per capita and child labor are determined simultaneously by each other. In the estimated model, child labor is partially determined by household income, but household income per capita is partially determined by child labor, as Table 7.23 illustrates. In addition, similar to the school participation model, a *municipio's* indigenous percentage is insignificant in determining child labor.

Though the *municipio* indigenous percent is insignificant in the two logit models, it should not be interpreted that indigenous areas do not differ from non-indigenous areas in educational attainment and in the probabilities of schooling and working. As Table 7.22 illustrates, mean levels of other significant determinants, such as mother's education, differ greatly between indigenous and non-indigenous areas, explaining much of the interethnic differential in the dependent variables. The lack of statistical significance of the *municipio* indigenous percent determinant shows that the differences in child education and child labor between indigenous and non-indigenous areas are due to differences in socioeconomic conditions. The presence of determinants measuring these conditions, such as mother's education, income per capita and number of siblings, "explain" much of the significance that would be attributed to a *municipio* determinant regressed on a simpler model. Any significance the *municipio* percentage determinant maintains is due to missing socioeconomic variables to which the *municipio* determi-

Table 7.23: Average Child Earnings

Variable	Mean Earnings (thousands of pesos per month)	Percent of Family Income	N
Age			
12 to 14	157.3	21.7	135
15 to 16	212.9	25.3	267
17 to 18	250.4	29.2	352
Schooling			
None	150.9	29.2	47
Incomplete Primary	183.7	27.0	197
Complete Primary	236.0	26.1	358
Incomplete Secondary	253.2	26.0	152
Male	219.4*	27.6	561
Female	223.7*	23.4	193
Non-indigenous (below 30%)	228.6	26.3	703
Indigenous (30% and above)	108.2	29.1	51

Source: INEGI 1989.
Note: For employed subsample aged 12 to 18 only.
   * Differences in mean earnings between males and females are not statistically significant at $\alpha = 0.10$.

nant is highly correlated. For the averages of those determinants that are significant to school participation and child labor, the indigenous subsample predicts lower probabilities of school participation and higher child labor than in the non-indigenous subsample. For example, the average difference in mother's educational level between the two areas is 2.7 years more in non-indigenous *municipios*. Based on the estimated model for school participation, this would mean, holding all other determinants of school participation constant, the average probability of school enrollment in non-indigenous areas is 13.4 percent greater than the probability of enrollment in indigenous areas.

The contribution of child labor income to total family income is substantial. Table 7.23 shows the percent contribution of child labor for age, educational attainment, gender and *municipio* indigenous percentage categories. As expected the percent contribution of child labor to family income increases with age. Increasing educational attainment reduces the contribution. Child income plays a slightly greater role in total family income in indigenous areas than in non-indigenous areas. It is interesting to note that male mean earnings are less than female mean earnings; this difference, however, is not statistically significant.

Conclusion

The examination of poverty at the *municipio* level reveals a consistent correlation between high degrees of socioeconomic poverty and the percentage of indigenous people living in a *municipio*. Income, earnings and assets are less in areas of greater indigenous concentration. For example, individuals in more indigenous *municipios* receive about 36 percent of the income that individuals in less indigenous *municipios* receive. This disparity persists even when comparing individuals with equivalent education, age, gender and other characteristics between "more" and "less" indigenous *municipios*. Gini coefficients suggest greater income equality within *municipios* grouped by indigenous and non-indigenous populations than for both populations together, indicating greater income inequality between ethnic groups.

Detailed decomposition of the earnings differentials shows that for the male sample, endowments of assessed characteristics account for 52 percent of the disparity between indigenous and non-indigenous workers' earnings. "Unexplained" factors such as variations in ability, quality of education, labor force participation, culture and labor market discrimination are responsible for the remaining 48 percent of the earnings gap. Thus there is considerable scope for policymakers to reduce overall earnings differentials between indigenous and non-indigenous people.

Large educational differences exist between indigenous and non-indigenous *municipios*, but there has been substantial improvement over the last several decades. Trends in average years of education show improvement over past years in indigenous and non-indigenous areas. Most notable has been the closing gap between genders within *municipio* groups. However, the gap between indigenous and non-indigenous areas is still large.

Primary school completion rates show significant variation along both ethnic and gender differences. Men in non-indigenous areas experience the highest rates of primary school completion. In contrast, women in indigenous areas experience the lowest rates of primary school completion.

Though the research in this report identifies individuals' ethnicity by the percentage of indigenous people in the *municipio* in which they reside, the empirical results consistently indicate lower earnings, lower standards of living and less educational attainment in *municipios* where indigenous people represent a greater percentage of the population than in *municipios* where they represent a smaller percentage.

The empirical results presented in this chapter show a clear socioeconomic disadvantage among those living in *municipios* with high percentages of indigenous people to those living in *municipios* with low percentages of indigenous people. Poverty assessments cannot afford to ignore the visible socioeconomic disparity presented by ethnicity. A priority for interventions is to target areas with high concentrations of indigenous people, since as the evidence shows, being indigenous is often synonymous with being poor. In what areas could such programs be further focused to maximize their economic rates of return? The analyses within this chapter offer several ideas. The following briefly summarizes two of the primary determinants of poverty found by this study, suggesting these determinants as guides for targeting mechanisms.

The apparent strong influence of education to ameliorate poverty and increase earnings, especially in indigenous areas, conveys a need to focus on improving access to education as an important development issue with significant and beneficial long-term socioeconomic repercussions. One of several frequently noted methods used to improve the access of indigenous populations to education is the implementation of bilingual education programs. Though the research within this report is unable to measure the effects of bilingual education, the benefits of bilingual education for indigenous populations have been well documented in Mexico and in other countries (see above). What the research within this chapter does is confirm the existing inequities of educational attainment and the critical value of education within and between ethnic groups in Mexico.

Large discrepancies in socioeconomic conditions between genders, especially pronounced within indigenous *municipios*, should also be noted when formulating policy. The large measured impact of mother's education on child labor, child educational attainment and poverty emphasizes the importance of gender awareness. Attempts at correcting gender biases in order to provide a more equitable distribution of access to education may, in the long run, reap the benefits of poverty alleviation that the empirical analyses would predict.

8

Peru

Donna Macisaac

In this chapter, individuals are identified as indigenous if they speak Quechua, Aymara or another indigenous language. Language is an important factor in Peru, and despite the fact that both Quechua and Aymara are officially recognized languages and are widely spoken, indigenous languages have low status. Many indigenous people are forced to reject their own language and culture in order to improve their socioeconomic position. The Peruvian social pyramid is such that the Spanish-speaking European descendants are at the top, followed in turn by the *mestizos* (who mostly speak only Spanish) and the *cholos* (roughly, Spanish-speaking indigenous people, and a negative term not used in the presence of the person to whom it is applied (see Bourricaud 1976)), while the monolingual indigenous language speakers are found at the bottom.

The purpose of this chapter is to document the socioeconomic conditions of the indigenous people of Peru. The analysis is based on the Peruvian 1991 Living Standards Measurement Study (PLSS). First, the identification of the indigenous population, including its location and socioeconomic profile, is discussed. The incidence of poverty among the indigenous and non-indigenous populations is examined, including an analysis of Peru's income distribution and the position of the indigenous population within this distribution. Also included are an analysis of earnings distribution across economic sectors, an examination of housing conditions and health status, and an evaluation of educational achievements with respect to age, location, gender and household head.

Estimates of labor force participation and the earnings of indigenous and non-indigenous men and women by economic sector and occupation are included. The earnings of working-aged males are estimated and decomposed in order to determine the existence and causes of the earnings differential between indigenous and non-indigenous workers. The factors affecting child schooling, school attendance and attainment, and labor force participation are empirically examined. Finally, an investigation is made of the migratory patterns of Peru's indigenous population.

Identifying Peru's Indigenous Population

Using PLSS information on language spoken, individuals are identified as indigenous if they speak Quechua, Aymara or another indigenous language. The resulting estimate of the Peruvian indigenous population is 11.3 percent of the total population. Quechua speakers account for the majority, or 63 percent, while Aymara speakers account for the remaining 37 percent (see Table 8.1). This estimate of the indigenous population is somewhat less than the 24.8 percent estimate from the latest (1981) census of Peru (CELADE 1992), and considerably less than the 47 percent estimate (9.3 million people) of the indigenous population reported for 1970 (Jordan Pando 1990).

Some of the difference in estimates can be attributed to the definition of indigenous people employed in each survey. The PLSS estimate is unable to classify bilingual native language speakers as indigenous people because language specification is mutually exclusive. Accordingly, PLSS estimates of the indigenous population are much smaller than other survey estimates, such as CELADE's, which allow for language combinations. Moreover, it is possible, given the low status awarded to indigenous people, that indigenous Peruvians who also speak Spanish chose to classify themselves as Spanish speakers. Equating ethnicity with language must be kept in mind when interpreting statistics on indigenous people; it is probable that the omitted Spanish-speaking indigenous people are in a better socioeconomic position than are native-speaking monolingual indigenous people.

Underestimates of the indigenous population also result from incomplete survey coverage. Due to security considerations, small farms and more remote households in the Sierra region were not surveyed. Consequently, the data from the Sierra region, and the Northern Sierra in particular, depict a population which is located in or near cities. In addition, the rural areas of the Coast and the entire Selva (which is primarily rural) are excluded from the survey. Given the rural and, more specifically, remote locations of indigenous people, it is likely that the indigenous population is underestimated. However, regardless of overall population estimates, the data from the LSMS include a wealth of information about the socioeconomic situation of the indigenous people of Peru.

Table 8.1: Language Distribution

Language Group	Number of Observations	Percent
Quechua	996	7.1
Aymara	520	4.2
Spanish	9,973	88.7
Total Indigenous	1,518	11.3

Source: PLSS 1991.

Socioeconomic Profile

While it appears that the indigenous population contains slightly more women than the Spanish-speaking population (52.3 percent versus 50.7 percent), it is likely that this is a result of linguistically defining the indigenous population, i.e., given their greater workforce participation rate, indigenous men are more likely to speak Spanish.

In general, indigenous households are more "traditional" than non-indigenous households. They are more likely to be headed by a man, more likely to contain married couples and also to have both the household head and her/his spouse present. While households are classified as indigenous if the household head speaks an indigenous language, closer examination reveals that not all individuals within households speak an indigenous language, and the proportion of the household which speaks an indigenous language varies considerably by rural/urban location. The average rural indigenous household contains 4.6 individuals, of which 4.1 people, or 89 percent, speak an indigenous language. An average indigenous household in the city contains 5.1 people, of which 2.2, or 43 percent, speak an indigenous language (see Table 8.2). Further examination of urban areas shows indigenous and non-indigenous households both average 5.1 individuals, 1.3 of which are children under 13 years of age, and are equally as likely to contain a woman who is either household head or married to the household head. Urban indigenous households, however, are more likely than Spanish-speaking households to contain a man who is either household head or married to the household head and, subsequently, are more likely to be dual-parented.

An average urban indigenous household contains fewer children under age 13 than an average rural indigenous household (at 1.3 versus 1.6 children), yet urban

Table 8.2: Household Description by Rural/Urban Location

Descriptor	Indigenous		Non-indigenous	
	Rural	Urban	Rural	Urban
Average Household Size	4.6	5.1	4.8	5.1
Average Indigenous Language Speakers	4.1	2.2	0.1	0.0
Average, Ages 13 and Under	1.6	1.3	1.5	1.3
Male Household Head or Spouse (%)	88.2	87.0	88.3	81.8
Female Household Head or Spouse (%)	92.2	92.9	86.9	92.6
Household Head and Spouse Present (%)	80.0	79.9	74.2	74.2
Female Household Head (%)	12.2	13.0	12.9	19.0
Average Persons Married	1.3	1.4	1.2	1.5
Average Family Income (million new *soles* per month)	72.5	176.8	113.6	286.9

Source: PLSS 1991.
Note: Ethnicity defined by household head's language.

indigenous households are much larger than rural indigenous households (5.1 people versus 4.6 people). Within urban indigenous households, the larger proportion of adults and the larger proportion of Spanish speakers contribute significantly to family income. Urban indigenous families earn an average of 176 million new *soles* per month as compared to 76 million new *soles* per month earned in rural indigenous households. The corresponding earnings for Spanish-speaking households are 287 and 144 million new *soles,* respectively.

The age composition of the population (see Table 8.3) is important due to the implications it has for education demand, employment and the economic dependence relation. The Peruvian indigenous population appears aged in comparison to the non-indigenous population. It is likely that this shift is the result of a strong socialization process whereby youngsters no longer speak the native language of their parents. However, as a significant proportion of the indigenous population is school-aged, the delivery of educational services becomes a primary concern. The relatively large proportion of elderly people within the indigenous population places similar linguistic demands on the delivery of social services, such as health care for the aged. Given that our sample of indigenous people includes only those who claim to be monolingual in an indigenous language and excludes bilingual indigenous people, it may be the case that indigenous people—given that they may have higher mortality rates—are not more aged than non-indigenous people; only that monolingual indigenous language speakers are more aged, probably due to the fact that younger people are more likely to go to school, learn Spanish and, over time, identify more with non-indigenous language speakers (even if they are bilingual).

Regional Distribution

Despite recent internal migration from rural to urban areas, and in particular to Lima, only 6.7 percent of the indigenous population is found in Lima, and 16.9

Table 8.3: Age Distribution
(percent)

Age Group	Indigenous	Non-indigenous
Younger than 5	8.3	8.8
5–14	22.0	23.4
15–29	24.6	31.6
30–44	18.9	17.3
45–59	16.1	11.2
Older than 59	10.3	7.8
Total	100.0	100.0

Source: PLSS 1991.
Note: Total of columns not exactly 100 percent because of rounding.

Table 8.4: Regional Distribution of Population
(percent)

Region	Indigenous	Non-indigenous
Lima	6.7	46.4
Other Urban	16.9	40.3
Coast North	0.4	18.2
Coast South	1.5	1.7
Sierra North	0.0	2.0
Sierra Central	2.5	8.7
Sierra South	12.5	9.7
Rural	76.4	13.3
Sierra North	6.4	7.3
Sierra Central	20.6	4.5
Sierra South	49.5	1.5
Total	100.0	100.0

Source: PLSS 1991.

percent is found in other urban areas (see Table 8.4). In contrast, 87 percent of Spanish speakers are located in urban areas: 46 percent in Lima and 40 percent in other urban areas.

An overwhelming majority, 76 percent, of indigenous people are located in rural areas, and half are located in rural areas of the south sierra. While indigenous people comprise 11 percent of the total Peruvian population, they account for 42 percent of rural Peruvians. Rural prevalence is important to keep in mind when interpreting information about the indigenous people of Peru. Indigenous people in urban areas have better access to services and more education than their rural counterparts; however, it is always the case that indigenous people fare worse than non-indigenous people in any given location.

Poverty Profile

A correlate of poverty is being indigenous. This section estimates the poverty incidence for indigenous people and assesses the position of indigenous people within the Peruvian income distribution. Comparisons of income distributions are undertaken by ethnicity and location. Finally, the monetary measures of poverty are complemented by an analysis of the housing, health and education situation of indigenous people.

Poverty Incidence

Using poverty lines which take into account urban/rural discrepancies, the distribution of poverty and extreme poverty among both indigenous and non-indigenous is examined. The poverty line is defined as the local currency equivalent of US$60 per month in 1985 purchasing power parity (PPP) dollars, and the extreme poverty line is US$30.

The Foster-Greer-Thorbecke (FGT) family of poverty rates (P_0, P_1 and P_2) using both poverty lines are presented in Table 8.5. The FGT P_0 measure gives the headcount index of poverty, which is the proportion of the population whose household per capita income is below the poverty line. Household per capita income is calculated by dividing the total household income by the number of people in the household (excluding household servants). FGT P_1 is the poverty gap index, which is the difference between the poverty line and the mean income of the poor, expressed as a ratio of the poverty line (known as the "income gap ratio"), and multiplied by the headcount index. FGT P_2 is an additive measure of the severity of poverty, whereby the poverty gaps of the poor are weighted by those poverty gaps in assessing poverty (see Ravallion 1992).

Table 8.5: Foster-Greer-Thornbecke (FGT) Family of Poverty Measures for Poverty Lines

Definition	Population	Location	Poverty Head Count Index (P_0)	Aggregate Poverty Gap Index (P_1)	FGT P_2 Index
Poverty	Indigenous	Urban	67.3	34.7	21.7
		Rural	82.6	52.8	38.0
		National	79.0	48.4	34.1
	Non-indigenous	Urban	47.4	18.5	9.8
		Rural	64.7	29.3	17.9
		National	49.7	19.9	10.8
	Overall	Urban	48.1	19.0	10.2
		Rural	72.3	39.1	26.3
		National	53.0	23.1	13.4
Extreme Poverty	Indigenous	Urban	32.4	14.4	7.8
		Rural	62.3	30.7	19.0
		National	55.3	26.8	16.3
	Non-indigenous	Urban	17.3	5.0	2.5
		Rural	30.0	11.9	7.2
		National	19.0	5.9	3.1
	Overall	Urban	17.8	5.4	2.7
		Rural	43.7	19.8	12.1
		National	23.1	8.3	4.6

Source: PLSS 1991.

At 79 percent, most of the indigenous population is poor and 55 percent is extremely poor. Indigenous people experience higher rates of poverty and extreme poverty than do non-indigenous people. Indigenous people are one and a half times as likely to be poor than are non-indigenous people, and almost three times as likely to be extremely poor. Consequently, indigenous people account for 11 percent of the Peruvian population, yet they comprise 19 percent of the poor and 27 percent of extremely poor Peruvians.

Both the aggregate poverty gap and the FGT P_2 indices give a picture similar to the headcount index. Indigenous people are the poorest of the poor. Indigenous people, whether urban or rural, have larger poverty gaps and suffer more severe levels of poverty than do Spanish speakers.

It is often argued that indigenous people are economically disadvantaged as a consequence of their prevalence in rural areas. However, as presented in Table 8.5, rural residence is not solely responsible for the low incomes of indigenous people. Comparison of average per capita incomes of rural dwellers shows the average income of Spanish speakers to be significantly greater than that of indigenous people. Moreover, rural indigenous people are 1.3 times as likely to be poor than are rural Spanish speakers, and twice as likely to be extremely poor.

Figure 8.1: National Household Income Distribution

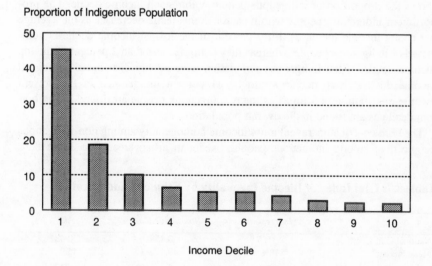

Proportion of Indigenous Population

Income Decile

Source: PLSS 1991.
Note: Household Per Capita Income = Total Household Income/Household Size.

Table 8.6: Indigenous Population Share in Each Income Decile

Income Decile	Mean Household Per Capita Income	Percent Indigenous in Each Decile	Multiple Factor of Indigenous Population Relative to Average
1	4.7	50.2	4.5
2	11.1	21.5	1.9
3	16.9	11.1	1.0
4	22.5	6.8	0.6
5	28.3	5.4	0.5
6	35.6	5.6	0.5
7	44.4	4.4	0.4
8	56.2	2.9	0.3
9	76.7	2.1	0.2
10	163.0	2.0	0.2

Source: PLSS 1991.
Note: Income is expressed in million new *soles* per month.

Income Distribution

The indigenous people of Peru are found primarily in the lowest income deciles. In fact, 74 percent of indigenous language speakers are found in the bottom 3 deciles and 45 percent are found in the bottom decile (see Figure 8.1). Table 8.6 shows the proportion of indigenous people within each income decile. The proportion of indigenous people within each income decile decreases as the average per capita income increases. Fifty percent of the lowest income decile is comprised of indigenous people, whereas they comprise less than 2 percent of the top income decile. If the indigenous population were evenly distributed among all income deciles, each decile would be 11 percent indigenous. In the present income distribution, 4.5 times as many indigenous people are found in the bottom decile as are found in the overall population.

The Gini coefficients reveal more income homogeneity among non-indigenous people than among indigenous people, except in urban areas (see Table 8.7).

Table 8.7: Gini Index of Income Inequality by Ethnicity and Location

	Indigenous	Non-indigenous	All
National Gini Coefficient	0.571	0.458	0.481
Mean Income[a]	18.1	49.4	45.9
Urban Gini Coefficient	0.430	0.438	0.439
Mean Income[a]	31.9	53.4	52.7
Rural Gini Coefficient	0.577	0.490	0.539
Mean Income[a]	13.7	23.0	19.1

Source: PLSS 1991.
a. Income is expressed in million new *soles* per month.

Figure 8.2: Per Capita Household Income Distribution

Cumulative Percent of Total Income

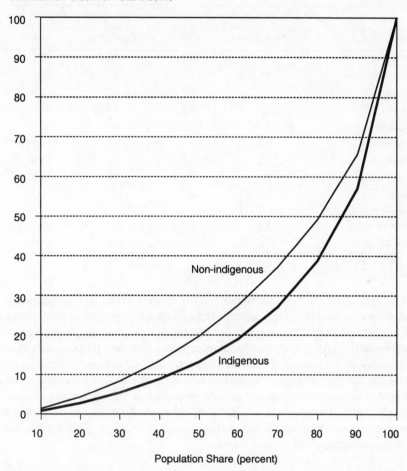

Population Share (percent)

Source: PLSS 1991.

Figure 8.2 illustrates the income distribution of both groups. The highest income decile of the indigenous population contains 43 percent of all indigenous income while the corresponding decile for the non-indigenous population contains 34 percent of income. The relatively large Gini coefficient for the indigenous people indicates there is greater income disparity among rural indigenous people.

Table 8.8 classifies income distribution by economic sector using worker earnings as the monetary measure of welfare. In support of previous observations on income inequality between groups, notice that in every sector, except agriculture, the Spanish-speaking population receives more than its proportionate share of earnings. Overall, 15 percent of the Peruvian workforce consists of indigenous people, yet this group receives only 6 percent of total earnings.

Table 8.8: Income Distribution by Economic Sector
(percent)

	Indigenous		Non-indigenous	
Industry	*Population*	*Income*	*Population*	*Income*
No Classification	0.0	0.0	0.3	0.2
Agriculture	9.6	1.3	10.7	5.3
Mining	0.1	0.0	1.3	3.9
Industry	0.9	0.5	13.6	14.9
Electrical	0.0	0.0	0.6	1.2
Construction	0.5	0.4	3.7	4.8
Commercial	2.3	1.7	25.6	26.6
Transportation	0.3	0.3	5.0	8.9
Finance	0.0	0.0	3.7	6.3
Services (including government)	1.5	1.5	20.3	21.9
Total Shares	15.2	5.8	84.8	94.2

Source: PLSS 1991.

The agricultural sector contributes heavily to the overall income inequality. Indigenous workers in the agricultural sector comprise 10 percent of Peru's workforce, yet these people receive only 1.3 percent of total earnings. While Spanish speakers in the agricultural sector also receive less than their proportionate share of earnings, at 5.3 percent of total earnings for their 10.7 percent presence in this sector, the earnings disparity is much less severe. Second to the agricultural sector, the industrial sector contributes to income inequality, as indigenous people within the industrial sector receive almost half their due share of earnings. Spanish speakers in the mining, transportation and finance sectors all acquire much more than their proportionate share of total income.

Housing Conditions

The previous two sections examine the interethnic distribution of economic inequality and poverty as defined by either income or consumption expenditure. However, other measures of welfare, such as housing conditions, educational attainment and access to and use of health care facilities, serve to complement these monetary measures and clarify the picture of individual well-being.

Table 8.9 shows the housing conditions for each group. While indigenous people are more likely to own their own home than non-indigenous people, the physical composition of these homes is consistently deficient in comparison to that of Spanish speakers. Of particular importance in health considerations is the availability of public water and sanitation facilities. Only 46 percent of indigenous homes have public water facilities, while 31 percent use wells and 15 percent use

Table 8.9: Housing Conditions

(percent of households)

Condition	Indigenous			Non-indigenous		
	Total	*Urban*	*Rural*	*Total*	*Urban*	*Rural*
Type of Dwelling						
Detached	97.5	92.7	100.0	85.8	83.5	100.0
Apartment	0.0	0.0	0.0	5.2	6.1	0.0
Several Houses in Courtyard	0.3	0.9	0.0	3.9	4.6	0.0
Dwelling in Compound	1.9	5.5	0.0	3.2	3.7	0.0
Improvised Dwelling	0.3	0.9	0.0	1.3	1.5	0.0
Other	0.0	0.0	0.0	0.5	0.6	0.0
Average Number of Rooms	2.8	3.2	2.6	3.5	3.6	3.0
Rooms per Capita	0.7	0.7	0.7	0.8	0.8	0.8
Tenure						
Squatter	3.0	5.8	1.5	3.0	3.1	1.9
Own Home	86.2	80.2	89.4	71.1	68.3	89.0
Rent	3.4	6.9	1.6	14.4	16.1	3.2
Other	7.4	7.1	7.6	11.5	12.4	5.9
Source of Water						
Public Water Supply	46.3	79.2	38.1	80.7	92.0	47.9
Public: Inside Dwelling	34.1	60.3	20.3	74.4	79.4	42.4
Public: Inside Building	12.2	12.2	12.2	6.3	7.0	2.3
Public: Outside Building	6.0	6.7	5.6	5.3	5.6	3.2
Well	30.8	16.1	38.6	3.2	2.1	10.0
River	14.8	0.0	22.6	5.4	0.1	39.0
Water Truck	0.9	2.6	0.0	3.0	3.4	0.2
Other	1.3	2.4	0.7	2.5	2.4	2.9
Sewage Facilities						
Public	21.4	54.7	3.7	71.6	81.0	12.2
Well/Septic	6.2	5.0	6.8	3.7	3.6	4.6
Latrine	39.1	24.2	47.0	10.9	7.9	29.7
None	33.4	16.1	42.6	13.8	7.5	53.5
Source of Lighting						
Electricity	41.8	75.2	24.0	88.3	96.3	37.4
Kerosene	48.0	15.3	65.4	9.3	2.3	53.8
Candles	9.6	8.7	10.2	2.1	1.0	8.9
None	0.3	0.9	0.0	0.1	0.1	0.0
Other	0.3	0.0	0.4	0.3	0.4	0.0
Telephone Services	2.2	5.3	0.5	18.0	20.8	0.0

Source: PLSS 1991.

the river as a source of water. Only 21 percent of indigenous homes have public waste disposal. Both of these factors contribute to intestinal disorders and may therefore be associated with the higher incidence of diarrhea (13 percent) among the indigenous population versus Spanish speakers (7 percent).

An examination of rural/urban differences provides some interesting observations. As indigenous households are less likely to have a public source of water in both rural and urban areas, indigenous people are much more likely to obtain water from wells. For instance, 16 percent of urban indigenous households and 39 percent of rural indigenous household have wells, whereas the corresponding proportions for Spanish households in these regions are only 2 and 10 percent, respectively. Among rural households, a larger proportion of Spanish homes use rivers as a water source. However, the rural prevalence of indigenous people results in a greater proportion of the indigenous population being exposed to the diseases associated with poor water quality.

Indigenous households are also less likely than their non-indigenous counterparts to have public sewage disposal both in rural and urban areas. Subsequently, latrines are more prevalent in the indigenous population. In both rural and urban areas, the proportion of indigenous households with latrines is significantly larger than the corresponding proportion of Spanish households. While 24 percent of indigenous households in urban areas have latrines, only 8 percent of urban Spanish households have latrines.

At 48 percent, an exceptionally large proportion of indigenous households use kerosene as a source of light; 88 percent of the homes of Spanish speakers use electricity. Within urban areas the use of kerosene is seven times greater in indigenous homes than in the homes of Spanish speakers. Because kerosene light creates airborne particulates, the average indigenous person is exposed to higher levels of indoor air pollution than the average Spanish speaker. Indoor air pollution is directly associated with respiratory disorders and cancers (World Bank 1992).

Furthermore, the relatively large proportion of urban indigenous households without public water, public sewage disposal and electricity, is evidence of a group of indigenous squatter settlements in urban areas. The survey indicates there is a larger incidence of squatter dwellings among the urban indigenous population (5.8 percent) than among the urban Spanish-speaking population (3.1 percent).

Health

Indigenous people are more likely to become ill than are non-indigenous people, but they are much less likely to consult a physician (Table 8.10). Perhaps as a result of poor initial health conditions, or as a result of neglecting treatment, the duration and severity of illness are greater among the indigenous population. The proportion of indigenous people hospitalized is almost twice that of the Spanish-speaking population. Although the average cost of both hospitalization and medicine is less for indigenous people, only 57 percent of indigenous people purchase medicine for their illness, in comparison to 81 percent of the non-indigenous population.

When indigenous people seek medical help they are more likely to see either a paramedic, pharmacologist or a traditional healer than a medical professional such as a doctor, dentist, obstetrician or nurse. Partially due to rural location, indigenous people are twice as likely to receive treatment in mobile clinics or at the home of the patient or doctor in comparison with Spanish speakers. Spanish

Table 8.10: Health Condition by Ethnicity

Status	Indigenous	Non-indigenous	All
Ill in Last 4 Weeks (%)	34.1	31.4	31.7
Days Ill in Last 4 Weeks	9.4	8.7	8.8
Days Incapacitated in Last 4 Weeks	2.9	2.1	2.2
Consulted Physician in Last 4 Weeks (%)	36.5	51.5	49.7
Consultation (%)			
Health	0.8	1.7	1.6
Medicine	1.3	1.1	1.1
None	97.9	97.1	97.1
Health Attendant (%)			
Doctor, Dentist, Obstetrician, Nurse	76.2	86.4	85.5
Paramedic	7.6	3.1	3.5
Pharmacologist Attended	11.8	9.2	9.4
Traditional Healer Attended	3.7	0.9	1.1
Where Treated (%)			
Hospital	37.2	36.2	36.3
Health Center	12.4	14.5	14.3
Mobile Clinic	11.5	5.0	5.6
Community Center	0.7	0.8	0.8
Clinic/Private Office	14.8	28.7	27.5
Pharmacy	11.4	9.3	9.5
House of Doctor	2.0	1.2	1.3
Own Home	4.1	2.8	3.0
Other	5.7	1.5	1.8
Transportation to Health Care Facility (%)			
Public	32.0	46.2	44.9
Motorized Private Vehicle	8.5	8.9	8.9
Walk	55.9	43.0	44.2
Time to Get to Doctor (minutes)	42.0	37.0	37.4
Time to Wait for Treatment (minutes)	69.5	61.4	62.1
Number of Times Seen for Same Illness	1.8	1.9	1.9
Cost for Agent Services (million new *soles*)	3.0	4.8	4.6
Hospitalized (%)	7.2	4.5	4.7
Nights Hospitalized	6.5	8.9	8.6
Cost for Hospitalization (million new *soles*)	9.1	63.3	55.1
Purchased Medicine (%)	57.4	81.3	78.4
Cost for Medication (million new *soles*)	7.2	11.8	11.4
Vaccinations Received (%)			
BCG, Polio, Triple and Measles	73.5	81.0	80.1
Some Vaccinations	24.2	17.9	18.7
No Vaccinations	2.1	0.5	0.7
Diarrhea in Last 15 Days (%)	12.5	6.8	7.5

Source: PLSS 1991.

speakers are twice as likely to receive treatment in a clinic or private office than indigenous language speakers. While public transport is the most common method of transportation to health clinics for the non-indigenous population (46 percent), 56 percent of the indigenous population walks to the treatment center. As a result of poor transportation, it takes indigenous language speakers longer to reach treatment facilities than Spanish speakers. Once at the clinic, indigenous people wait longer than Spanish speakers to receive treatment.

In terms of preventative health care, 73 percent of the indigenous population has received BCG (Bacillus of Calmette and Guerin), polio, triple and measles vaccinations in comparison to 81 percent of the non-indigenous population. Two percent of the indigenous population has not received any vaccinations, which is four times the rate for the non-indigenous population.

Education

The national education system of Peru consists of 6 years of compulsory primary schooling, 5 years of secondary schooling, and university or non-university post-secondary education. According to UNESCO (1989) statistics, only 66 percent of Peruvians enter primary school by age 6, although 97 percent of Peruvians enter school at some point in their lives. Without grade repetition or prolonged absence from school, secondary school begins at age 12 and continues through to age 16; post-secondary education follows at age 17. On average, it takes five years to complete a university undergraduate degree.

Table 8.11: Years of Schooling Attained by Age and Location

Age Group	Mean Years of Schooling		Non-indigenous versus Indigenous Education Advantage Ratio
	Indigenous	Non-indigenous	
Adult Population			
20–29	7.7	11.0	1.43
30–39	6.6	10.5	1.59
40–49	5.6	9.1	1.63
50–59	4.7	7.7	1.64
60 and Over	4.8	6.7	1.40
All Ages	5.5	8.1	1.47
School-aged Population in Urban Areas			
6–11	2.4	2.2	0.91
12–16	5.9	7.0	1.20
17–21	8.9	10.0	1.18
22–25	10.5	11.4	1.14
School-aged Population in Rural Areas			
6–11	1.8	1.8	1.03
12–16	5.9	6.1	1.03
17–21	7.9	8.4	1.05
22–25	7.4	9.0	1.22

Source: PLSS 1991.

Table 8.11 presents the average years of schooling for selected age groups according to ethnicity and urban/rural location. Concerning the adult population, the data indicate that in recent years the difference between indigenous and non-indigenous people's educational attainment has narrowed. On average, non-indigenous people have 47 percent more education than indigenous people, although in the past 20 years this schooling advantage has been reduced to less than 20 percent. Moreover, within rural areas, school-aged non-indigenous children have almost no educational advantage over indigenous children. Notwithstanding similar levels of schooling for ethnic groups in rural areas, rural dwellers have less education than urban dwellers.

In urban areas, primary school-aged indigenous children have more education than their non-indigenous counterparts. However, among secondary school-aged urban children, the educational advantage favors Spanish speakers. Given this analysis, we can conclude that a larger proportion of urban indigenous children are either dropping out of school or repeating grades.

At present, 40 percent of the non-indigenous population is enrolled in school in comparison to 36 percent of the indigenous population. It is probable, therefore, that without intervention, Spanish speakers will retain an educational advantage.

Illiteracy rates by language and location are presented in Table 8.12. Individuals are considered to be illiterate if they cannot read or write and are at least 14 years of age. Illiteracy rates are much higher for indigenous people than for non-indigenous people, at 5.2 and 0.3 percent, respectively. Although a relatively small proportion of the indigenous population speaks Aymara, they comprise the majority of the illiterate indigenous population. The prevalence of illiteracy among Aymara speakers may be partially attributed to their history of geographic isolation (Escobar 1988). Rural areas often have higher illiteracy rates than urban areas as their low population density makes schools less accessible and, additionally, there has been less emphasis on schooling for traditional rural occupations. However, at present, larger proportions of illiterate Aymara speakers are found in urban areas (10.9 percent) than in rural areas (6.2 percent). For both Quechua and Spanish speakers, higher rates of illiteracy are found in rural areas.

Not only is the indigenous population less educated and less literate than the Spanish-speaking population, but it also lags behind the non-indigenous popula-

Table 8.12: Distribution of Illiteracy by Language and Location
(percent)

Language	Total	Urban	Rural
Total Indigenous	5.2	4.1	5.8
Quechua	3.9	1.2	5.6
Aymara	7.3	10.9	6.2
Non-indigenous	0.3	0.2	0.8

Source: PLSS 1991.

Table 8.13: Highest Educational Achievement of Household Head
(percent)

Highest Level of Education Reached	Indigenous	Non-indigenous
None/Initial	1.7	0.5
Incomplete Primary	29.8	14.3
Primary	28.9	22.6
Incomplete Secondary	15.5	13.8
Secondary	18.4	27.3
Non-university Higher	0.5	4.8
Incomplete University	1.5	4.0
Complete University	3.8	12.2
Postgraduate University	0.3	0.7
Total	100.0	100.0

Source: PLSS 1991.
Note: Total of columns is not exactly 100 percent because of rounding.

tion in terms of training courses. Only 8 percent of indigenous people report having taken a training course in comparison to 28 percent of Spanish speakers.

The difference in educational achievements between household heads of ethnic groups is substantial. Table 8.13 shows that only 40 percent of indigenous household heads have education in excess of primary school. In contrast, 41 percent of Spanish-speaking household heads have some secondary school education and 22 percent have some post-secondary education. Only 6 percent of indigenous household heads have some post-secondary education.

Analysis of education levels by gender and ethnic group shows that educational gaps have been slowly decreasing over time, both between groups as well as between genders (see Figure 8.3). For all individuals born before 1980, there is a stable pattern of mean years of schooling based on ethnic group and gender. Non-indigenous males have more education than non-indigenous females who, in turn, have more education than indigenous males who are succeeded by indigenous females. In all birth cohorts, indigenous people have less education than Spanish speakers and indigenous women have the least amount of education.

The same relationship of ethnicity and gender to mean years of schooling is found with literacy rates but the disparities are more pronounced. Decreasing rates of literacy are found in succession: non-indigenous males, non-indigenous females, indigenous males and indigenous females.

Educational attainment by language and gender is presented in Table 8.14. The gap in educational achievements is larger between women than between men. The proportion of indigenous females with primary school education or less is 74 percent, almost double the corresponding proportion of Spanish-speaking females. Concomitantly, there has been a greater reduction in educational differences

Figure 8.3: Formal Education by Birth Cohort

Years of Schooling

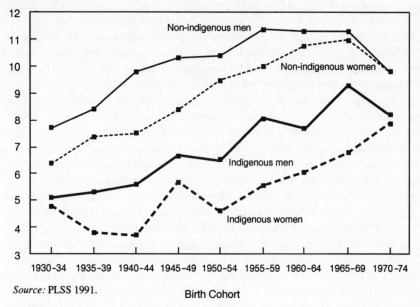

Source: PLSS 1991.

Birth Cohort

Table 8.14: Highest Educational Achievement
(percent)

Highest Level of Education Reached	Women		Men	
	Indigenous	*Non-indigenous*	*Indigenous*	*Non-indigenous*
None/Initial	6.9	3.2	5.4	3.5
Incomplete Primary	43.2	21.6	31.3	19.1
Primary	23.4	16.3	23.0	14.0
Incomplete Secondary	16.4	19.9	19.7	22.0
Secondary	6.4	24.1	15.6	22.9
Non-university Higher	0.9	5.2	1.5	5.2
Incomplete University	0.6	3.7	1.0	5.3
Complete University	2.3	5.8	2.4	7.4
Postgraduate University	0.0	0.3	0.2	0.5
Total	100.0	100.0	100.0	100.0

Source: PLSS 1991.
Note: Total of columns is not exactly 100 percent because of rounding.

between genders of non-indigenous people as compared to the indigenous population. In fact, in the present population of primary school-aged Spanish speakers, girls have more education than boys. In comparison, primary school-aged indigenous boys still receive 11 percent more education than indigenous girls.

Before concluding that indigenous people believe education to be less important for girls than for boys, the factors which affect schooling decisions must first be understood. One aspect of the schooling decision is consumption, in which people acquire education regardless of its financial benefits. Another aspect, and perhaps the main consideration, is investment, which values education according to its financial returns. If greater earnings are a function of greater levels of schooling, there is more incentive to obtain education. Unfortunately, more subjective considerations affect the education of women versus men as each culture places a risk premium on women's education. Such a premium is based on cultural perceptions of a woman's role or the probability that she will remain in the labor market. In summary, differences in school achievements for boys and girls occur because of differences in the value parents place on children or because the culture may be such that the net return to educating boys is higher than that for educating girls.

In a study of the relationship between gender and education in rural Peru, Gertler and Glewwe (1992) find parents are less willing to pay for girls' schooling relative to boys. As this study shows, the average income of indigenous rural households is less than that of non-indigenous households in rural areas, 51 and 72 million new *soles* per month, respectively. Therefore, it may be more difficult for indigenous households to afford to pay for schooling. Furthermore, in many low and middle income Peruvian families, such as the majority of indigenous households, "parents prefer to send their sons to school and give their daughters the bare minimum of education and then put them in charge of domestics tasks" (Vargas 1987). Families in rural areas of Peru, "maintain preferential attitudes toward boys and discriminatory ones towards girls" (Fernandez 1986). While the socio-historical status of indigenous people of Peru is such that women and men once had equal status, it appears that indigenous parents are now more predisposed to educating their sons than their daughters (Gálvez Barrera 1980).

Earnings Projections

In this section we develop a model of individual earnings based on economic and other factors. The primary purpose of this model is to examine the existence, and causes of, an earnings differential between indigenous and non-indigenous people.

Toledo (Carnoy 1979) presented an earnings model based on 1961 and 1972 income data for the purpose of examining changes in the (overall) Peruvian income distribution. He found that the income gap widened in the 1960s, not as much due to changes in the characteristics of the workforce itself, but more due to the "payoff" levels of these characteristics (changes in the wage rate for different occupations). This study explains, in part, the exacerbation in the indigenous/non-indigenous income distribution, as we know that indigenous people have been less mobile and less likely to change jobs out of the (discounted) agriculture sector. We also note that, as would be expected given the results of our study, dummy variables for indigenous languages are negatively correlated with earnings in Toledo's model.

Adult Labor Force Participation

In order to describe the Peruvian labor market and, more specifically, the position of indigenous people in the labor market, a sample of the PLSS is selected which represents the potential labor force. In general, the potential labor force is composed of individuals who are eligible for work. Given the high labor force participation rate for young Peruvians, our potential labor force sample contains individuals of ages 12 to 65, and excludes those who work less than 30 hours per week while attending school.

Using the PLSS data, labor income is defined as any income derived from both primary and secondary jobs under*taken during the last seven days, or any income derived from both primary or secondary jobs undertaken during the last year. This income is expressed in millions of new *soles* per month. Employment categories are similarly defined according to work undertaken in either the last seven days or, if unspecified, that undertaken during the last year.

Labor force participants are usually defined as individuals who are presently employed or searching for work. However, there are many Peruvians who report being employed and yet do not receive labor earnings. Thus, we analyze the employment categories of individuals who receive labor income separately from those who do not receive labor income. In doing so, we define labor force participants as work-aged individuals who receive labor income and, subsequently, divide the sample of potential labor force participants into labor force participants and non-labor force participants. Table 8.15 presents the earnings and occupational distribution for each ethnic group.

Two important observations can be made from this data. First, a larger proportion of the non-indigenous population is gainfully employed compared with the indigenous population, at 64 and 54 percent, respectively. Second, labor earnings are consistently higher for non-indigenous workers than for indigenous workers; the average earnings of Spanish-speaking workers are more than double the average earnings of indigenous workers.

The relative proportions of Spanish-speaking workers are higher than indigenous workers in the private sector (23 percent versus 10 percent), the public sector (11 percent versus 7 percent), and among those self-employed (26 percent versus 15 percent). In stark contrast, the farming sector contains 54 percent of the indigenous, and only 7 percent of the Spanish-speaking labor force.

Among occupations, the largest income disparity occurs between indigenous and non-indigenous farmers. For example, 29 percent of indigenous farmers do not receive labor income, while the corresponding figure for non-indigenous farmers is 3 percent. From this we may infer that there is a large group of the indigenous subsistence farmers who are, consequently, exceptionally poor. Among

Table 8.15: Labor Force Participation, Ages 12 to 65

Employment Category	Indigenous			Non-indigenous		
	Number	Percent	Average Income	Number	Percent	Average Income
Public Sector Worker	(18)	2.0	87.2	97	1.8	190.8
Private Sector Worker	80	8.8	58.4	632	12.5	101.7
Public Sector Professional	40	4.5	149.3	490	9.2	152.7
Private Sector Professional	(7)	0.7	100.7	524	10.5	165.1
Home Worker	(4)	0.4	56.6	52	1.0	50.3
Self-employed	102	12.4	101.6	1162	22.7	148.9
Farm-employed	236	25.1	38.0	258	4.2	82.0
Total Labor Force	490	54.2	67.6	3,287	63.5	137.5
Self-employed	(19)	2.2	n.a.	167	3.1	n.a.
Farm-employed	270	29.2	n.a.	211	3.6	n.a.
Total Non Labor Force	416	45.8	n.a.	1,884	36.5	n.a.
Potential Labor Force	906	100.0	n.a.	5,171	100.0	n.a.

Source: PLSS 1991.
( ) Insignificant cell count.
n.a. Not applicable.

farmers who report employment earnings, the average indigenous farmer receives less than half the income of an average Spanish-speaking farmer.

Within the public sector, the earnings differential is dependent on employment as either a worker or a professional. Indigenous public sector workers receive only 46 percent of the wages of non-indigenous workers. Given the positive association between education and job placement in the public sector, it appears that indigenous public sector workers are educationally restricted to lower level or menial jobs. In contrast, public sector indigenous professionals have virtual wage parity with Spanish-speaking public sector professionals, and their educational difference is minimal. Within the private sector, indigenous workers and professionals receive 58 and 61 percent of non-indigenous labor earnings, respectively.

In the conventional concept of unemployment, the unemployed are defined as individuals who have no employment, are available for work, and have recently engaged in job seeking activities. If we apply this definition of unemployment and, therefore, include those Peruvians who report having looked for work in the past 7 days as part of the labor force, the Spanish-speaking labor force has a higher rate of unemployment than the indigenous labor force, 4.8 percent versus 1.2 percent. However, there are reasons that the definition of unemployment above understates the unemployment of indigenous people. First, it is likely that the informal network in indigenous communities provides excellent employment information so that indigenous adults do not actively seek work because they are aware that no work is available. Second, it is possible that indigenous people are more likely to accept periods of intermittent unemployment as a fact of life and therefore rely on family support while pursuing community and family obligations. In the North American context, in response to these problems, some researchers classify any indigenous work-aged person who does not hold a wage job as unemployed (Kleinfeld and Kruse 1982). Since this ignores the informal sector, which makes up a large portion of the working population of Peru, we therefore apply a similar definition of unemployment that includes informal sector workers. The findings are that a larger proportion of the indigenous population is "unemployed" than the Spanish-speaking population—46 percent of the indigenous population versus 37 percent of the non-indigenous population.

The low average earnings of indigenous people are not only associated with their participation in farming activities, but are also a consequence of their employment in seasonal work. For example, 11 percent of work-aged indigenous people are involved in seasonal work and their average income is only 42 million new *soles* per month. While 4.4 percent of work-aged Spanish speakers are seasonal workers, their average earnings are much more substantial, 158.6 million new *soles* per month. Presumably, indigenous seasonal workers are employed in low paying agricultural activities, whereas the average earnings of Spanish seasonal workers suggest more professional employment.

The distribution of the Peruvian population by industry and gender is presented in Table 8.16. The agriculture industry depends heavily on the labor of indigenous people—69 percent of indigenous women and 58 percent of indigenous men are involved in agricultural activities. Yet, on average, indigenous women and men earn only one-third the salary of non-indigenous workers employed in agriculture. One explanation could be that the Spanish speakers control the land and the non-Spanish speakers work on it. Clearly, this is an area for further research.

The occupational distribution reflects a social structure that avails to Spanish speakers the high social status occupations and most lucrative incomes. The primary employer for the Spanish-speaking population is the commercial sector, which employs 42 percent of women and 22 percent of men. This sector is the second largest employer of indigenous women, at 21 percent, and the third largest employer of indigenous men, at 10 percent. The earnings differential within the commercial sector is only marginally in favor of non-indigenous people with non-indigenous women earning 1.2 times the salary of indigenous women and non-indigenous men earning 1.5 times the salary of indigenous men. Including almost a quarter of the Spanish-speaking population, the service sector is their second largest employer. It is also the second largest employer of indigenous men at 13 percent and ranks third for indigenous women at 7 percent. The fourth largest employer of indigenous workers is industry, which contains 3 percent of women and 8 percent of men. The average salary for these women is half that of both non-indigenous women and indigenous men, and almost one-fourth the average salary of non-indigenous men.

Table 8.16: Economic Sector by Gender and Ethnicity

	Women				Men			
	Indigenous		*Non-indigenous*		*Indigenous*		*Non-indigenous*	
Economic Sector	*Percent*	*Average Income (pesos)*	*Percent*	*Average Income (pesos)*	*Percent*	*Average Income (pesos)*	*Percent*	*Average Income (pesos)*
No Classifi- cation	0.0	n.a.	0.4	86.7	0.3	55.0	0.2	139.1
Agriculture	69.2	18.0	11.1	52.0	58.1	36.2	13.7	105.4
Mining	0.0	n.a.	0.3	323.3	0.7	96.5	2.4	353.4
Industry	3.3	40.8	15.1	87.4	7.8	85.1	16.8	151.0
Electrical	0.0	n.a.	0.2	156.0	0.6	119.3	1.0	241.5
Construction	0.0	n.a.	0.3	68.0	6.9	87.1	7.3	147.5
Commercial	20.6	84.0	41.6	100.4	9.6	114.7	22.1	166.4
Transportation	0.0	n.a.	1.9	178.9	3.6	108.8	8.7	202.5
Finance	0.0	n.a.	2.9	162.6	0.0	n.a.	5.4	202.7
Services (including government)	6.9	73.4	26.2	88.9	12.6	136.3	22.4	151.5
Total	100.0	57.1	100.0	97.3	100.0	71.9	100.0	163.0

Source: PLSS 1991.
n.a. Not applicable.

The finance sector is composed exclusively of Spanish speakers. It also provides some of the highest salaries in Peru. The highest earnings advantage is found between males, as non-indigenous males earn 2.3 times the wage of indigenous males. The next highest earnings advantage is found between genders of the Spanish-speaking population; on average non-indigenous men earn 1.7 times the wage of non-indigenous women. The wage differential is somewhat smaller between women workers, yet is still in favor of non-indigenous women who receive 1.5 times the wage of indigenous women. The smallest earnings differential is found between genders of the indigenous population—men receive 1.3 times the average earnings of women. Despite greater wage parity between genders of indigenous people versus non-indigenous people, we conclude that not only are earnings less for the indigenous population, but they are markedly less for indigenous women.

The indigenous working population is concentrated in farming. For instance, 66 percent of indigenous women and 52 percent of indigenous men are farmers or farm workers (see Table 8.17). In comparison, Spanish speakers are working in a much wider variety of occupations. Better paying jobs in trade, transportation, teaching and clerical fields are dominated by Spanish speakers.

Table 8.17: Occupation by Gender and Ethnicity

| | Women | | | | Men | | | |
| | Indigenous | | Non-indigenous | | Indigenous | | Non-indigenous | |
Occupation	Percent	Average Income (pesos)	Percent	Average Income (pesos)	Percent	Average Income (pesos)	Percent	Average Income (pesos)
Teachers	2.2	82.0	8.3	106.2	3.0	225.0	3.9	160.5
Clerical	0.4	471.5	11.2	107.7	1.8	71.0	6.3	173.2
Trade: Self-employed	10.6	99.2	18.4	98.9	3.7	99.5	7.5	199.3
Sales	0.7	..	4.2	65.4	0.5	177.1	3.2	89.9
Street Vendor	7.9	60.3	11.0	107.6	4.4	116.1	5.3	122.1
Cook/Waiter/Restaurant	2.0	89.3	5.9	78.2	0.5	83.6	1.2	67.9
Farmers	65.5	16.7	10.6	48.7	52.0	33.6	9.6	95.4
Farm Workers	4.3	24.6	0.7	57.9	5.9	51.0	2.3	60.0
Tailors	0.5	19.6	5.9	81.0	1.1	103.4	1.3	122.5
Trades: crafts-persons/electric workers	0.0	n.a.	0.4	62.3	3.1	104.0	10.4	151.6
Construction	0.3	..	0.0	n.a.	7.5	84.6	5.0	133.3
Transportation	0.0	n.a.	0.4	276.0	4.2	106.3	7.1	174.8

Source: PLSS 1991.
.. Not available.
n.a. Not applicable.

Second to farming, a large proportion of indigenous women are self-employed in trade (11 percent), and 8 percent of indigenous women work as street vendors. While these occupations have a high level of compatibility with household responsibilities, the low earnings associated with such occupations result in little financial independence for indigenous women. Non-indigenous women are employed in a wider variety of occupations than indigenous women, yet are focused in traditionally female occupations which pay less than traditional male occupations. The major occupation of Spanish-speaking women is self-employment in trade, at 18.4 percent. After trade, equal proportions of non-indigenous women are farmers, street vendors and secretaries.

The occupational distribution of indigenous men differs substantially from Spanish-speaking men. More than half of working indigenous men are farmers, whereas less than 10 percent of Spanish-speaking men are farmers. While Spanish-speaking men are more evenly distributed throughout various occupations, relatively larger proportions of Spanish-speaking men work in the better paid occupations of tradesmen, transportation equipment operators and clerks. In general, indigenous men are paid less than Spanish-speaking men in similar occupations.

Decomposition of Earnings Differentials

In order to fully understand the position of indigenous people in the labor market, it is necessary to examine the respective roles of ethnicity and personal endowments, such as schooling and experience, in determining the level of worker earnings.

The Data.   Given the high labor force participation rate of young Peruvians, labor market analysis is undertaken for adults between the ages of 12 and 65. However, due to the complex relationship between earnings and school attendance,[1] all individuals who are presently attending school are excluded from the analysis. The sample contains 2,180 males who reported labor earnings within the past year.

Because we are specifically interested in the factors which contribute to the earnings differential between groups, we limit the analysis to males and, in doing so, present an "upper bound" estimate of discrimination due to indigenous origin. This limitation avoids compounding the results with gender discrimination. Unfortunately, the sample of indigenous women who reported employment earnings is insufficient to generate confident estimates of female earnings equations.

Mean characteristics of indigenous and non-indigenous males are presented in Table 8.18. Average earnings in the sample are 152.3 million new *soles* per month. Indigenous workers earn less than half the income of non-indigenous workers. The level of educational attainment of the two groups differs substantially. Indigenous men have only 6.7 mean years of schooling relative to 10.0 mean years of schooling for Spanish-speaking men. In terms of levels attained, nearly 60 percent of the indigenous group has not exceeded primary school education, whereas only 23 percent of the non-indigenous group belongs to this category. Only 5 percent of indigenous workers have post-secondary education as compared to 25 percent of non-indigenous workers.

Although the PLSS contains information on experience in present occupation, a Mincerian measure of experience (age – schooling – 6) is also created. The average months of experience reported in the survey are dramatically greater for indigenous people; on average indigenous workers have almost twice the experience of non-indigenous people. Mincerian experience is also greater among indigenous workers but the difference between groups is less pronounced.

The prevalent occupation for indigenous people is farming, which contains 50 percent of indigenous males. This sector contains only 8 percent of non-indigenous males. In contrast, the private sector employs the largest proportion of non-indigenous males, at 41 percent, while it contains only 21 percent of indigenous males. Indigenous workers are also half as likely to be self-employed and less likely to work in the public sector than are non-indigenous workers. The majority of indigenous workers are located in rural areas, at 68 percent, whereas the major-

Table 8.18: Mean Characteristics by Ethnicity

Characteristic	Indigenous (N=315)	Non-indigenous (N=1,858)	All (N=2,174)
Employment Earnings	70.6	164.7	152.3
Years of Schooling	6.7	10.0	9.6
Highest Educational Attainment (%)			
No Education	1.4	0.3	0.5
Incomplete Primary	26.5	7.9	10.2
Completed Primary	28.8	15.0	16.8
Incomplete Secondary	16.4	16.8	16.8
Completed Secondary	21.6	35.1	33.4
Non-university Higher	2.0	8.2	7.4
University	3.3	16.6	14.9
Training Course (%)	11.3	33.0	30.1
Mincerian Experience (years)	25.9	21.4	22.0
Reported Experience (years)	17.3	9.8	10.8
Hours Worked per Month	222.3	204.0	206.4
Economic Sector (%)			
Farming	50.1	7.7	13.3
Public	12.9	18.4	17.7
Private	20.8	40.9	38.3
Self-employed	15.1	30.8	28.7
Other Employment	1.1	2.2	2.0
Seasonal Work (%)	9.2	4.0	4.7
Age	39.3	37.6	37.8
Married (%)	64.0	55.7	56.8
Region (%)			
Lima	8.9	51.5	45.9
Rural	67.8	11.1	18.5
Social Security (%)	51.6	65.5	64.4
Union (%)	34.3	37.3	37.0

Source: PLSS 1991.

ity (52 percent) of non-indigenous workers are located in Lima. The measures of average age, hours worked and percent married are marginally higher among indigenous workers.

Results. The results of earnings function estimates are presented in Table 8.19. The coefficient on years of schooling can be interpreted as the percentage increase in earnings associated with an extra year of schooling. Estimation of a basic earnings function gives an overall rate of returns to education of 5.7 percent. However, as shown in Table 8.20, including other variables which capture regional location and economic sector reduces the returns to education to 4.2 per-

Table 8.19: Basic Earnings Functions by Ethnicity

Variable	All	Indigenous	Non-indigenous
Years of Schooling	0.0571	0.0256	0.0617
	(12.07)	(1.69)	(12.56)
Years of Experience	0.0412	–0.0116	0.0462
	(8.87)	(1.19)	(9.12)
Years of Experience-squared	–0.0009	–0.0000	–0.0010
	(7.55)	(0.04)	(6.72)
Hours Worked (log)	0.3818	0.1793	0.4185
	(8.96)	(1.47)	(9.31)
Indigenous	–0.8353		
	(14.67)		
Constant	1.9536	2.9441	1.6723
N	2,180	316	1,863
Adjusted R^2	0.2115	0.0603	0.1455

Source: PLSS 1991.
Note: The dependent variable is the natural logarithm of earnings. Numbers in parentheses are t-ratios. Numbers greater than 1.96 are significant at the 5 percent level and numbers greater than 1.65 are significant at the 10 percent level or better.

cent. This can be explained by the positive association between schooling and obtaining a job in a well-paying sector. In effect, the coefficient for schooling in the simple equation represents not only the direct effect on earnings but also schooling's indirect effect (via economic sector) on earnings. The basic equation is important from a policy perspective because it indirectly points to the importance of schooling in gaining access to better paying jobs.

While schooling is the strongest determinant of earnings in the extended equation, when estimated over both groups, all other factors are statistically significant at the 1 percent level. Moreover, the magnitude and influence of each factor are intuitive. This equation tells us, other things being equal, that indigenous people earn 44 percent less than Spanish speakers. In other words, even if indigenous people had the same amount of education and experience or, more importantly, the same proportion of workers in farming and rural locations as non-indigenous people, they would still earn about one-half that of non-indigenous people.

Estimation of the expanded equation for each group provides some interesting results. The average rate of returns to schooling for Spanish-speaking workers is 3 times that of indigenous workers, at 4.8 and 1.6 percent, respectively. Moreover, schooling is not a significant contributor to the earnings of indigenous men but it is a significant factor in the earnings of non-indigenous men. This is a very low estimate of the returns to schooling. It is low for Peru itself, and in comparison to other Latin American countries (Psacharopoulos 1994). It is also a very low estimate for indigenous people, as presented in the chapters in this volume. One sim-

Table 8.20: Extended Earnings Functions by Ethnicity

Variable	All	Indigenous	Non-indigenous
Years of Schooling	0.0425	0.0156	0.0479
	(9.04)	(1.10)	(9.62)
Years of Experience	0.0281	−0.0007	0.0309
	(6.17)	(0.05)	(6.17)
Years of Experience-squared	−0.0005	−0.0001	−0.0005
	(4.51)	(0.26)	(3.99)
Hours Worked (log)	0.3562	0.2019	0.3827
	(8.91)	(1.83)	(8.98)
Indigenous	−0.4380		
	(7.43)		
Married	0.3064	0.0515	0.3288
	(8.40)	(0.49)	(8.52)
Farm Employment	−0.3975	−0.4013	−0.2555
	(5.02)	(2.55)	(2.64)
Public Employment	0.1046	0.5113	0.0504
	(2.04)	(2.85)	(0.95)
Self-employment	0.2464	0.3737	0.2315
	(5.93)	(2.19)	(5.46)
Lima	0.1168	0.4062	0.1086
	(3.09)	(2.11)	(2.83)
Rural	−0.3756	−0.2321	−0.4414
	(5.36)	(1.54)	(5.44)
Constant	2.0210	2.8183	1.8072
N	2,174	315	1,858
Adjusted R^2	0.3257	0.2549	0.2565

Source: PLSS 1991.
Note: The dependent variable is the natural logarithm of earnings. Numbers in parentheses are t-ratios. Numbers greater than 1.96 are significant at the 5 percent level and numbers greater than 1.65 are significant at the 10 percent level or better.

ple explanation for this very low estimate is that the sample of indigenous people is exclusively those individuals who claim to be monolingual speakers of an indigenous language. Therefore, more acculturated and integrated segments of the indigenous population—bilingual indigenous people—are not included. Similarly, non-indigenous men receive positive yet diminishing returns to labor market experience; indigenous men are not rewarded for labor market experience. This suggests that the experience reported by indigenous men represents time trapped in low paying sectors.

The factors which are significant in predicting earnings of indigenous men are location-based and job-specific. Employment in the public sector, self employment and living in Lima increase the earnings of the indigenous population, while

employment in the farming sector negatively affects earnings. The relative proportions of indigenous to non-indigenous people in the areas above support the
distinct earnings advantage found for Spanish speakers.

It is also interesting to note the differential effect of marriage on the earnings of
indigenous and non-indigenous populations. Marriage increases the earnings of
non-indigenous men by 3.3 percent while marriage has no effect on the earnings
of indigenous men.

Unfortunately, because there are fewer observations for the union and social
security variables, these variables are not incorporated in the final earnings equations. Their independent impact on earnings, however, is more positively associated with the earnings of non-indigenous people than it is with the earnings of
indigenous people.

In the basic earnings equation, years of schooling contribute significantly to
increase the earnings of both ethnic groups. However, when regional and job
related variables are added, both the magnitude and significance of the schooling
variable are reduced. In fact, schooling is insignificant in the extended earnings
equation estimated for indigenous people.

An extended earnings function is estimated and the results presented in Table
8.21. Three points are noteworthy. First, the explanatory power of all equations
increases in comparison to similar equations with the years of schooling variable.
Second, the impact of the employment sector is less in these equations. From both
these points we can conclude that education level is associated with employment
sector, which in turn affects earnings. Third, while higher levels of education provide higher earnings, obtaining some university experience is the only significant
educational factor in obtaining increased earnings for indigenous men. Again, the
results for indigenous people reflect the nature of the sample—monolingual indigenous language speakers. Schooling would appear to be (have been) less effective
for those individuals claiming to be monolingual indigenous language speakers.
This would imply, among other possibilities, that these individuals did not learn
much from their schooling, and/or that they do not use their schooling—including
their knowledge of the Spanish language—in their daily activities.

Decomposition Results. The Oaxaca (1973) decomposition method described
above in Chapter 4 is used to decompose the indigenous/non-indigenous male
workers' earnings differential (see Table 8.22).

The proportion of this differential that is due to the productive characteristics of
individuals is equivalent to about 50 percent of the differential in log of earnings
between indigenous and non-indigenous men. In other words, if indigenous workers were endowed with the same productive characteristics as non-indigenous
workers, the earnings differential between them would narrow by 50 percent. The
remaining difference in wages is "unexplained." This component also contains
any unmeasured factors which contribute to the earnings differential such as ability, health, the quality of education, labor force attachment and culture.

The contribution of each variable to the overall earnings differential between
indigenous and non-indigenous males is shown in Table 8.23. A positive entry

Table 8.21: Extended Earnings Functions by Ethnicity with Schooling Levels

Variable	All	Indigenous	Non-indigenous
Completed Primary	0.0425*	−0.1546*	0.1152*
	(0.65)	(1.18)	(1.50)
Some Secondary School	0.1041	−0.0700*	0.1744
	(1.72)	(0.54)	(2.50)
Non-university Higher	0.3199	0.3640*	0.3924
	(3.81)	(0.99)	(4.34)
Some University	0.6206	0.5245	0.6929
	(8.42)	(1.70)	(8.58)
Years of Experience	0.0274	−0.0006*	0.0297
	(6.05)	(0.05)	(5.95)
Years of Experience-squared	−0.0005	−0.0001*	−0.0005
	(4.67)	(0.36)	(4.00)
Hours Worked (log)	0.3597	0.2215	0.3828
	(9.07)	(2.00)	(9.06)
Indigenous	−0.4415		
	(7.54)		
Married	0.2872	0.0670*	0.3072
	(7.91)	(0.64)	(7.98)
Farm Employment	−0.4119	−0.4142	−0.2726
	(5.24)	(2.63)	(2.84)
Public Sector Employment	0.0763*	0.4533	0.0292
	(1.50)	(2.49)	(0.555)
Self-employment	0.2327	0.3654	0.2167
	(5.64)	(2.13)	(5.15)
Lima	0.1224	0.4164	0.1139
	(3.25)	(2.18)	(2.98)
Rural	−0.3907	−0.2032	−0.4721
	(5.63)	(1.34)	(5.85)
Constant	2.2669	2.8624	2.0641
N	2,174	315	1,858
Adjusted R^2	0.3369	0.2617	0.2681

Source: PLSS 1991.
Note: The dependent variable is the natural logarithm of earnings. Numbers in parentheses are t-ratios. Numbers greater than 1.96 are significant at the 5 percent level and numbers greater than 1.65 are significant at the 10 percent level or better; * Insignificant.

indicates an advantage in favor of the non-indigenous population, and a negative entry indicates an advantage in favor of the indigenous population. On the endowments side, much of Spanish speakers' earnings advantage can be explained by their education, particularly at the university level, and location. Rural location is a major disadvantage to the economic well-being of indigenous people.

Much of the "unexplained" portion of the earnings differential is due to hours worked and experience; that is, for the same amounts of work and market experi-

Table 8.22: Indigenous Workers' Earnings Disadvantage and Its Decomposition

Indigenous Worker's Earnings	Overall Differential	Amount Attributed To:	
		Endowments	Wage Structure
Gap (in current *soles*)	94.1	46.9	47.2
As Percent of Overall Differential	100.0	49.8	50.2
As Percent of Non-indigenous Earnings	42.9	21.4	21.5

Source: Calculated from Table 8.21.

ence, indigenous people are paid less than non-indigenous people. In addition, as married indigenous language speakers do not receive as large an earnings premium as married Spanish speakers, part of the "unexplained" earnings differential is due to marriage. With respect to education, indigenous people are paid less than

Table 8.23: Variable Contributions

Variable	Contribution of Variable to Earnings Differential		Contribution as Percentage of Total Earnings Differential	
	Endowment $b_n(X_n-X_i)$	Pay Structure $X_i(b_n-b_i)$	"Explained" Endowments	"Unexplained" Endowments
Constant	0.00000	-0.79828	0.00000	-85.64431
Primary School	-0.01592	0.07805	-1.70803	8.37372
Some Secondary	0.02399	0.09324	2.57328	10.00326
Non-university Higher	0.02456	0.00056	2.63474	0.05994
Some University	0.09261	0.00554	9.93570	0.59486
Years of Experience	-0.06814	0.29952	-7.309999	32.13362
Hours Worked (log)	-0.03478	0.85930	-3.73163	92.19178
Married	-0.02296	0.15216	-2.46315	16.32420
Farm Employment	0.11487	0.06992	2.32361	7.50099
Public Employment	0.00143	-0.05873	0.15330	-6.30046
Self-employed	0.03284	-0.02360	3.52284	-2.53160
Lima	0.04814	-0.02897	5.16518	-3.10822
Rural	0.26765	-0.18090	28.71475	-19.40837
Subtotal	0.46428	0.46781	49.81059	50.18941
Total	0.93208		100.0	

Source: Computed from Table 8.21.

non-indigenous people for both their primary and secondary education, but they receive equal compensation for their university education. Rural location affects the earnings of Spanish-speaking workers more negatively than it affects the earnings of indigenous men. Conversely, indigenous men receive greater economic rewards for their urban location than do Spanish-speaking men.

Schooling and Work Activities of Peruvian Youth

An examination of the determinants of either schooling or work must take into account their non-exclusive nature, particularly in the case of indigenous children who are less schooled and more likely to work than non-indigenous children. With the objective of studying work and school attendance decisions, and years of schooling for young indigenous Peruvians, we select a sample of children aged 7 to 16. The overall sample contains 2,751 observations, 322 of which are indigenous youths; the remaining 2,429 are non-indigenous youths. Table 8.24 presents the mean characteristics of the sample.

The average indigenous child is just over 11 years of age, has 3.1 siblings and comes from a family with an average per capita income of 9.5 million new *soles* per month. In terms of education, 96 percent of indigenous children attend school (almost exclusively public school, and none of these children received scholarships). On average these children have 3.9 years of schooling. With regards to labor, 54 percent of children are working—workforce participation is defined as greater than zero hours worked and includes paid and unpaid work.

As 93 percent of the indigenous sample is located in rural areas, it is interesting to compare the indigenous sample to the rural Spanish-speaking sample to see whether differences in educational achievements and work participation are due to location or ethnicity. A much higher proportion of indigenous children work, yet the rate of school attendance is greater for indigenous children than for rural Spanish-speaking children. Indigenous children have similar levels of education as rural Spanish-speaking children (who are slightly younger), but are less educated than urban Spanish-speaking children (who are slightly older). While indigenous children are more likely to work, their mean hours of work, both at home and in the labor market, are similar to those of Spanish-speaking children.

The proportion of the child workers who are paid for their work is slightly higher for indigenous children than for Spanish-speaking children (3.1 percent versus 2.5 percent), but the earnings are similar at 34 million new *soles* per month. However, family wealth, in terms of family income and other household-based proxies such as rooms per capita, is much lower for the indigenous population. The average household per capita income of indigenous children is less than half that of rural, and less than one-quarter that of urban, non-indigenous children. Indigenous households are also more crowded. Both parents of Spanish-speaking children are better educated than their indigenous counterparts. This is especially true of Spanish-speaking mothers. Schooling costs are significantly lower for

Table 8.24: Mean Characteristics by Ethnicity and Location, Children Aged 7–16

Characteristic	Indigenous	Non-indigenous		
		Total	*Urban*	*Rural*
Quechua (%)	57.4	0.0	0.0	0.0
Aymara (%)	42.6	0.0	0.0	0.0
Age (years)	11.3	11.6	11.6	11.2
Male (%)	48.1	50.0	49.7	51.6
Rural (%)	93.0	15.4	0.0	100.0
Lima (%)	0.4	43.9	51.9	0.0
Mother's Schooling (years)	3.8	7.5	7.9	4.9
Father's Schooling (years)	5.5	8.8	9.3	6.1
Child Working (%)	53.6	11.5	7.5	33.3
Child Attending School (%)	95.7	97.1	97.6	94.4
Schooling (years)	3.9	4.7	4.9	3.9
Number of Siblings	3.1	2.8	2.8	2.9
Income per Capita (millions new *soles*)	9.5	41.1	44.7	20.8
Rooms per Capita	0.45	0.59	0.60	0.55
Hours of Work per Week	22.6	22.8	23.0	22.4
Hours of Chores per Week	9.4	8.0	7.7	9.7
Cost of School (millions of new *soles*)	9.2	36.3	39.5	18.1
Public School (%)	99.6	83.5	81.1	97.0
Scholarship (%)	0	1.6	1.8	0.2
N	322	2,429	1,976	453

Source: PLSS 1991.

indigenous children than for non-indigenous children, mainly due to the limited presence of indigenous children in private schools.

It is clear that indigenous children have less schooling and a higher rate of work participation than non-indigenous children. The succeeding analysis will examine the differences *between* different groups of indigenous youths. Tables 8.25, 8.26 and 8.27 show the factors which affect the years of schooling, school attendance and work participation of indigenous Peruvian youths.

Years of Schooling

Aymara-speaking children have significantly more education than Quechua-speaking children. While schooling increases with age, male children have slightly more education and urban children have an educational advantage over rural children.

Table 8.25: Means of Parent/Child Characteristics for Indigenous Children

Characteristic	Schooling (years)	School Attendance (%)	Work (%)	Sample Size
Quechua	3.1	94.2	67.8	199
Aymara	4.8	97.6	34.7	123
Female	3.7	95.1	46.0	164
Male	4.0	96.3	61.9	158
Age				
7 to 9	1.8	98.5	36.4	106
10 to 12	3.5	98.5	59.1	102
13 and Over	6.2	90.5	65.5	114
Parents Married	4.1	97.6	50.5	226
Parents Not Married	3.3	90.3	59.4	67
Mother Present	3.9	96.1	55.1	304
Mother Not Present	4.5	88.4	29.0	(18)
Father Present	3.9	96.0	65.7	295
Father Not Present	4.1	92.7	52.5	(27)
Mother's Schooling				
0–6 Years	3.7	95.3	55.3	298
7–11 Years	5.6	100.0	33.1	(24)
Father's Schooling				
0–6 Years	3.7	94.9	56.9	254
7–11 Years	4.3	100.0	46.5	58
12 or More Years	6.4	88.2	11.8	(10)
Mother's Employment				
None	4.6	92.9	43.4	40
Public Sector Worker	1.4	100.0	0.0	(5)
Private Sector Worker	4.7	100.0	100.0	(3)
Self-employed	4.9	100.0	17.7	(11)
Farmer	3.7	96.3	59.8	245
Father's Employment				
None	2.3	100.0	71.3	(4)
Public Sector Worker	5.0	100.0	77.6	(7)
Private Sector Worker	3.0	83.8	46.0	33
Public Sector Professional	5.8	100.0	0.0	(10)
Private Sector Professional	4.0	100.0	0.0	(1)
Self-employed	5.2	100.0	33.2	(9)
Farmer	3.8	96.9	55.6	230
Unemployed	1.0	100.0	0.0	(1)

Source: PLSS 1991.
( ) Insignificant cell count.

Children of well educated parents are also better educated, but the influence of parental education is greater for mothers than for fathers. The least educated children have mothers who farm and fathers who either farm or are private sector

Table 8.26: Means of Household Characteristics for Indigenous Children

Characteristic	Schooling (years)	School Attendance (%)	Work (%)	Sample Size
Number of Siblings				
0 to 2	3.9	95.2	46.2	112
3 to 6	4.0	97.0	57.4	175
6 and Over	3.4	91.1	59.3	35
Income per Capita				
0 to 4	3.6	96.4	62.0	133
5 to 9	4.1	98.2	49.4	105
10 and Over	4.1	91.4	45.8	84
Rooms per Capita				
0 to 0.24	2.8	87.3	77.6	44
0.25 to 0.49	3.6	97.0	53.9	163
0.50 and Over	4.6	96.8	44.9	115
Rural	3.9	95.4	57.3	303
Urban	4.0	100.0	5.3	(19)
Public Sewer	4.8	100.0	0.0	(13)
No Public Sewer	3.8	95.5	55.6	303
Public Water	3.7	99.3	53.5	110
No Public Water	4.0	93.9	53.7	212
Own Home	4.1	95.9	52.3	277
Do Not Own Home	2.4	94.6	62.7	45

Source: PLSS 1991.
( ) Insignificant cell count.

workers. Schooling is positively affected by family income. Income correlates, such as home ownership, public water source and crowding, also affect years of schooling. In addition, children are better educated if they come from homes where the parents are married.

Children who are employed, either at home or in the work place, have a schooling advantage; more hours of work are associated with more years of schooling. This important finding has implications for the child labor debate.

School facilities affect the educational attainment of indigenous children. Lack of water and sewage facilities at school, lack of transportation to school other than walking, and poor access to books and supplies all contribute to reducing the number of years of schooling for the average indigenous child.

School Attendance

Among indigenous children, language and rural location are reflected in school attendance. School attendance is greater among Aymara speakers than Quechua speakers, and greater among urban children. Boys are more likely to attend school than girls, and school attendance decreases as children get older. Concerning parents' education, children whose mother or father has some secondary edu-

Table 8.27: Means of School Characteristics for Indigenous Children

Characteristic	Schooling (years)	School Attendance (%)	Work (%)	Sample Size
Work (hours per week)				
1 to 9	3.0	100.0	100.0	50
10 to 19	3.2	97.1	100.0	52
20 to 29	3.7	91.5	100.0	30
30 and Over	5.6	88.1	100.0	46
Household Chores (hours per week)				
1 to 4	3.3	97.0	48.1	29
5 to 9	3.9	98.8	51.9	125
10 and Over	4.3	91.5	59.3	114
Seasonally Employed	5.1	93.0	100.0	(17)
Not Seasonally Employed	3.8	94.4	100.0	161
School Facilities				
Public Water	4.2	96.5	44.3	165
Public Sewer	4.3	98.1	54.9	89
No Water or Sewer	2.6	89.1	78.1	52
Transportation to School				
Public Transport	7.3	100.0	27.2	(8)
Private Transport	10.0	100.0	100.0	(1)
Walk	3.8	99.5	53.0	282
Book Access				
Access to All Books	3.4	100.0	47.3	73
Access to Less than 50 Percent	4.0	100.0	55.5	38
Share Books in Household	3.8	100.0	50.7	34
Share Books Outside Household	4.0	98.7	50.1	63
Use Library	5.1	100.0	52.8	62
No Book Access	2.0	95.2	77.3	(20)
Changed School	4.9	73.1	29.4	(7)
Did Not Change School	3.9	100.0	52.8	283
Cost for School (millions of new *soles*)				
0 to 2	3.4	83.8	63.1	87
3 to 6	3.1	100.0	50.5	65
6 and Over	4.4	99.5	49.7	170

Source: PLSS 1991.
( ) Insignificant cell count.

cation are most likely to attend school; lower attendance rates are found if either parent has only primary school education. Having a father who is employed as a private sector worker or a mother who does not work both decrease the likelihood that a child will attend school.

Attendance rates are higher among households where the parents are married, and where the household has a public water source or public sewage disposal.

School attendance does not, however, increase continually with family income or other income proxies such as rooms per capita. This implies that there is a certain household income threshold, which is reflected in the household infrastructure, above which children are sent to school.

School attendance is affected by child labor both in the home and in the market place; as work hours increase, school attendance decreases. This observation, along with the finding reported above, suggests that working may increase school attainment for some. For others, working in the labor market detracts from schooling. This issue requires further study.

Finally, school facilities influence school attendance. Lack of school water and sewage facilities, limited book access and the necessity of walking to school are all correlated with lower school attendance.

Work Participation

Ethnicity is a major determinant of child workforce participation. Quechua speakers are much more likely to work than are Aymara speakers. Workforce participation is also greater for older children, males and children who live in rural areas. Both parental employment and education affect the work decision of indigenous children. Children of less educated parents and children whose parents are employed as farmers are more likely to work. The parents of working children are less likely to be married. Working children come from larger, low income families, and they live in crowded homes which are not owned by their families.

High opportunity costs for schooling increase the likelihood that a child will work. Children who have poor book access, whose schools lack water and sewer facilities, and whose monetary investment in schooling is low have higher rates of workforce participation.

Migration

Indigenous people are less likely to leave their place of birth than non-indigenous people. Table 8.28 shows the distribution of each ethnic population by birth place as well as the proportion of migrants from each of these locations. The table can

Table 8.28: Migration from Place of Birth
(percent)

	Country	Hamlet	Town	City	Other	Total
Indigenous Birthplace	13.8	42.0	22.6	12.6	9.0	100.0
Indigenous Migration	25.4	10.3	57.7	46.4	7.7	27.4
Non-indigenous Birthplace	4.4	7.4	22.0	65.6	0.7	100.0
Non-indigenous Migration	43.6	37.9	70.9	24.3	27.3	36.4

Source: PLSS 1991.

be interpreted as follows: while 42 percent of the indigenous population was born in a hamlet, only 10 percent of these people left their place of birth. Of the Spanish-speaking people who were born in a hamlet, 38 percent relocated. The table shows that most of the indigenous population was born in a hamlet and that most of the Spanish-speaking population was born in a city.

Of the 23 percent share of the indigenous population born in a town, 58 percent left their birth place. As a result, town-born indigenous people constitute the largest group, 48 percent, of indigenous migrants. Similarly, city-born Spanish speakers form the largest share of Spanish-speaking migrants, at 44 percent, a share closely followed by the proportion of Spanish-speaking migrants born in towns (43 percent).

The reasons for migration reported by each group are presented in Table 8.29. The primary reason for indigenous migration is job search. This is particularly true for the large group of indigenous town-born migrants; 46 percent of these migrants leave in order to find work. Marriage is the second most influential incentive for indigenous people to migrate from rural areas. Schooling is a factor in the decision to migrate among the small population of country-born indigenous migrants, as well as among the relatively larger group of city-born indigenous migrants. However, in all birth places, but more so in hamlets and towns, non-indigenous people are more likely than indigenous people to migrate in order to study. Almost equal proportions of both ethnic groups leave their birth place for monetary reasons, but money is not a dominant concern for either population.

Indigenous migrants are much older than non-indigenous migrants; the average age of indigenous migrants is 18 years, whereas the average age of non-

Table 8.29: Determinants of Migration from Birthplace
(percent)

Reason for Leaving	Country	Hamlet	Town	City
Indigenous Migrants				
More Money	0.0	13.7	3.7	8.3
Work	38.8	22.3	45.9	39.0
Study	15.4	5.3	8.2	17.0
Marriage	15.6	21.5	10.1	7.5
Terrorism	0.0	0.0	0.5	0.0
Other	30.2	37.7	31.7	28.2
Total	100.0	100.0	100.0	100.0
Non-indigenous Migrants				
More Money	6.5	8.7	8.0	6.0
Work	29.4	27.4	21.2	17.4
Study	17.3	11.8	18.5	18.4
Marriage	5.0	7.5	5.3	5.7
Terrorism	0.0	0.0	0.2	0.1
Other	41.8	44.6	47.0	52.3
Total	100.0	100.0	100.0	100.0

Source: PLSS 1991.

Table 8.30: Migration to Present Location
(percent)

	Indigenous	Non-indigenous	All
Status			
Moved and Returned to Present Residence	13.5	13.0	13.1
Lived in Present Residence 12 Months	93.2	95.3	95.1
Moved for Seasonal Work	2.8	9.4	8.5
Reason for Locating in Present Residence			
More Money	3.1	9.1	8.5
Work	34.3	23.5	24.6
Study	6.9	12.4	11.8
Marriage	17.8	6.9	8.0
Terrorism	0.0	0.1	0.2
Other	37.8	48.0	47.0

Source: PLSS 1991.

indigenous migrants is 15 years (see Table 8.30). While indigenous people are less likely to move to their present location in order to obtain seasonal work, they are more likely to leave their present residence for work reasons than are non-indigenous people.

Work is the primary reason for the location of both indigenous and non-indigenous populations, at 34 and 24 percent, respectively. After work, marriage remains a decisive factor for the present residence of the indigenous population. The proportion of the indigenous population that lives in its present location for reasons of marriage is more than double the corresponding proportion of the non-indigenous population. Schooling and monetary concerns play a greater role in the location decisions of the Spanish-speaking population than for the indigenous population.

Conclusion

Indigenous people receive negligible and non-significant returns to their investments in education, except at the university level. Indigenous people are heavily concentrated in agriculture, where they experience higher wage differentials than elsewhere, compared with non-indigenous people. In addition, indigenous people are at the bottom of the Peruvian income distribution. Most of the indigenous population is poor, at 79 percent, and more than half is extremely poor. Moreover, indigenous people account for 11 percent of the sample population, yet they comprise 19 percent of the poor and 27 percent of extremely poor Peruvians.

The impoverished situation of indigenous people is directly reflected in both poor housing conditions (lack of public water, sewer facilities and electricity) and health status. While indigenous people are more likely to own their own homes, the physical composition of these homes is consistently deficient in comparison to those of Spanish speakers. Of particular importance is the availability of public water and sanitation facilities. Only 46 percent of indigenous homes have public water facilities, while 31 percent use wells and 15 percent use the river as a source of water; only 21 percent of indigenous homes have access to public waste disposal. An examination of rural/urban differences further highlights the indigenous population's deprivation.

In Peru, indigenous people are more likely to become ill than non-indigenous people, but they are much less likely to consult a physician. Perhaps as a result of poor initial health conditions, or as a result of neglecting treatment, the duration and severity of illness are greater among the indigenous population. Although the average cost of both hospitalization and medicine is less for indigenous people, only 57 percent of indigenous people purchase medicine for their illness, in comparison to 81 percent of the non-indigenous population.

Analysis of education levels by gender and ethnicity shows that educational gaps have been slowly decreasing over time, both between ethnic groups as well as between genders. Still, as a group, non-indigenous people have 47 percent more education than indigenous people. Not only is the indigenous population less educated and less literate than the Spanish-speaking population, but it also lags behind the non-indigenous population in terms of training. Similarly, the difference in educational achievements of household heads is substantial. Only 40 percent of indigenous household heads have education in excess of primary school, and only 6 percent have some post-secondary education. In contrast, 41 percent of Spanish-speaking heads of household have some secondary school education and 22 percent have some post-secondary education.

On average, the earnings of indigenous people are less than half those of Spanish speakers. Better paying occupations are dominated by Spanish speakers. While sections of the indigenous population have moved to new occupations like wage laborer, teacher, and tradesperson, the majority of the population remains involved in agricultural work. Seventy percent of indigenous people are involved in agricultural work, yet those who are paid for their work receive less than half the wages of their Spanish-speaking counterparts. Thirty percent of indigenous people are subsistence farmers.

Estimation of earnings functions by ethnic group shows that the average rate of returns to schooling for Spanish-speaking workers is 3 times that of indigenous workers, at 4.8 and 1.6 percent. It is also found that returns to schooling are insignificant for indigenous people, unless we differentiate by level, whereby university education is then profitable for indigenous people. Indigenous men are not rewarded for labor market experience, suggesting that the experience reported by indigenous men represents time trapped in low paying sectors. It should be kept in mind that the indigenous population in Peru is defined as monolingual Aymara and Quechua speakers. Consequently, these groups are not competing in the same segment of the labor market as the non-indigenous population (or the bilingual indigenous working population). Although higher levels of education provide higher earnings, schooling at the university level is the only significant educational factor which leads to increased earnings for indigenous men in Peru.

In Peru, the proportion of the overall earnings differential that is due to the productive characteristics of individuals is equivalent to 50 percent. In other words, if indigenous workers were endowed with the same productive characteristics as non-indigenous workers, the earnings differential between them would narrow by 50 percent. The remaining difference in wages is "unexplained," and may include any unmeasured factors which contribute to the earnings differential such as ability, health, the quality of education, labor force attachment and culture. However, wage discrimination against the indigenous population may account for as much as 50 percent of the overall earnings differential.

An analysis of the contribution of each variable to the overall earnings differential between indigenous and non-indigenous workers indicates that much of the Spanish speakers' earnings advantage can be explained by education at the university level. Rural location is a major disadvantage to the economic well-being of indigenous people. Yet, rural location does not affect Spanish speakers as negatively as it does indigenous language speakers, with the result of indigenous people being unduly penalized for their location. Much of the "unexplained" portion of the earnings differential is due to hours worked and experience; that is, for the same amounts of work and labor market experience, indigenous people are paid less than non-indigenous people.

Note

1. Earnings of youths are negatively associated with school attendance whereas earnings of older individuals are positively associated with education. Presumably, youths are attending school full-time and older workers are attending school part-time.

9

Conclusion

George Psacharopoulos and Harry Anthony Patrinos

This study presents the results of an empirical analysis of the socioeconomic conditions of Latin America's indigenous population. The primary focus is descriptive, supplemented with analyses of specific issues. The analyses rely on microdata from national survey sources from the late 1980s and early 1990s. A review of the literature on indigenous people in Latin America, as well as the much richer literature on the subject in industrial countries, reveals that empirical studies of the socioeconomic conditions of Latin America's indigenous people are scarce. The present study, therefore, is an attempt to help fill this void. It is confirmed that the incidence of poverty among indigenous people in the countries under investigation is very high. To a very large extent, being of indigenous origin is synonymous with being poor. Nevertheless, equalization of income-generating characteristics would boost the productivity of the indigenous population in their market and non-market activities and lead to a considerable reduction in inequality and poverty among the indigenous population, although the actual estimates vary from country to country.

Indigenous populations make up a significant portion of the poor. In terms of targeting, the indigenous poor do differ from the non-indigenous poor, especially in terms of language and culture. Since ethnic inequalities are affected by public policies, it is critical to understand how, by how much, and under what circumstances these inequalities are influenced. The results presented in this study can feed into country poverty assessments, poverty profiles, analyses of poverty incidence, and examinations of the interethnic distribution of income and social indicators. The commitment to analyze poverty and devise strategies for its reduction cannot exclude the indigenous and ethnic components.

Definitions of indigenous people differ from country to country due to the use of different survey instruments. This fact makes it difficult to attempt any cross-national comparisons. Given available data, three different variables identify indigenous respondents: (i) language spoken, (ii) self-perception, and (iii) geographic concentration. In this analysis, language defines the indigenous populations in Bolivia and Peru. In Bolivia, it is possible to distinguish between monolingual and bilingual (Spanish and indigenous language) individuals, while in Peru, only monolingual indigenous or Spanish speakers can be isolated. The self-identification or self-perception method of defining the reference population is used in the case of Guatemala. The geographic location or concentration of the indigenous population, in combination with language identity, is used in order to include Mexico, a country with a large absolute number of indigenous people (see Table 9.1).

This study shows that most indigenous people live in conditions of extreme poverty. The main findings follow.

Principal Conclusions

Poverty among Latin America's indigenous population is pervasive and severe. In Bolivia, while more than half of the total population is poor, over two-thirds of the bilingual indigenous population and almost three-quarters of the monolingual indigenous population are poor. The majority, 66 percent, of the population of Guatemala is poor, with 38 percent of all households below the extreme poverty line. The indigenous population, however, is disproportionately poor; 87 percent of all indigenous households are below the poverty line and 61 percent are below the extreme poverty line.

In Mexico, in *municipios* with a less than 10 percent indigenous population, the poverty headcount index is 18 percent; in *municipios* 10 to 40 percent indigenous, 46 percent of the population is poor; and in *municipios* over 70 percent indigenous, over 80 percent of the population is poor.

Most of the indigenous population of Peru is poor, at 79 percent, and more than half is extremely poor. In fact, indigenous people are one and a half times as likely to be poor than are non-indigenous people, and almost three times as likely to be

Table 9.1: Indigenous Population

Country	In Thousands	As a Percentage of the Total Population
Countries in This Study		
Bolivia (1988)	2,642	51.3
Guatemala (1981)	2,536	41.8
Mexico (1990)	5,282	7.4
Peru (1981)	3,627	24.8
Other Countries		
Colombia (1985)	238	0.8
Honduras (1988)	49	1.3
Paraguay (1981)	39	1.2
Venezuela (1982)	141	0.9

Source: EIH 1989, INEGI 1989, Gnerre 1990, PLSS 1991, CELADE 1992.

extremely poor. Consequently, indigenous people account for 11 percent of the sample population, yet they comprise 19 percent of the poor and 27 percent of extremely poor Peruvians.

In Guatemala, the degree of income inequality among the combined indigenous and non-indigenous populations in each region is greater than the estimated income inequality for separate groups. This proves that income inequality is clearly an interethnic problem (see Table 9.2).

The results of a statistical analysis of the determinants of poverty in Mexico reveal that a 1 percent increase in the indigenous population of a *municipio* leads to an increase in an individual's probability of being poor by approximately 0.5 percent. This variable has considerable impact given the potential range of indigenous population concentration, 0 to 100 percent. Living in a 50 percent indigenous *municipio* increases one's probability of being poor by a substantial 25 percent, marking a greater potential increase in the marginal probability of being poor than is possible with any other observed factor.

In Bolivia, being indigenous increases the probability of being poor by 16 percent. The probability of poverty increases by almost 45 percent for household members whose head of household is unemployed. This suggests that being employed is more important than being indigenous in terms of reducing poverty. Among indigenous heads of household, participation in the labor force leads to a 40 percent reduction in the incidence of poverty.

The living conditions of the indigenous population are generally abysmal, especially when compared to those of the non-indigenous population. In Guatemala, the majority of the population does not have access to such public services as water, sanitation and electricity. Less than one-third of all indigenous households have water piped to their homes for their exclusive use, compared with almost half of non-indigenous households. The study also shows that approximately half of all indigenous households have no sanitary services, and three-fourths have no electricity.

In Bolivia, households headed by a non-indigenous person have a higher number of rooms and more rooms per capita than households headed by an indigenous person. And although the indigenous group has a much higher level of home own-

Table 9.2: Poverty in Latin America
(percent of population below poverty line)

Country	Indigenous	Non-Indigenous
Bolivia	64.3	48.1
Guatemala	86.6	53.9
Mexico	80.6	17.9
Peru	79.0	49.7

Source: EIH 1989, ENSD 1989, INEGI 1989, PLSS 1991.

ership, this says little about the quality of housing, which is lower for the indigenous group. This is reflected in the lower rate of sewage facility connections to indigenous households, and the lower prevalence of latrines. An important finding is the substantially higher prevalence of land ownership among indigenous people. This could indicate that indigenous people maintain ties to rural areas, allowing them to maintain already established support networks.

In the less indigenous areas of Mexico, material possessions such as televisions, refrigerators and automobiles are more plentiful than in the more indigenous areas. Services such as piped water, electricity and telephone service are also more common in less indigenous areas. In contrast, home ownership is more prevalent in more indigenous areas, but a closer examination reveals a clear disparity in the physical composition of homes between more and less indigenous *municipios*. Homes in less indigenous areas are built from higher quality materials; 71 percent are constructed with concrete and brick compared with only 29 percent in more indigenous areas. A larger percentage of homes in indigenous areas are built with wood than in less indigenous areas (21 percent versus 6 percent).

While indigenous people are more likely to own their homes in Peru, the physical composition of these homes is also consistently deficient in comparison to that of Spanish speakers. Of particular importance is the availability of public water and sanitation facilities. Only 46 percent of indigenous homes have public water facilities, while 31 percent use wells and 15 percent use the river as a source of water; only 21 percent of indigenous homes have public waste disposal. An examination of rural/urban differences further highlights the indigenous population's deprivation. As indigenous households are less likely to have a public source of water in both rural and urban areas, indigenous people are much more likely to obtain water from wells; 16 percent of urban indigenous households and 39 percent of rural indigenous households have wells, whereas the corresponding proportions of Spanish households are only 2 and 10 percent. While the proportion of rural Spanish households that use rivers as their water source is larger than rural indigenous households, the rural prevalence of indigenous people results in a greater proportion of the indigenous population being exposed to the diseases associated with poor water quality. Almost half of all indigenous households rely on kerosene as a source of light; 88 percent of the homes of Spanish speakers use electricity. Within urban areas the use of kerosene is seven times greater in indigenous homes than in the homes of Spanish speakers. The relatively large proportion of urban indigenous households without public water, public sewage disposal and electricity is evidence of a group of indigenous squatter settlements in the urban areas.

There is a very strong correlation between schooling attainment and indigenous origin, and between schooling attainment and poverty category. In Bolivia, the schooling levels of indigenous people are approximately three years less, on average, than for non-indigenous individuals. The difference is even greater for indigenous females, suggesting that they are the most disadvantaged in Bolivian society.

In Guatemala, the majority of indigenous people have no formal education and of those who do, the majority have only primary education. On average, indigenous people have only 1.3 years of schooling and only 40 percent are literate.

Access to formal education in Mexico has expanded in recent years, and improvements have occurred in indigenous areas. Nevertheless, educational levels remain higher in non-indigenous areas. Illiteracy continues to be an important problem for some states, especially those which are predominantly indigenous. The rate of illiteracy increases for both males and females as *municipio* indigenous percentages rise. The disparity is greatest in the female subsample, where the illiteracy rate is more than four times greater in the "high" indigenous *municipio* category than in the "low" indigenous *municipio* category. In addition, it is interesting to note that the gender disparity in the illiteracy rate increases as the *municipio* indigenous percentage increases. For the least indigenous *municipios*, the male/female difference is only 2 percent; but for the "high" indigenous *municipios*, the difference is 16 percent, showing a pattern of increasing male/female educational inequities as the *municipio* indigenous concentration increases. The higher the proportion of indigenous people in a *municipio*, the lower the average level of schooling of its population. Males have almost 7 years of schooling in those *municipios* with less than a 10 percent indigenous population, whereas males in those *municipios* with a 40 percent or more indigenous population have only 3.5 years of schooling.

For the adult population of Peru, the data indicate that in recent years the difference between indigenous and non-indigenous people's educational attainment has narrowed. Still, non-indigenous people have 20 percent more education than indigenous people. Not only is the indigenous population less educated and less literate than the Spanish-speaking population, but it also lags behind the non-indigenous population in terms of training. Differences in educational levels of indigenous and non-indigenous individuals are substantial. Only 40 percent of indigenous heads of household have education in excess of primary school. In contrast, 41 percent of Spanish-speaking heads of household have some secondary school education, and 22 percent have some post-secondary education. Only 6 percent of indigenous heads of household have some post-secondary education. Educational gaps between the indigenous and non-indigenous populations, as well as between genders, have been decreasing over time.

The parents' skills and educational attainment are reflected in the schooling and other human capital characteristics of their children. In Guatemala, 9 percent of non-indigenous children and 21 percent of indigenous children are reported as being employed. The children of indigenous origins are born with many socioeconomic disadvantages and are unable to keep up with their non-indigenous peers. Indigenous children are more likely to repeat grades at the primary level and are more likely to drop out of school altogether.

In Bolivia, non-indigenous children aged 6 to 18 are still much more likely to be enrolled in school than indigenous children. Interestingly, the poorer children are actually *more* likely to be enrolled than the non-poor children. In terms of years of schooling attainment among the in-school population, non-indigenous children receive more schooling than indigenous children regardless of gender. Multivariate analysis shows that being indigenous has a strong effect on schooling attainment. In terms of school enrollment, the participation rate is slightly higher among males, with a greater percentage of non-indigenous youths attending school than indigenous youths.

In Peru, 40 percent of non-indigenous children are enrolled in school, as compared to 36 percent of indigenous children. The effects of language and rural location are reflected in school attendance; school attendance is greater among Aymara speakers than Quechua speakers, and greater among urban children. School attendance is also affected by child labor, both in the home and in the labor market; as hours worked increase, school attendance decreases. Being indigenous is a major determinant of child workforce participation. Quechua speakers are much more likely to work than Aymara speakers. In addition, both parental employment and education affect the work decision of indigenous children. Children of less educated parents, children of fathers who are employed as farmers, and children of mothers who are not in the labor force are more likely to work. With regards to child labor, similar results are found for Guatemala, but this is not the case in Mexico.

In Mexico, enrollment rates are higher in non-indigenous areas. The gap in enrollment rates between indigenous and non-indigenous areas widens with age, reaching a peak at 17 years, when the non-indigenous enrollment rate is approximately twice the indigenous rate. Child labor force participation is greater in indigenous areas than in non-indigenous areas, but not if one holds other factors constant. This can be partially explained by the rural concentration of the indigenous population. Parental education plays an important role in average educational levels among children. The average increase in school attainment for a child with a mother with secondary or greater education, as opposed to a mother with no education, is 3.5 years in non-indigenous areas. Similar differences exist in indigenous areas. Where comparisons are available, the impact of parental education is greatest in less indigenous *municipios*. The employment conditions of the head of the household also has a clear impact on a child's average educational attainment. Heads of household who work in non-agricultural pursuits in either indigenous or non-indigenous areas have children with higher levels of educational attainment than do heads of household who are otherwise employed. The contribution of the income of working children to total family income is substantial. As expected, the contribution of child labor to family income increases with age, while increasing educational attainment reduces the contribution. Child income plays a slightly greater role in total family income in indigenous areas than in non-indigenous areas.

The health problems of indigenous groups are severe. In Bolivia, indigenous people are more likely to have been sick or injured in the previous month than are non-indigenous people. There is a higher tendency among indigenous individuals for their disability to be sufficiently severe to keep them out of work for more than a week. Furthermore, indigenous persons are less likely to seek medical help for their ailments. Regarding an important preventive measure, the vaccination rate against yellow fever for non-indigenous individuals is double the rate for indigenous individuals. Indigenous women are in a substantially inferior position with respect to comprehensive maternal health care. Surprisingly, while the poor are less likely to receive professional attention at birth in a medical establishment, effectively targeted programs through public clinics have actually led to *higher* provision rates of certain preventive health procedures—such as tetanus vaccination—for poor women than for non-poor women.

In Peru, as in Bolivia, indigenous people are more likely to become ill than non-indigenous people, but they are much less likely to consult a physician. Perhaps as a result of poor initial health conditions, or as a result of neglected treatment, the duration and severity of illness are greater among the indigenous population. The proportion of indigenous people hospitalized is almost twice that of the Spanish-speaking population. Although the average cost of both hospitalization and medicine is less for indigenous people, only 57 percent of indigenous people purchase medicine for their illness, as compared to 81 percent of the non-indigenous population.

Labor force participation is higher and the rate of unemployment is lower for indigenous people, who are concentrated in particular sectors of the economy. In Bolivia, a greater percentage of all indigenous persons participate in the labor force, and a lower percentage of the indigenous labor force is unemployed (usual definition). Indigenous workers are more likely to have a second job, and they tend to work more hours than their non-indigenous counterparts. Yet bilingual indigenous workers earn, on average, less than two-thirds the salary of non-indigenous persons. Therefore, a high proportion of the indigenous poor are "working poor." Approximately one-half are self-employed, while the majority of non-indigenous individuals work as employees. Poorer individuals are more likely to be self-employed, and less likely to be an employee or a business owner. About 40 percent of both bilingual indigenous and monolingual Spanish employees are likely to work in the public sector, while the remaining 60 percent work in the private sector. Monolingual indigenous speakers, however, are far more likely to work in the private sector.

In Guatemala, most indigenous people work in the agricultural sector where wages are lower than in any other sector. The workforce is composed primarily of males for both the indigenous and non-indigenous populations. Indigenous workers are more likely than non-indigenous workers to be self-employed.

Noting the importance of organized labor in Mexico, unions are nearly two times more prevalent in less indigenous *municipios* than in more indigenous *municipios*. Unionization, however, is more important for indigenous workers, as it helps pull them out of poverty.

In Peru, the agricultural industry depends heavily on the labor of indigenous people. For example, 70 percent of indigenous women, and 63 percent of indigenous men, are involved in agricultural activities. Yet, on average, indigenous women and men earn only one-third the salary of non-indigenous workers employed in agriculture.

Indigenous people have much lower levels of schooling relative to the non-indigenous population, but equalizing schooling attainment would result in a considerable increase in relative earnings. Much of the earnings disadvantage of indigenous workers is due to lower human capital endowments. While the monetary benefits of schooling are lower for the indigenous population, an increase in schooling levels would lead to a significant increase in earnings in all countries except Peru. The relative magnitude, however, differs from country to country. In Bolivia, there is a significant negative effect on earnings associated with being indigenous. Examining the determinants of earnings separately for indigenous and non-indigenous workers, the average increase in earnings associated with an extra year of schooling is higher for non-indigenous males than for indigenous males by almost 3 percentage points, at 8.6 and 5.7 percent (Table 9.3). Similarly, non-indigenous workers receive higher returns to labor market experience. Hours worked per week have a higher payoff for non-indigenous workers by a margin of 8 percentage points.

The rate of returns to schooling in Guatemala is 11 percent for indigenous workers and 12 percent for non-indigenous workers. The rate of returns to schooling is higher for female workers, both indigenous and non-indigenous. In Mexico there is very little difference in the marginal payoff to schooling for individuals in more or less indigenous *municipios*.

In Peru, the increase in earnings associated with an extra year of schooling for Spanish-speaking workers is 3 times that of indigenous workers, at 4.8 and 1.6 percent. Indigenous men are not rewarded for labor market experience, suggesting that the experience reported by indigenous men represents time trapped in low paying sectors. While higher levels of schooling provide higher earnings, obtaining some university education is the most significant factor leading to increased earnings for indigenous men in Peru. It should also be kept in mind that the target

Table 9.3: Educational Attainment and the Increase in Earnings Associated with an Extra Year of Schooling

Country	Male Indigenous Workers		Male Non-indigenous Workers	
	Mean Years of Schooling	Increase in Earnings (%)	Mean Years of Schooling	Increase in Earnings (%)
Bolivia	7.4	5.7	10.1	8.6
Guatemala	1.8	9.1	4.9	10.5
Mexico	3.8	8.7	7.3	9.3
Peru	6.7	2.6	10.0	6.2

Source: Calculated from Tables 5.31, 5.32, 6.10, 6.28, 7.13, 7.14, 8.18, 8.19.

population in Peru is defined as the monolingual Aymara and Quechua speakers. In general, these groups do not compete in the same segment of the labor market as the non-indigenous population (or the bilingual indigenous working population). Also, the omission of externalities associated with increased schooling may lead to an underestimation of the "true" benefits of schooling.

One of the primary concerns of this report is the question of whether the equalization of human capital and other productive characteristics would result in the virtual elimination of socioeconomic inequalities, or whether the support of affirmative action programs would have the desired effect of nullifying such inequalities. Differential outcomes, of course, may be due to outright discrimination. Discrimination against indigenous people may deleteriously affect their access to schooling, the quality of schooling they receive and their labor market performance.

The statistical decomposition of the earnings differential between indigenous and non-indigenous workers produces mixed results. In Bolivia, for example, the portion of the overall earnings differential due to disparities in the productive characteristics of indigenous and non-indigenous working males is 72 percent. In other words, based on observed characteristics, the earnings differential between indigenous and non-indigenous workers would narrow by 72 percent if each group were endowed with the same productive characteristics. The remaining 28 percent difference in earnings is "unexplained," and reflects both measurement error and unaccounted factors such as disparities in ability, quality of education, labor force participation, culture and labor market discrimination. Therefore, discrimination could only account for 28 percent of the overall earnings differential between indigenous and non-indigenous workers in the urban Bolivian labor market. This very low estimate of the upper bound of discrimination in explaining ethnic earnings differentials in Bolivia is, no doubt, at least partly due to the fact that the sample is urban. However, a previous study of the extent of discrimination against indigenous people in rural Bolivia found no evidence of discrimination (Kelley 1988).

In Guatemala, however, approximately one-half of the earnings differential can be attributed to differences in endowments. For females, as much as three-fourths of the differential is due to differences in human capital. These upper bound estimates of discrimination indicate that up to 50 percent of the overall differential could be due to discrimination against the indigenous working population.

In Peru, the proportion of the overall earnings differential that is due to the productive characteristics of individuals is equivalent to 50 percent. In other words, if indigenous workers were endowed with the same productive characteristics as non-indigenous workers, the earnings differential between them would narrow by 50 percent. The remaining difference in wages is "unexplained," and may include any unmeasured factors which contribute to the earnings differential. Therefore, wage discrimination against the indigenous population could account for as much as 50 percent of the overall earnings differential. An analysis of the contribution of each variable to the overall earnings differential between indigenous and non-indigenous workers indicates that much of the Spanish-speaking workers' earnings advantage can be explained by education at the university level. Rural location is a major disadvantage to the economic well-being of indigenous people. Yet, rural location does not affect Spanish speakers as negatively as it does indigenous language speakers, with the result being that indigenous people are unduly penalized for their location. Much of the "unexplained" portion of the earnings differential is due to hours worked and experience; that is, for the same amounts of work and labor market experience, indigenous people are paid less than nonindigenous people.

In Mexico, the portion of the differential that is due to the productive characteristics or endowments of individuals is equivalent to 52 percent of the differential in earnings between workers in indigenous and non-indigenous areas. In other words, if those in indigenous areas were endowed with the same amounts of productive characteristics as those in non-indigenous areas, the difference in earnings between them would narrow by 52 percent. However, the remaining 48 percent difference in earnings is "unexplained." Therefore, discrimination against those in indigenous areas may explain up to 48 percent of the wage differential, thus forming the "upper bound" of discrimination. For the differential in earnings due to "explained" factors or endowments, higher educational attainment plays a large role in explaining the non-indigenous earnings advantage. However, the largest contribution to the non-indigenous advantage stems from non-agricultural employment, reflecting the predominance of non-agricultural workers in non-indigenous areas. The table below summarizes potential wage discrimination in each of the countries covered in this study.

Country	Discrimination (percent)
Bolivia	28
Guatemala	52
Mexico	48
Peru	50

Lessons Learned

There is, fortunately, an unrealized potential. This is evident, for example, in the case of Bolivia, where the educational level of the population has been increasing rapidly over the last few decades. The average schooling level of indigenous males has increased continuously over time, with a sharp rise for individuals born in 1959 and later. For indigenous women, the increase is even more dramatic, particularly for the post-1952 Revolution population. The statistical results show that by equalizing human capital characteristics, much of the earnings differential between indigenous and non-indigenous workers would disappear. These findings suggest that the socioeconomic condition of indigenous people in Bolivia can be improved because policy-influenced variables such as education and occupation are largely responsible for earnings differences. This provides considerable hope for the future. The question that remains, however, is how to improve the productive capabilities of the indigenous population. One obvious solution is to raise their educational level.

For education projects, knowledge about the indigenous population can aid in determining the location of new schools, targeting those with poor performance, and—when and if appropriate and in demand—providing bilingual education. The apparent strong influence of education to ameliorate poverty and increase earnings, especially in indigenous areas, conveys a need to focus on improving access as an important development issue with significant and beneficial long term socioeconomic repercussions. One of several frequently noted methods for improving access to education among the indigenous population is the implementation of some form of bilingual education.

The involvement of indigenous people can aid in the improvement of the design and implementation of development projects. First, agreement on what must be done should be reached between the interested parties. It is necessary to decide on the goals of the intervention from the outset. Is it reform? And if so, what is meant by reform? In the case of indigenous people, is the goal assimilation, integration and the erasure of indigenous culture? Or the preservation of indigenous culture through policies designed with the participation of indigenous people? In the case of education, the lack of meaningful participation by indigenous people could result in the loss of their culture and language.

Institutional issues associated with the functioning of labor markets are also important considerations. To some extent, indigenous people receive lower earnings and have a higher incidence of poverty because they are locked into the secondary sector of the economy. This information can aid in the creation of appropriate employment generation schemes. While many poor and non-poor workers are located in the informal sector of the economy, the location of the indigenous poor in this sector is especially important. This information points to an appropriate sector to target in any poverty reduction strategy.

More extensive knowledge about the indigenous population can aid in the design of health interventions in the region. For example, access to medical care for pregnant women is essential for the preservation of the mother's life and the healthy development of the newborn child. Among indigenous women, however, this medical attention is lacking. An important challenge is to devise strategies to extend health care to indigenous people.

A very important finding in this report is that fertility and child mortality levels in urban Bolivia decline significantly in response to greater education for both mothers and fathers. Lower fertility, in turn, is associated with higher participation in the labor force for women, thereby reflecting one indirect effect of education on earnings. Education demonstrates the strongest effect in reducing fertility. More importantly, ethnicity and household income levels are not significantly associated with fertility once education is controlled for. This implies that fertility behavior is not an insurmountable cultural datum, but rather is susceptible to change through policy-based interventions such as increased access to education.

The western model of development views traditional cultures as poor, so that efforts are directed at improving their standard of living. This is based on the ideology that all cultures must achieve a certain level of material acquisition in order to be developed. There is the belief that tribal cultures are unable to satisfy the material needs of their people. Some argue that all people share a desire for what is defined as material wealth, prosperity and progress. Others, it is believed, have different cultures only because they have not yet been exposed to the superior technological alternatives offered by industrial civilization. The problem with this reasoning is that the materialistic values of the industrialized countries of the world are not cultural universals. Indigenous populations *are* different, and taking this into account means not imposing non-indigenous values. Any attempt to improve the conditions of indigenous populations would benefit from the consideration of "traditional" customs and expertise. Traditional community values have persisted among Amerindians. Prior to European contact, these included entrepreneurial activity, which was crushed by the European immigrants. When this entrepreneurial spirit again became active, it was community- rather than individually-based. This reflects the importance indigenous people place on the kinship system (*comuneros*).

Future Research

There is a lack of empirical studies regarding the socioeconomic conditions of Latin America's indigenous population. Important issues to be tackled include defining the target population, solving the problem of scarce data and designing appropriate research methodologies.

While many countries in the region have sizeable indigenous populations, few include questions to identify the ethnolinguistic characteristics of individuals in their household or labor force surveys. To identify the reference population in this study, it was necessary to make do with surveys that provide single indicators. However, what are needed are multiple indicators—as used in the United States and Canada census. The whole range of indicators is necessary, including language, self-identification or self-perception, geographic location or concentration, ancestry and, possibly, dress (as in the Guatemala 1993 census).

Therefore, what are needed are better data, including panel data, so that in the future researchers can undertake more in-depth analyses and include a larger number of countries. In addition, longitudinal research could be conducted; that is, an attempt should be made to answer questions such as "What was the level of discrimination 10, 20 and 30 years ago?" "What will it be 5, 10, 15 years from now?" "What were the effects of past policies and programs?" "What will be the effects of present policies and programs?"

It may also be useful to study the experiences of developed countries with indigenous populations. Their treatment of the "indigenous question" could prove useful, especially in terms of analyzing what these countries did successfully and what efforts were unsuccessful. The information at their disposal, as well as how they use it and collect it, could also be examined.

A future research project on indigenous people could combine the quantitative approach taken here with qualitative analysis, such as the participatory-observation research approach (or participatory poverty assessment) (Salmen 1987; see also Stanley 1978). The idea is to combine comprehensive empirical work with field-work and micro-survey techniques. For example, if it is found that indigenous people in the cities of Bolivia are working as self-employed individuals who earn less than non-indigenous individuals with the same levels of schooling, then in-depth interviews with these groups of individuals should be conducted in order to ascertain the reasons for the income discrepancy. Without this qualitative data, probable reasons for the discrepancy, including race, access to training and cultural values, are merely speculative. Such sophisticated differences are difficult to assess using only empirical analysis, generally based upon less than perfect data sets.

Many indigenous people living in urban areas maintain ties with the rural com-munities to their mutual advantage. Resources are constantly exchanged between town and country. This transfer of resources is important and not always ade-quately captured in household survey data. The complex social networks can only be examined with a qualitative research approach. An examination of informal safety nets can be accommodated through a participatory research exercise.

The unpaid but productive activities of indigenous people living and working in rural communities are often misrepresented as unemployment or underemploy-ment. Many peasants, however, are often involved in a variety of activities that provide income, although these are not easily observed, especially with aggregate household data. Apparently idle peasants are in most cases heavily involved in many activities, but these are not easily categorized. This type of information can only be obtained through direct observation. The information collected, however, can be quantified and analyzed. This can aid in the design of rural development efforts with indigenous components.

There is much useful information regarding the manifestations of poverty that individuals are usually not open to disclosing. This may include information about their health, sanitation practices, attitudes and behavior regarding birth control, income or discrimination. A new approach, therefore, is necessary to supplement conventional sources. Conversational interviews can be used to ascertain not only the people's income and ability to pay, but also their values with regard to lan-guage, history and culture. It may be most effective to involve the target popula-tions in the design of surveys and projects, and to discuss with target groups the purpose of these initiatives, possibly through "participatory rural appraisals."

The purpose is to tie in future research with the goal of poverty reduction. The ultimate goal of the link between empirical and qualitative work, therefore, is to assist in the development of overall poverty reduction strategies. The participatory research method is designed to "listen to poor people" in order to learn how they assess their own poverty and existing poverty reduction strategies, how their own survival strategies operate, which official poverty reduction strategies they prefer, and which are they prepared to support. These assessments are intended to refo-cus, elaborate or validate conclusions drawn from conventional analysis. Such an approach would contribute towards ensuring that the ultimate poverty reduction strategy not only be country specific, but also be specific to the different categories of poor people.

The division between empirical work (usually done by an economist) and field survey work (usually done by an anthropologist) is probably not the best method for achieving the goal of making the poverty assessment more practical and more meaningful. There is a need to move beyond conceptual and methodological barriers and to transcend dichotomies (anthropologist-economist). Therefore, an individual or a team of economists/sociologists/anthropologists could assist each other in the preparation of both the empirical work and the verifying field work. This way, both aspects of the work feed into each other and the divisions between quantitative and qualitative research methodologies are much less severe. And, most importantly, the efforts to reduce poverty will be enhanced.

References

Adamson, R. 1992. "Investing in Indigenous Knowledge." *Akwe:kon Journal* 9(2): 50–51.

Altimir, O. 1987. "Income Distribution Statistics in Latin America and Their Reliability." *Review of Income and Wealth* 33(2): 111–155.

Alverson, H. 1979. "The Roots of Time: A Comment on Utilitarian and Primordial Sentiments in Ethnic Identification." In R. Hall, ed., *Ethnic Autonomy-Comparative Dynamics: The Americas, Europe and the Developing World*. New York: Pergamon Press.

Anand, S. 1977. "Aspects of Poverty in Malaysia." *Review of Income and Wealth* 23(1): 1–16.

Arcos, C. and C. Marchán. 1978. "Guaytacama y Cusubamba: Dos Modalidades de Desarrollo de la Agricultura Serrana." *Revista Ciencias Sociales* 2(5): 13–51.

Armitage, J. and R. Sabot. 1991. "Discrimination in East Africa's Urban Labor Markets." In Nancy Birdsall and Richard Sabot, eds., *Unfair Advantage: Labor Market Discrimination in Developing Countries*. Washington, D.C.: The World Bank.

Armstrong, R., J. Kennedy and P. R. Oberle. 1990. *University Education and Economic Well-Being: Indian Achievement and Prospects*. Ottawa: Indian and Northern Affairs Canada, Quantitative Analysis and Socio-Demographic Research.

Arrow, K. 1973. "Higher Education as a Filter." *Journal of Public Economics* 2(3): 193–216.

Banerjee, B. and J. B. Knight. 1985. "Caste Discrimination in the Indian Labour Market." *Journal of Development Economics* 17(3): 277–307.

Barsky, O. 1978. "Iniciativa Terrateniente en las Transformaciones de la Sierra Ecuatoriana: 1959–1964." Master's Thesis, PUCE-FLACSO, Quito.

BCE (Banco Central del Ecuador) and FODERUMA (Fondo de Desarrollo Rural Marginal). 1978. *Indian Community El Panecillo*. Quito.

Beals, R. 1952. "Acculturation, Economics, and Social Change in an Ecuadorean Village." In S. Tax, ed., *Acculturation in the Americas*. Proceedings and Selected

Papers of the XXIXth International Congress of Americanists. Chicago: University of Chicago Press.

————. 1966. *Community in Transition: Nayón-Ecuador.* Los Angeles: University of California.

Becker, G. S. 1971. *The Economics of Discrimination.* Chicago: University of Chicago Press.

————. 1975. *Human Capital.* New York: National Bureau of Economic Research.

Beghin, F. J. 1964. "Informe Sobre las Condiciones de Servidumbre Vigentes en las Haciendas del Oriente Ecuatoriano." *Humanitas* 5: 112–128.

Bensusan, G. 1988. "Mexico." In E. Mendelievich, ed., *Children at Work.* Geneva: International Labour Office.

Bhattacherjee, D. 1985. "A Note on Caste Discrimination in a Bombay Automobile Firm." *Industrial Relations* 24(1): 155–159.

Bigsten, A. 1988. "Race and Inequality in Kenya, 1914–1976." *Eastern Africa Economic Review* 4(1): 1–11.

Birdsall, N. and R. Sabot, eds. 1991. *Unfair Advantage: Labor Market Discrimination in Developing Countries.* Washington, D.C.: The World Bank.

Blinder, A. S. 1973. "Wage Discrimination: Reduced Form and Structural Estimates." *Journal of Human Resources* 8: 436–465.

Bodley J. H. 1990. *Victims of Progress.* Mountain View, CA: Mayfield Publishing Company.

Bound, J. and R. B. Freeman. 1992. "What Went Wrong? The Erosion of Relative Earnings and Employment among Young Black Men in the 1980s." *Quarterly Journal of Economics* 107(1): 201–232.

Brascoupé, S. 1992. "Indigenous Perspectives on International Development." *Akwe:kon Journal* 9(2): 6–17.

Brosnan, P. 1984. "Age, Education and Maori-Pakeha Income Differences." *New Zealand Economic Papers* 18: 49–61.

Brosnan, P. and C. Hill. 1983. "Income, Occupation and Ethnic Origin in New Zealand." *New Zealand Economic Papers* 17: 51–57.

Brownrigg, L. A. 1972. "The Nobles of Cuenca: The Agrarian Elite of Southern Ecuador." Ph.D. Dissertation, Columbia University, New York.

Brush, S. B. 1977. "The Myth of the Idle Peasant: Employment in a Subsistence Economy." In R. Halperin and J. Dow, eds., *Peasant Livelihood: Studies in Economic Anthropology and Cultural Ecology.* New York: St. Martin's Press.

Burger, J. 1987. *Report from the Frontier: The State of the World's Indigenous Peoples.* London: Zed Books Ltd.

————. 1990. *The Gaia Atlas of First Peoples: A Future for the Indigenous World.* New York: Anchor Books.

Burgos Guevara, H. 1970. *Relaciones Interétnicas en Riobamba.* Ediciones Especiales No. 55. Mexico: Instituto Indegenista Interamericano.

Carnoy, M. 1979. *Can Educational Policy Equalise Income Distribution in Latin America?* Westmead: Saxon House, for the International Labour Office.

————. 1980. "Segmented Labour Markets: A Review of the Theoretical and Empirical Literature and its Implications for Educational Planning." In M. Carnoy et al., eds., *Education, Work and Employment* Volume II. Paris: UNESCO, International Institute for Educational Planning.

Carvajal, M. J. and F. K. Morris. 1989/1990. "Educacion Formal: ¿Vehiculo de Integracion Economica y Social del Indio Guatemalteco." *Revista de la Integracion y el Desarrollo de Centroamerica* 45/46: 95–110.

Casagrande, J. B. 1974. "Strategies for Survival: The Indians of Highland Ecuador." In D. B. Heath, ed., *Contemporary Cultures and Societies of Latin America*, 2nd ed. New York: Random House. Spanish translation: "Estrategias para Sobrevivir: Los Indígenas de la Sierra del Ecuador." *América Indígena* 36(January, 1976): 95–114.

CELADE (Latin American Demographic Center). 1992. *Demographic Bulletin* 25(50). Santiago, Chile.

Center for Applied Linguistics and the World Bank. 1975. *Perú: A Profile of Languages and their Use*. Washington, D.C.

CEPAL (United Nations Economic Commission for Latin America and the Caribbean). 1991. *Magnitud de la Pobreza en America Latina en los Años Ochenta*. Estudios e Informes de la CEPAL 81. Santiago, Chile.

Chayanov, A. V. 1966. "On the Theory of Non-Capitalist Economic Systems." In D. Thorner, ed., *The Theory of Peasant Economy*. Homewood, IL: Richard D. Irwin, Inc.

Chiswick, B. R. 1987. "Race Earnings Differentials." In George Psacharopoulos, ed., *Economics of Education: Research and Studies*. Oxford: Pergamon Press.

CIDA (Comité Interamericano de Desarrollo Agrícola). 1965. *Tenencia de la Tierra y Desarrollo Socio-económico del Sector Agrícola—Ecuador*. Washington, D.C.: PAU.

———. "Differences in Education and Earnings Across Racial and Ethnic Groups: Tastes, Discrimination, and Investments in Child Quality." *Quarterly Journal of Economics* 103(3): 571–597.

Clatworthy, S. J. 1981a. "The Effects of Education on Native Behaviour in the Urban Labour Market." Report to the Federal Task Force on Labour Market Development, Canada Department of Employment and Immigration, Ottawa.

———. 1981b. "Issues Concerning the Role of Native Women in the Winnipeg Labour Market." Institute of Urban Studies, Winnipeg.

———. 1981c. "Patterns of Native Employment in the Winnipeg Labour Market." Report to the Federal Task Force on Labour Market Development, Canada Department of Employment and Immigration, Ottawa.

Colburn, F. 1989. *Every Day Forms of Peasant Resistance*. New York: M. E. Sharpe, Inc.

Collins, J. L. 1983. "Fertility Determinants in a High Andes Community." *Population and Development Review* 9(1): 61–75.

Cornell University, Department of Anthropology. 1965. *Indians in Misery: A Preliminary Report on the Colta Lake Zone, Chimborazo, Ecuador*. Prepared in collaboration with the Ecuadorean Institute of Agrarian Reform and Colonization. Quito: USAID/Ecuador.

————. 1966. E. Maynard, ed., *The Indians of Colta: Essays on the Colta Lake Zone, Chimborazo (Ecuador)*. Quito: USAID/Ecuador.

Crespi, M. 1968. "The Patrons and Peons of Pesillo: A Traditional Hacienda System in Highland Ecuador." Ph.D. Dissertation, University of Illinois, Urbana.

Cycon, D. E. 1991. "When Worlds Collide: Law, Development and Indigenous Peoples." *New England Law Review* 25(3): 761–794.

Darity, W. A. 1982. "The Human Capital Approach to Black-White Earnings Inequality: Some Unsettled Questions." *Journal of Human Resources* 17(1): 72–93.

Davis, P. M. 1981. "What We Have Learned from the Peruvian Experiment." In M. L. Larson and P. M. Davis, eds., *Bilingual Education: An Experience in Peruvian Amazonia*. Dallas: Summer Institute of Linguistics.

Davis, Shelton H., ed. 1993. *Indigenous Views of Land and the Environment*. Discussion Paper 188. Washington, D.C.: The World Bank.

de Villalobos, R. and A. Monares. 1990. "Poverty Profile for Ecuador." Working Paper No. 100. The International Fund for Agricultural Development, Rome.

del Aguila, W. 1987. "Educational Effects of Multilingualism in Guatemala." *Journal of Multilingual and Multicultural Development* 8(4): 379–382.

Deprez, P. 1973. "Education and Economic Development: The Case of Indian Reserves in Canada." In *Two Papers on Canadian Indians* Series 5: Occasional Papers Nos. 5 and 6. Winnipeg: University of Manitoba.

DGEI (Dirección General de Educación Indígena). 1993. *Informacion de Alumnos, Maestros y Escuelas de Educacion Inicial, Preescolar y Primaria Indigena por Entidad y Grupo Etnico*. Mexico D.F.: Secretaria de Educacion Publica.

Dhesi, A. S. and H. Singh. 1989. "Education, Labour Market Distortions and Relative Earnings of Different Religion-Caste Categories in India (A Case Study of Delhi)." *Canadian Journal of Development Studies* 10(1): 75–89.

Doeringer, P. B. and M. J. Piore. 1972. *Internal Labor Markets and Manpower Analysis*. Lexington, MA: D.C. Heath.

Duncan, O. D. 1968. "Inheritance of Poverty or Inheritance of Race?" In D. P. Moynihan, ed., *On Understanding Poverty*. New York: Basic Books.

Dutcher, N. 1982. *The Use of First and Second Languages in Primary Education: Selected Case Studies*. World Bank Staff Working Papers, No 504. Washington, D.C.: The World Bank.

Ecuador, Grupo de Evaluación de la Reforma Agraria (IERAC, JUNAPLA, MAG). 1977. *Evaluación del Proyecto Sectorial Cayambe*. Quito: CENCOTAP.

Escobar, A. 1988. "Bilingualism in Peru." In C. B. Paulston, ed., *International Handbook of Bilingualism and Bilingual Education*. New York: Greenwood Press.

Evans, G. 1992. "Internal Colonialism in the Central Highlands of Vietnam." *Sojourn* 7(2): 274–304.

Farley, R. 1990. "Blacks, Hispanics, and White Ethnic Groups: Are Blacks Uniquely Disadvantaged?" *American Economic Review* 80(2): 237–241.

Fernandez, H. 1986. "Women's Educational Situation in Peru." Mimeo. Instituto Nacional de Investigacion y Desarrollo de la Educación, Lima, Peru.

Filer, R. K. 1983. "Sexual Difference in Earnings: The Role of Individual Personalities and Tastes." *Journal of Human Resources* 18(1): 82–99.

Gálvez Barrera, A. 1980. "The Historical Status of Women in Peru." *Impact of Science on Society* 30(1): 7–9.

Gerber, L. M. 1990. "Multiple Jeopardy: A Socio-Economic Comparison of Men and Women Among the Indian, Metis and Inuit Peoples of Canada." *Canadian Ethnic Studies* 3: 69–84.

Gertler, P. and P. Glewwe. 1992. "The Willingness to Pay for Education for Daughters in Contrast to Sons: Evidence from Rural Peru." *The World Bank Economic Review* 6(1): 171–188.

Gnerre, M. 1990. "Indigenous Peoples in Latin America." Working Paper No. 30. International Fund for Agricultural Development, Rome.

Godoy, R. 1992. "The Effect of Rural Education on the Use of the Tropical Rain Forest by the Sumu Indians of Nicaragua: Possible Pathways, Qualitative Findings, and Policy Options." Cambridge, MA: Harvard Institute for International Development.

Goldin, C. and S. Polachek. 1987. "Residual Differences by Sex: Perspectives on the Gender Gap in Earnings." *American Economic Review* 77(2): 143–151.

———. 1992. "Work and Ideology in the Maya Highlands of Guatemala: Economic Beliefs in the Context of Occupational Change." *Economic Development and Cultural Change* 41(1): 103–123.

Granja B., A. M. 1977. "Reforma Agraria en Ichubamba de Cebadas: Un Estudio de Caso." Documentos de Trabajo No. 3. Thesis for Licentiate in Anthropology, PUCE, Quito.

Gunderson, M. 1989. "Male-Female Wage Differentials and Policy Responses." *Journal of Economic Literature* 27(1): 46–72.

Gwartney, J. D. and J. E. Long. 1978. "The Relative Earnings of Blacks and Other Minorities." *Industrial and Labor Relations Review* 31(3): 336–346.

Hagen, E. E. 1962. *On the Theory of Social Change: How Economic Growth Begins*. Homewood, IL: Dorsey Press, Inc.

———. 1968. *The Economics of Development*. Homewood, IL: Richard D. Irwin, Inc.

Hahn, D. R. 1991. *The Divided World of the Bolivian Andes: A Structural View of Domination and Resistance*. New York: Crane Russak.

Halvorsen, R. and R. Palmquist. 1980. "The Interpretation of Dummy Variables in Semilogarithmic Equations." *Journal of Human Resources* 17(1): 72–93.

Hammer, J., J. Cercone, and I. Nabi. 1992. "Distributional Effects of Social Sector Spending in Malaysia, 1974–1989." Paper presented at the World Bank Conference, "Public Expenditures and the Poor: Incidence and Targeting," Washington, D.C.

Handy, J. 1984. *Gift of the Devil: A History of Guatemala*. Boston: South End Press.

Hanratty, D. 1990. *Paraguay: A Country Study*. Washington, D.C.: Government Printing Office.

Hardman, M. J. 1981. "Introductory Essay." In M. J. Hardman, ed., *The Aymara Language in Its Social and Cultural Context: A Collection of Essays on Aspects of Aymara Language and Culture*. Gainesville: University Presses of Florida.

Harrison, B. and L. Gorham. 1992. "Growing Inequality in Black Wages in the 1980s and the Emergence of an African-American Middle Class." *Journal of Policy Analysis and Management* 11(2): 235–253.

Hawkins, J. N. 1983. "Educational Demands and Institutional Response: Dowa Education in Japan." *Comparative Education Review* 27(2): 204–226.

Hawthorn, H. B. 1967. *A Survey of the Contemporary Indians of Canada: Economic, Political, Educational Needs and Policies*. Volume II. Ottawa: Indian Affairs Branch.

Hernandez, I. 1988. "Identidad Indígena y Educacion." *Desarrollo Economico* 28(109): 121–137.

Heyneman, S. 1979. "Primary Education in Bolivia: What's Wrong?" Education Department, The World Bank, Washington, D.C.

Hicks, J. F., H. E. Daly, S. H. Davis and M. de Lourdes de Freitas. 1990. *Ecuador's Amazon Region: Development Issues and Options*. Discussion Paper 75. Washington, D.C.: The World Bank.

Hill, M. S. 1979. "The Wage Effects of Marital Status and Children." *Journal of Human Resources* 14(4): 579–594.

Hirsch, B. T. 1980. "The Determinants of Unionization: An Analysis of Interarea Differences." *Industrial and Labor Relations Review* 33(2): 147–161.

Hirsch, B. T. and J. Addison. 1986. *The Economic Analysis of Unions: New Approaches and Evidence*. Boston: Allen & Unwin.

Hirschman, C. 1983. "Labor Markets and Ethnic Inequality in Peninsular Malaysia, 1970." *Journal of Developing Areas* 18(1): 1–20.

Hirschman, C. and M. G. Wong. 1984. "Socioeconomic Gains of Asian Americans, Blacks, and Hispanics: 1960–1976." *American Journal of Sociology* 90(3): 584–607.

Hornberger, N. 1992. "Literacy in South America." *Annual Review of Applied Linguistics* 12: 190–215.

Hull, J. 1987. *An Overview of the Educational Characteristics of Registered Indians in Canada*. Ottawa: Indian and Northern Affairs Canada.

IERAC (Instituto Ecuatoriano de Reforma Agraria y Colonización), IEAG (Instituto Ecuatoriano de Antropología y Geografía), and JUNAPLA (Junta Nacional de Planificación y Coordinación Económica). 1965. *Zula*. Prepared by A. C. Samaniego, field work by C. S. García. Quito.

IFAD (International Fund for Agricultural Development). 1992. *The State of World Rural Poverty: An Inquiry into Its Causes and Consequences*. New York: New York University Press.

ILO (International Labour Office). 1949. *Conditions of Life and Work of Indigenous Populations of Latin America Countries*. Geneva.

———. 1953. *Indigenous Peoples: Living and Working Conditions of Aboriginal Populations in Independent Countries*. Studies and Reports No. 35. Geneva.

INAH (Instituto Nacional de Antropología e Historia). 1987. *Dinámica de la Población de Habla Indígena (1900–1980)*. Mexico, D.F.

INEGI (Instituto Nacional de Estadística Geografía e Informatica). 1991. "Continua la Entrega del Censo de Población de 1990." *Información Económica y Social. Revista Internacional del INEGI* 3(3): 26–53.

————. 1992a. *XI Censo Nacional de Población y Vivienda, 1990.* Mexico, D.F.

————. 1992b. *Perfil Sociodemografico. Censo Nacional de Población y Vivienda, 1990.* Mexico, D.F.

INI (Instituto Nacional Indigenista). 1991. "Programa Nacional de Desarrollo de los Pueblos Indígenas, 1991–1994." *Comercio Exterior* 41(3): 304–317.

Institute for Resource Development/Macro Systems. 1987. *Encuesta Nacional de Salud Materno Infantil, 1987: Guatemala.* Columbia, MD.

————. 1989. *Maternal and Child Health in Bolivia: Report on the In-depth DHS Survey in Bolivia 1989.* Columbia, MD.

Jacobson, C. K. 1984. "Internal Colonialism and Native Americans: Indian Labor in the United States from 1871 to World War II." *Social Science Quarterly* 65(1): 158–171.

Jensen, K. 1984. "Civilization and Assimilation in the Colonized Schooling of Native Americans." In P. G. Altbach and G. P. Kelly, eds., *Education and the Colonial Experience.* New York: Advent Books.

Jordan Pando, R. 1990. *Desarrollo en Poblaciones Indígenas de América Latina y El Caribe.* Mexico City: Instituto Indigenista Interamericano and FAO.

Jorgensen, J. G. 1977. "Poverty and Work among American Indians." In H. R. Kaplan, ed., *American Minorities and Economic Opportunity.* Itasca, IL: F. E. Peacock.

Junankar, P. N. and C. A. Kapuscinski. 1991a. "Aboriginal Employment and Unemployment: An Overview." Discussion Paper No. 255. Australian National University, Centre for Economic Policy Research.

————. 1991b. "The Incidence of Long Term Unemployment in Australia." *Australian Bulletin of Labour* 17(4): 325–352.

Kelley, J. 1988. "Class Conflict or Ethnic Oppression? The Cost of Being Indian in Rural Bolivia." *Rural Sociology* 53(4): 399–420.

Kelley, J. and H. S. Klein. 1981. *Revolution and the Rebirth of Inequality: A Theory of Revoluation Applied to the National Revolution in Bolivia.* Berkeley: University of California Press.

Kitagawa, E. M. 1955. "Components of a Difference between Two Rates." *Journal of the American Statistical Association* 50(272): 1168–1194.

Klein, H. 1982. *Bolivia, the Evolution of a Multi-Ethnic Society.* New York: Oxford University Press.

Kleinfeld, J. and J. A. Kruse. 1982. "Native Americans in the Labor Force: Hunting for an Accurate Measure." *Monthly Labor Review* July: 47–51.

Klitgaard, R. 1991. *Adjusting to Reality: Beyond "State Versus Market" in Economic Development.* San Francisco: ICS Press.

Klitgaard, R. and R. Katz. 1983. "Overcoming Ethnic Inequalities: Lessons from Malaysia." *Journal of Policy Analysis and Management* 2(3): 333–349.

Knight, J. B. and R. H. Sabot. 1982. "Labor Market Discrimination in a Poor Urban Economy." *Journal of Development Studies* 19(1): 67–97.

Kuo, C.-Y. 1976. "The Effect of Education on the Earnings of Indian, Eskimo, Metis, and White Workers in the Mackenzie District of Northern Canada." *Economic Development and Cultural Change* 24(2): 387–398.

Lachman, D. and K. Bercuson, eds. 1992. "Economic Policies for a New South Africa." Occasional Paper No. 91. International Monetary Fund, Washington, D.C.

Lautard, E. H. 1982. "Occupational Segregation and Inequality between Native and non-Native Canadians, 1971." *The Canadian Journal of Native Studies* 2(2): 303–320.

López, L. E. and L. D'Emilio. 1992. "Bilingual Education beyond National Frontiers. Bolivian-Peruvian Cooperation." *The Major Project of Education in Latin America and the Caribbean Bulletin* 27:41–56.

Lourié, S. 1982. "Inequalities in Education in Rural Guatemala." In *Inequalities in Educational Development: Papers Presented at an IIEP Seminar.* Paris: UNESCO, International Institute for Educational Planning.

Lundahl, M. 1992. *Apartheid in Theory and Practice: An Economic Analysis.* Boulder: Westview Press.

Luzuriaga, C. C. and C. Zuvekas. 1983. *Income Distribution and Poverty in Rural Ecuador, 1950–1979: A Survey of the Literature.* Tempe, AZ: Arizona State University.

Martínez, G. and A. Dubly. 1967–68. *Diagnóstico Socio-Económico del Medio Rural de la Provincia de Pichincha.* Quito: JUNAPLA.

Masferrer, E. 1983. "La Situacion Social de los Grupos Indigenas de America Latina." In N. J. Rodríguez, E. Masferrer, and R. Vargas Vega, eds., *Educacion, Etnias y Descolonizacion en America Latina: Una Guía para la Educación Bilingue Intercultural* Volume II. Mexico D.F.: UNESCO.

McClave, J. and P. Benson. 1991. *Statistics for Business and Economics.* San Francisco: Dellen Publishing Co.

Medina, C. 1977a. "The Legal Status of Indians in Bolivia." Mimeo Institute for the Development of Indian Law, Washington, D.C.

————. 1977b. "The Legal Status of Indians in Brazil." *American Indian Journal* 3(9): 12–24.

Micklin, M. 1990. "Guatemala." In C. B. Nam, W. J. Serow and D. F. Sly, eds., *International Handbook on Internal Migration.* New York: Greenwood Press.

Miller, P. W. 1989. "The Structure of Aboriginal and Non-Aboriginal Youth Unemployment." *Australian Economic Papers* 28(52): 39–56.

Miller, R. 1982. "The Mexican Approach to Developing Bilingual Materials and Teaching Literacy to Bilingual Students." *The Reading Teacher* April: 800–804.

Mincer, J. 1974. *Schooling, Experience and Earnings.* New York: National Bureau of Economic Research.

Mincer, J. and S. Polachek. 1974. "Family Investments in Human Capital: Earnings of Women." *Journal of Political Economy* 82(2): S76–S108.

————. 1978. "Women's Earnings Reexamined." *Journal of Human Resources* 8(1): 118–134.

Modiano, N. 1973. *Indian Education in the Chiapas Highlands.* New York: Holt, Rinehart and Winston, Inc.

————. 1988. "Public Bilingual Education in Mexico." In C. B. Paulston, ed., *Handbook of Biligualism and Bilingual Education.* New York, Greenwood Press.

Moll, P. G. 1992. "The Decline of Discrimination against Colored People in South Africa, 1970 to 1980." *Journal of Development Economics* 37(2): 289–307.

Mondloch, J. 1979. "Guía Antropológica sobre la Planificación Familiar Areas Indígenas." Report prepared for the Asociación Pro-Bienestar de la Familia, Guatemala.

Mörner, M., ed. 1970. *Race and Class in Latin America.* New York: Columbia Press.

Morren, R. C. 1988. "Bilingual Education Curriculum Development in Guatemala." *Journal of Multilingual and Multicultural Development* 9(4): 353–370.

Munzel, M. 1973. "The Aché Indians: Genocide in Paraguay." International Work Group for Indigenous Affairs, Copenhagen.

Myers, W. E. 1989. "Urban Working Children: A Comparison of Four Surveys from South America." *International Labour Review* 128(3): 321–335.

Nyrop, Richard, ed. 1983. *Guatemala: A Country Study.* Washington, D.C.: The American University.

Oaxaca, R. L. 1973. "Male-Female Wage Differences in Urban Labor Markets." *International Economic Review* 14(1): 693–701.

Oaxaca, R. L. and M. R. Ransom. 1989. "Overpaid Men and Underpaid Women: A Tale of the Gender Specific Wage Effects of Labor Market Discrimination." Paper presented at the International Economic Association World Congress, Athens, August 28–September 1, 1989.

Ovalle, I. and A. Cantu. 1982. *Necesidades Esenciales en México. Situación Actual y Perspectivas al Año 2000.* Mexico: Editorial Siglo XXI.

PAHO (Pan-American Health Organization). 1990. *Health Conditions in the Americas.* Washington, D.C.: The World Health Organization.

Palafox, J. C., J. Prawda and E. Velez. 1994. "Primary School Quality in Mexico." *Comparative Education Review.* 38: 167–180.

Paredes Barros, C. H. 1967. "Incidencia Económica y Social del Proceso de Liquidación del Huasipungo en la Provincia de Pichincha." Thesis for degree of Economista, PUCE, Quito.

Parkyn, L. K. 1989. "The Ladinoization of the Guatemalan Urban Indigena—An Ethnographic Study of the Processes of Sociocultural Change in Santa Cruz del Quiche." Ph.D. Thesis, Temple University, Philadelphia.

Parsons, T. 1954. *Essays in Sociological Theory.* New York: Free Press.

Patrinos, H. A. and G. Psacharopoulos. 1992. "Socioeconomic and Ethnic Determinants of Grade Repetition in Bolivia and Guatemala." Working Paper WPS 1028. World Bank, Latin America and the Caribbean Technical Department, Washington, D.C.

————. 1993. "Schooling and Non-Schooling Activities of Peruvian Youth." Mimeo. World Bank, Latin America and the Caribbean Technical Department, Washington, D.C.

Patrinos, H. A. and C. N. Sakellariou. 1992. "North American Indians in the Canadian Labour Market: A Decomposition of Wage Differentials." *Economics of Education Review* 11(3): 257–266.

————. 1993. "Decomposing Aboriginal/Non-Aboriginal Earnings Differentials in Canada: Culture versus Discrimination." Mimeo. University of Sussex.

Pearse, A. 1975. *The Latin American Peasant.* The Library of Peasant Studies, No. 1. London: Frank Cass.

Plaza, P. 1990. "Towards Standardization of Language for Teaching in the Andean Countries." *Prospects* 20(3): 377–384.

Polachek, S. W. 1975. "Potential Biases in Measuring Male-Female Discrimination." *Journal of Human Resources* 10(2): 205–229.

Poston, D. L. and J. Shu. 1987. "The Demographic and Socioeconomic Composition of China's Ethnic Minorities." *Population and Development Review* 13(4): 703–722.

PREDESUR (Programa Regional para Desarrollo del Sur del Ecuador). 1978. *Características Socio-económicas del Grupo Shuar, Valles de Nangaritza-Zamora, Yacumbí, Provincia de Zamora Chinchipe.* Final Report. Quito.

Preston, R. 1987. "Education and Migration in Highland Ecuador." *Comparative Education* 23(2): 191–207.

Psacharopoulos, George 1994. "Returns to Investment in Education: A Global Update." *World Development* (September).

————. 1993. "Ethnicity, Education, and Earnings in Bolivia and Guatemala." *Comparative Education Review* 37(1): 9–20.

Psacharopoulos, George, et al. 1992. "Poverty and Income Distribution in Latin America: The Story of the 1980s." Report No. 27. World Bank, Latin America and the Caribbean Technical Department, Regional Studies Program, Washington, D.C.

Psacharopoulos, George. and Zafiris Tzannatos. 1992. *Women's Employment and Pay in Latin America: Overview and Methodology.* Washington, D.C.: The World Bank.

Psacharopoulos, George. and Maureen Woodhall. 1985. *Education for Development.* New York: Oxford University Press.

Ravallion, Martin. 1992. *Poverty Comparisons: A Guide to Concepts and Methods.* Living Standards Measurement Study Working Paper No. 88. Washington, D.C.: The World Bank.

Reimers, C. W. 1983. "Labor Market Discrimination against Hispanic and Black Men." *Review of Economics and Statistics* 65(4): 570–579.

Rens, J. 1961. "The Andean Programme." *International Labour Review* 84(6): 423–459.

————. 1963. "The Development of the Andean Programme and Its Future." *International Labour Review* 86(6): 547–563.

Richards, M. F. 1987. *Seasonal Migration and Physiological Risk in a Guatemalan Maya Community.* Ph.D. Dissertation, University of Wisconsin, Madison.

Richards, M. and J. Richards. 1990. "Languages and Communities Encompassed by Guatemala's National Bilingual Education Program." USAID in conjunction with the Ministerio de Educación de Guatemala.

Rojas, E. 1991. "Factores que Explican los Niveles de Escolaridad Media de los Hijos en Guatemala." UNESCO-OREALC, Santiago.

Rosenhouse, S. 1992. "Políticas y Programas de Población ante la Diversidad Étnica: Diferencias Culturales o Insensibilidad Política." *Revista Mexicana de Sociología.*

Saavedra, C. 1981. "Social and Cultural Context of the Aymara in Bolivia Today." In M. J. Hardman, ed., *The Aymara Language in Its Social and Cultural Context: A Collection of Essays on Aspects of Aymara Language and Culture.* Gainesville: University Presses of Florida.

Sáenz Andrade, Á. 1978. "El Proceso de Transformación de la Estructura Agraria, Estructura Ocupacional y Migraciones en la Parroquia Cutuglahua en el Período 1950–1974." Thesis for Licentiate in Sociology, PUCE-CLACSO, Quito.

Sagarin, E. and J. Moneymaker. 1979. "Language Nationalist, Separatist, Secessionist Movement." In R. Hall, ed., *Ethnic Autonomy-Comparative Dynamics: The Americas, Europe and the Developing World.* New York: Pergamon Press.

Salmen, L. F. 1987. *Listen to the People: Participant-Observer Evaluation of Development Projects.* New York: Oxford University Press for The World Bank.

Sandefur, G. D. 1986. "American Indian Migration and Economic Opportunities." *International Migration Review* 20(1): 55–68.

Sandefur, G. D. and J. Jeon. 1991. "Migration, Race and Ethnicity, 1960–1980." *International Migration Review* 25(2): 392–407.

Sandefur, G. D. and A. Pahari. 1989. "Racial and Ethnic Inequality in Earnings and Educational Attainment." *Social Service Review* 63(2): 199–221.

Sandefur, G. D. and A. Sakamoto. 1988. "American Indian Household Structure and Income." *Demography* 25(1): 71–80.

Sandefur, G. D. and W. J. Scott. 1983. "Minority Group Status and the Wages of Indian and Black Males." *Social Science Research* 12: 44–68.

Sandefur, G. D., S. McLanahan and R. A. Wojtkiewicz. 1989. "Race and Ethnicity, Family Structure, and High School Graduation." Discussion Paper No. 893–89. University of Wisconsin-Madison, Institute for Research on Poverty.

Schultz, T. P. 1991. "Labor Market Discrimination: Measurement and Interpretation." In Nancy Birdsall and Richard Sabot, eds., *Unfair Advantage: Labor Market Discrimination in Developing Countries.* Washington, D.C.: The World Bank.

Schultz, T. W. 1961. "Investment in Human Capital." *American Economic Review* 51:1–17.

Scott, K. 1992. "Women in the Labor Force in Bolivia: Participation and Earnings." In George Psacharopoulos and Zafiris Tzannatos, eds., *Case Studies on Women's Employment and Pay in Latin America.* Washington, D.C.: The World Bank.

Segal, B. 1979. "Ethnicity Where the Present Is the Past." In R. Hall, ed., *Ethnic Autonomy-Comparative Dynamics: The Americas, Europe and the Developing World.* New York: Pergamon Press.

Semyonov, M. 1986. "The Socioeconomic Status of Noncitizen Arab Workers in the Israeli Labor Market: Cost and Benefits." *Social Science Quarterly* 67(2): 411–418.

Serafino, N.M. 1991. "Latin American Indigenous Peoples and Considerations for U.S. Assistance." (96-663F) Congressional Research Service, The Library of Congress, Washington, D.C.

Shimahara, N. 1984. "Toward the Equality of a Japanese Minority: The Case of Burakumin." *Comparative Education* 20(3): 339–353.

Shyrock, H., et al. 1976 *The Methods and Materials of Demography*. San Diego, CA: Academic Press.

Siegel, P. M. 1965. "On the Cost of Being a Negro." *Sociological Inquiry* 35:41–57.

SIL (Summer Institute of Linguistics). 1988. *Ethnologue Languages of the World*. Dallas.

————. 1992. *Ethnologue Languages of the World*. Dallas.

Silva, N. V. 1985. "Updating the Cost of Not Being White in Brazil." In P.-M. Fontaine, ed., *Race, Class and Power in Brazil*. Los Angeles: University of California.

Silvers, A. 1980. *Rural Development and Urban-bound Migration in Mexico*. Washington, D.C.: Resources for the Future.

Sinclair, V. and G. Trah. 1991. "Child Labour: National Legislation on the Minimum Age for Admission to Employment or Work." *Conditions of Work Digest* 10(1): 19–38.

Smith, C. 1992. *Guatemalan Indians and the State: 1540 to 1988*. Austin: University of Texas.

Smith, G. H. 1990. "The Politics of Reforming Maori Education: The Transforming Potential of Kura Kaupapa Maori." In H. Lauder and C. Wylie, eds., *Towards Successful Schooling*. London: The Falmer Press.

Smith, J. P. 1984. "Race and Human Capital." *American Economic Review* 74(4): 685–698.

Smith, J. P. and F. R. Welch. 1977. "Black-White Male Wage Ratios: 1960–70." *American Economic Review* 67(3): 323–338.

Snipp, M. 1988. "On the Costs of Being an American Indian: Ethnic Identity and Economic Opportunity." In J. H. Johnson, Jr. and M. L. Oliver, eds., *Proceedings of the Conference on Comparative Ethnicity: Ethnic Dilemmas in Comparative Perspective*. University of California, Los Angeles, June 1–3, 1988.

————. 1989. *American Indians: The First of this Land*. New York: Russell Sage Foundation.

Snipp, M. and G. D. Sandefur. 1988a. "Earnings of American Indians and Alaskan Natives: The Effects of Residence and Migration." *Social Forces* 66(4): 994–1008.

————. 1988b. "Small Gains for Rural Indians Who Move to Cities." *Rural Development Perspectives* 5(1): 22–25.

Stabler, J. C. 1989. "Dualism and Development in the Northwest Territories." *Economic Development and Cultural Change* 37(2): 805–839.

————. 1990. "A Utility Analysis of Activity Patterns of Native Males in the Northwest Territories." *Economic Development and Cultural Change* 39(1): 47–60.

Stanley, S., ed. 1978. *American Indian Economic Development*. Paris: Mouton Publishers.

Stephen, D. and P. Wearne. 1984. *Central America's Indians*. London: Minority Rights Group.

Stephen, L. 1991. "Culture as a Resource: Four Cases of Self-managed Indigenous Craft Production in Latin America." *Economic Development and Cultural Change* 40(4): 101–130.

Stevens, S. M. 1978. "Passamaquoddy Economic Development in Cultural and Historical Perspective." In S. Stanley, ed., *American Indian Economic Development.* Paris: Mouton Publishers.

Swetnam, J. 1980. "Disguised Employment and Development Policy in Peasant Economies." *Human Organization* 39(1): 32–39.

———. 1989. "What Else Did Indians Have to Do with Their Time? Alternatives to Labor Migration in Prerevolutionary Guatemala." *Economic Development and Cultural Change* 38(1): 89–112.

Takaaki, M. 1987. "Ainu, The Invisible Minority." *Japan Quarterly* April–June: 143–148.

Townsend, J. and B. Newman. 1985. "Bilingual Education Project in Guatemala: Preliminary Results on the Test of Principal Hypothesis during 1983." Nutrition Institute for Central America and Panama (INCAP), Guatemala City.

Treadgold, M. 1980. "Aboriginal Incomes: An Aggregative Analysis of the 1976 Census Results." *Australian Bulletin of Labour* 7(1): 31–46.

Trosper, R. L. 1980. "Earnings and Labor Supply: A Microeconomic Comparison of American Indians and Alaskan Natives to American Whites and Blacks." Publication No. 55. Boston College, Social Welfare Research Institute.

Tujab, G. 1987. "La Política de Revitalizatión de las Lenguas Mayas." *América Indígena* 47(3): 535–45.

Tzannatos, Zafiris 1991. "Reverse Racial Discrimination in Higher Education in Malaysia: Has It Reduced Inequality and at What Cost to the Poor?" *International Journal of Educational Development* 11(3): 177–192.

UNESCO (United Nations Educational, Scientific and Cultural Organization). 1964. *Statistical Yearbook: 1963.* Paris.

———. 1989. *Statistical Yearbook: 1989.* Paris.

UNICEF (United Nations Children's Fund). 1992. *Children of the Americas: Child Survival, Protection and Integrated Development in the 1990s.* Santafe de Bogotá, Colombia.

United Nations. 1983. "Study of the Problem of Discrimination against Indigenous Populations." Report E/CN.4/Sub.2/1983/21/Add.5. Economic and Social Council, Commission on Human Rights, Subcommission on Prevention of Discrimination and Protection of Minorities. New York.

Urban, G. and J. Sherzer. 1992. *Nation-States and Indians in Latin America.* Austin: University of Texas.

USAID (United States Agency for International Development). 1977. *Statistics for the Analysis of the Education Sector: Mexico.* Washington, D.C.

van den Berghe, P. L. 1992."Education, Class, and Ethnicity in Southern Peru: Revolutionary Colonialism." In P. G. Altbach and G. P. Kelly, eds., *Education and the Colonial Experience.* 2nd Revised Edition. New York: Advent Books.

van Ginneken, W. 1980. *Socio-economic Groups and Income Distribution in Mexico*. A Study Prepared for the ILO World Employment Programme. New York: St. Martin's Press.

Vargas, V. 1987. "Reflecting on Women's Education in Peru." Mimeo. Centro Flora Tristan, Lima, Peru.

Villavicencio, G. 1973. *Relaciones Interétnicas en Otavalo, Ecuador.* Serie de ediciones especiales, No. 64. México D.F.: Instituto Indigenista Interamericano.

Waggoner, D. 1991. *Undereducation in America: The Demography of High School Dropouts.* New York: Auburn House.

Wali, A. and S. Davis. 1992. "Protecting Amerindian Lands: A Review of World Bank Experience with Indigenous Land Regularization Programs in Lowland South America." Report No. 19. World Bank, Latin America and the Caribbean Technical Department, Regional Studies Program, Washington, D.C.

Walter, L. E. 1976. "Interaction and Organization in an Ecuadorean Indian Highland Community." Ph.D. Dissertation, University of Wisconsin—Madison.

Warnam, A. 1992. *Cuadernos de Demografía Indígena*. Mexico, D. F.: Instituto Nacional Indígenista.

Weber, M. 1947. *The Theory of Social and Economic Organizations*. New York: Oxford University Press.

Webster, P. L. and J. W. Dwyer. 1988. "The Cost of Being Nonwhite in Brazil." *Sociology and Social Research* 72(2): 136–142.

Welch, A. R. 1988. "Aboriginal Education as Internal Colonialism." *Comparative Education* 24(2): 203–215.

Whetten, N. L. 1961. *Guatemala, The Land and the People*. New Haven: Yale University Press.

Whitten, N. E. 1976. *Sacha Runa: Ethnicity and Adaptation of Ecuadorian Jungle Quechua*. Urbana: University of Illinois Press.

Wong, M. G. 1982. "The Cost of Being Chinese, Japanese, and Filipino in the United States: 1960, 1970, 1976." *Pacific Sociological Review* 25(1): 59–78.

World Bank. 1990. *World Development Report 1990: Poverty*. New York: Oxford University Press.

———. 1992. *World Development Report 1992: Development and the Environment*. New York: Oxford University Press.

World Commission on Environment and Development. 1987. *Our Common Future* (Brundtland Report). New York: Oxford University Press.

Zolezzi, G and J. Riester. 1987. "Lenguas Indígenas de Oriente Boliviano. Clasificación Preliminar." *América Indígena* 3:425–435.